Natural Hazards, UnNatural Disasters

Natural Hazards, UnNatural Disasters

The Economics of Effective Prevention

 THE UNITED NATIONS

 **THE WORLD BANK**
Washington, DC

ISBN: 978-0-8213-8050-5
eISBN: 978-0-8213-8141-0
DOI: 10.1596/978-0-8213-8050-5

Library of Congress Cataloging-in-Publication Data

Natural hazards, unnatural disasters : the economics of effective prevention / The World Bank and The United Nations.
   p. cm.
Includes bibliographical references and index.
ISBN 978-0-8213-8050-5 — ISBN 978-0-8213-8141-0 (electronic)
  1. Disasters—Economic aspects.   2. Natural disasters—Economic aspects.
  3. Emergency management. I. World Bank. II. United Nations.
HC79.D45N416 2011
363.34'7—dc22

                                        2010031475

Cover art: The cover art is based on a Madhubani painting depicting the destruction caused by the 2004 tsunami. This piece was created by Amrita Das, a female artist from Madhubani District, Bihar, India, and is part of a private art collection.

For centuries, women from the Mithila region of Bihar have passed down through generations the tradition of floor and wall painting. This art form is linked historically with disasters. It became popular after a severe drought hit the region between 1966 and 1968. The Indian government, in an attempt to help develop sources of income other than agriculture, encouraged local women to paint on paper (rather than on floors and walls) to allow their artwork to be sold. This art form is now recognized internationally.

Cover design: Serif Design Group

Praise for
Natural Hazards, UnNatural Disasters
The Economics of Effective Prevention

"This report synthesizes our knowledge about the effects of natural hazards on human welfare, particularly in its economic aspects. It is a remarkable combination of case studies, data on many scales, and the application of economic principles to the problems posed by earthquakes, abnormal weather, and the like. It provides a deep understanding of the relative roles of the market, government intervention, and social institutions in determining and improving both the prevention and the response to hazardous occurrences."

—KENNETH J. ARROW, Nobel Prize in Economics, 1972

"This excellent and timely study is a wake-up call to all of us responsible for managing and mitigating floods, earthquakes, and other natural hazards."

—BRUCE BABBIT, Former Secretary of the Interior, USA

"This book on natural hazards and unnatural disasters is very well done on a topic of supreme and immediate importance. I particularly like the chapters on how quickly countries and regions do recover from disasters—a topic discussed at least ever since John Stuart Mill—and how good markets are in responding in terms of land and other values to the prospect of disasters. I strongly recommend this book to non-economists as well as economists, and to government officials who must cope with floods, oil spills, earthquakes, and other disasters."

—GARY S. BECKER, Nobel Prize in Economics, 1992

"Three keywords come to mind after reading this World Bank report: prevention, strong international cooperation, and priority on helping human beings affected by disasters with compassion and dignity. With this report the World Bank highlights what international actors, national governments, local authorities, and individuals should constantly consider when discussing prevention measures. Governments must take the lead in implementing preventive actions both directly, by allocating efficiently public resources, and indirectly, by showing people how to protect themselves. This is the real challenge that not only the World Bank but all of us have to face. This is the dream that we have and it can become true if we are ready to pay the (political) price to achieve it. This ideal mirrors the belief and the actions undertaken by the Italian Civil Protection."

—GUIDO BERTOLASO, Head of the Italian Civil Protection

"How is it that some communities are able to soften the blows they face when rare natural events hit them, whereas others experience huge suffering? *Natural Hazards, UnNatural Disasters* contains the tightest analytical and empirical investigation into the question. It's a terrific book."

—SIR PARTHA DASGUPTA, Frank Ramsey Professor of Economics,
University of Cambridge

"It is a sad commentary on how aid is media-driven that official aid agencies and NGOs will make a huge effort for disaster relief and virtually no effort for prevention. This report courageously makes the case for redressing the balance. It dramatizes as never before that "natural disasters" are not so natural—prevention failures cost myriad lives, usually among the poorest. It issues a challenge: reverse the shameful neglect of prevention so as to save those lives."

—WILLIAM EASTERLY, author of The White Man's Burden (2006)

"It is the moral and ethical duty of all humanitarian and development workers to ensure that every dollar is well spent. Thus this study is an essential primer for all policy makers and practitioners concerned with disaster risk reduction and recovery—even more so in this age of frugal necessity. In building community safety and resilience, sensible spending, greater transparency, and accountability are essential to do more, do better, and reach further in tackling the most significant vulnerabilities that confront humanity. This report highlights the need for increased resources and innovative partnerships, in line with the Red Cross and Red Crescent experience, which shows that it really pays to invest in disaster prevention."

—BEKELE GELETA, Secretary General of the International Federation of Red Cross and Red Crescent Societies

"This book is a must-read for policy makers and concerned individuals all over the world. For too long, leaders have done too little to prevent the transformation of natural hazards into (un)natural disasters, and then moved too slowly once they occur. And now the risks are growing with rapid urbanization and climate change. This book organizes vast amounts of material into compelling analyses and clear messages, and the authors put forward pragmatic policy suggestions that blend market incentives with 'smart' regulation and sound governance principles. They need to be taken seriously."

—SRI MULYANI INDRAWATI, Managing Director, World Bank; Former Minister of Finance, Indonesia

"Warning people of impending hazards saves lives and livelihoods. But we can still do better as shown in this excellent report! With clear arguments, statements, and evidence, it is a convincing call for governments the world over to improve the detection and forecasting of hazards risks, and to develop better warnings for sectoral planning to reduce human and economic losses that are setting back socio-economic development. Improvement of early warning systems is clearly an investment in sustainable development, as demonstrated in many countries where benefits exceed costs many times over."

—MICHEL JARRAUD, Secretary General of the World Meteorological Organization

"When a natural hazard strikes innocent victims, people from around the world pitch in to help. It is incumbent on policy makers to make sure that this generosity is well-used. This report is one of the first to treat hazards from an economic perspective of value-for-money. That lens—dismal at it may seem—provides crucial insights on why we should spend more on preventive action (and why we don't), on why reliance on formal rules and planning does not always work, and on why we need to think of disaster risk prevention in broader developmental terms. The report provides a detailed, welcome, and timely blueprint for reducing disasters in a period when natural hazards appear to be on the rise."

—HOMI KHARAS, Senior Fellow, Brookings Institution

"I have just read your report and find it both fascinating and right on target! The deep problems result from . . . terrible governance over a long time, which then destroys the trust that individuals have in their government and in each other. Rebuilding is not just of the physical world but also the much tougher job of rebuilding trust and social capital. I wish that the steps toward achieving that tough job were easy and quick, but they are not. You are doing very important work."

—ELINOR OSTROM, Nobel Prize in Economics, 2009

"Neither adverse economic shocks nor natural hazards are avoidable, but citizens, economic agents and governments can do a lot to limit or mitigate their worst effects through an intelligent combination of prevention, insurance, and sensible coping. This book is a primer on how to deal with natural hazard risks so they do not become natural 'disasters,' as is aptly suggested by the title. It emphasizes what governments can do to promote effective prevention. . . . It also examines the role of catastrophic insurance and shows that in spite of its key importance, market and government failures are quite pervasive in this area."

—GUILLERMO PERRY, Former Minister of Finance and Public Credit, Colombia

"This book-length report by staff of the World Bank on the economics of preventing (un)natural disasters is as nearly a definitive treatment of the subject as we are likely to obtain. The combination of economic analysis with factual description, personal narratives, charts, data, photographs, and references makes a compelling multidisciplinary case for different kinds of preventive efforts targeted on the specific causes and likely consequences of potential disasters in every part of the globe."

—RICHARD POSNER, author of Catastrophe: Risk and Response (2004)

"This report is a gem. The language is clear and simple; the organization is logical; the verbal illustrations are impressive; the maps and diagrams are comprehensible; the theoretical discussions are easily understood; and the subject is compelling: how to understand hazards and how to cope, in advance and after, with earthquakes, storms, floods, droughts, and extreme events. It is a model to be studied and emulated. It is a team effort, contradicting the popular notion that a camel is a horse described by a committee. I don't remember reading any other 248 pages on a deadly serious subject that were so informative and so easily digested. Congratulations to the authors and all their advisors and reviewers."

—THOMAS C. SCHELLING, Nobel Prize in Economics, 2005

"This is an excellent piece of work with really practical lessons that will influence the way disasters are handled—and indeed prevented. The report could inform and illuminate policy analyses in a way that would make a gigantic difference to the lives of vulnerable people. I welcome it warmly."

—AMARTYA SEN, Nobel Prize in Economics, 1998

"The main thesis of this report, that prevention matters and requires just as much intelligence as funds, is correct. But not all risks can be prevented, and the report does a brilliant job of analyzing how we share or cope with residual risk. I recommend this report to any reader who wants to understand the true nature of catastrophe risk and insurance markets beyond the relatively mundane issues of supply, demand, and the market-clearing price for risk. This report might even help students of the subprime mortgage debacle understand what really went wrong as that market lost all sight of the principles laid out in this terrific report."

—JOHN SEO, Co-founder, Fermat Capital Management, LLC;
Former State-Appointed Advisor to the Florida Hurricane Catastrophe Fund

"I happened to read this careful, thoughtful, studious report near the beginning of hurricane season. There will be another hurricane season next year and the year after. There will also be droughts, floods, and earthquakes. Responses will be more effective, before and after the event, and damage will be less if governments, relief organizations, and others learn from this study. Ignorance is not bliss in hurricane season."

—ROBERT M. SOLOW, Nobel Prize in Economics, 1987

"*Natural Hazards, UnNatural Disasters* provides policy makers with a new and valuable approach that focuses on the economics of reducing deaths and destruction from natural hazards. In a critical analysis across a range of topics, the report takes on a number of sacred cows by emphasizing the critical role of incentives (both private and public), freely functioning markets, the free flow of information, institutional arrangements, and the possibilities and limits to governmental actions. The report lays out the economics of hazards reduction for the non-specialist, draws on the latest literature, and supplements that literature with numerous supporting new empirical and analytical studies. It will be a standard reference in the hazards policy and research community."

—RODNEY WEIHER, Former Chief Economist, NOAA

"This book represents the first systematic analysis of the management of extreme risks from a worldwide comparative perspective. It is a major contribution to an increasingly important field."

—MARTIN WEITZMAN, Professor of Economics, Harvard University

"The world is continually beset with so-called natural disasters, with triggering events ranging from shaking earth and scorching weather, to severe storms and surging rivers. Such disasters impose a massive toll of human suffering, particularly on the poor. But the losses come not primarily from the actions of nature. Rather, as this wide ranging and insightful analysis demonstrates, they derive from the synergy of natural forces and misguided choices by humans. We enhance risks by channeling rivers and spewing greenhouse gases, and expose ourselves to the risks that prevail by building cities in flood zones and in manners vulnerable to earthquakes. And where dangers do exist, we often deal ineffectively by choosing recovery over prevention when the latter would be far less costly, and by failing to meld public and private mitigation efforts in cost-effective fashion. This study, remarkable for its clear thought and thorough documentation, could change the way we cope with the calamities."

—RICHARD ZECKHAUSER, Frank P. Ramsey Professor of Political Economy,
Harvard University

"As someone who repeatedly had to deal with the devastating consequences of severe natural hazards at the highest level of responsibility, I can appreciate the enormous value of this volume. It is long overdue. Its sound analysis and sensible policy prescriptions make this report mandatory reading for any person with duty, or plain interest, in this field."

—ERNESTO ZEDILLO, Former President of Mexico;
Director, Yale Center for the Study of Globalization

Contents

Figures

Tables

Acknowledgments

The report has been prepared by a team led by Apurva Sanghi, comprising S. Ramachandran, Alejandro de la Fuente, Martina Tonizzo, Sebnem Sahin, and Bianca Adam. S. Ramachandran made major contributions to the writing of the report. An extended team comprising individuals from more than 25 organizations contributed to relevant background work: Jose-Miguel Albala-Bertrand, Javier Baez, Daniel Bitran, Brian Blankespoor, Henrike Brecht, Shun Chonabayashi, Luc Christiansen, Maureen Cropper, Jesus Cuaresma, Uwe Deichmann, Sergio Dell'anna, Stefan Dercon, Amod Dixit, Kerry Emanuel, Jocelyn Finlay, Thomas Fomby, Jed Friedman, Suzette Galinato, Maryam Golnaraghi, Lucy Hancock, Stefan Hochrainer, Yuki Ikeda, Nick Ingwersen, George Joseph, Hemang Karelia, Shyam KC, Philip Keefer, Charles Kenny, Carolyn Kousky, Randall Kuhn, Daniel Kull, Howard Kunreuther, Somik Lall, Stephen Ling, Joanne Linnerooth-Bayer, Norman Loayza, Ramon Lopez, Olivier Mahul, Anil Markandya, Reinhard Mechler, Robert Mendelsohn, Rina Meutia, Erwann Michel-Kerjan, Sanket Mohapatra, Robert Muir-Wood, Francis Muraya, Eric Neumayer, Eduardo Olaberria, Thomas Pluemper, Agnes Quisumbing, Nicola Ranger, Paul Raschky, Dilip Ratha, Jamele Rigolini, Olga Rostapshova, Gokay Saher, Indhira Santos, Manijeh Schwindt, John Seo, A.R. Subbiah, Thomas Teisberg, Michael Toman, Pantea Vaziri, Hyoung Gun Wang, Rodney Weiher, Ben Wisner, Chris Woodruff, Futoshi Yamauchi, Okuyama Yasuhide, Jaime Yepez, Yisehac Yohannes, Michael Young, Ricardo Zapata, and Richard Zeckhauser. We are grateful to Zoubida Allaoua, Milan Brahmbhatt, Marianne Fay, John Holmes, Saroj Jha, Kathy Sierra, Michael Toman, and Margareta Wahlstrom for their supervision and guidance.

We benefited greatly from periodic discussions with our core reviewers and advisors: Milan Brahmbhatt, Shanta Devarajan, Bekele Geleta, Indermit

Gill, Daniela Gressani, Michel Jarraud, Werner Kiene, Homi Kharas, Justin Yifu Lin, Frank Lysy, Vikram Nehru, Richard Posner, Muhammad Saidur Rahman, Richard Somerville, and Eric Werker. In addition, World Bank country directors Ellen A. Goldstein (Bangladesh), Kenichi Ohashi (Ethiopia and Sudan), Yvonne Tsikata (Haiti), Johannes Zutt (Comoros, Eritrea, Kenya, Rwanda, Seychelles, and Somalia), and Ulrich Zachau (Turkey) provided insightful comments on the country spotlights. We also thank Elinor Ostrom for her perceptive remarks on the Haiti spotlight. We have benefited from many consultations, meetings, and workshops, and thank participants in these events, which included representatives from academia, government, civil society, and private sector organizations.

We thank our many colleagues, both internally and externally, who provided helpful comments, reviews, and stimulated discussions on various aspects of the report: Issam A. Abousleiman, Roberto Adam, Jean-Christophe Adrian, Edward Charles Anderson, Mir Anjum Altaf, Jorge Saba Arbache, Enrique Blanco Armas, Margaret Arnold, Elif Ayhan, Edward Barbier, Scott Barrett, Reid Basher, Joanne Bayer, Sofia U. Bettencourt, Rosina Bierbaum, Sanjay Bhatia, Anna Bjerde, Aurelia Blin, Jan Bojo, Alex Bowen, Eduardo Cavallo, Alison C.N. Cave, Raffaello Cervigni, Poulomi Chakarbarti, Shubham Chaud-huri, Ajay Chhibber, Loic Chiquier, Kenneth Chomitz, Linda Cohen, Richard Damania, Julie Dana, Saurabh Suresh Dani, Jishnu Das, Susmita Dasgupta, Ian Davis, James Douris, Edgardo Favaro, Wolfgang Fengler, Achim Fock, Jorge Garcia-Garcia, Ross Alexander Gartley, Francis Ghesquiere, Stuart Gill, Xavier Giné, Iwan Gunawan, Eugene Gurenko, Hongjoo J. Hahm, Pedro Hallal, Stephane Hallegatte, Kirk Hamilton, Sonia Hammam, Johu Harding, Nagaraja Rao Harshadeep, Andrew Healy, Rafik Fatehali Hirji, Niels B. Holm-Nielsen, Monika Huppi, Zahid Hussain, Stephen Hutton, Ahya Ihsan, Kremena Ionkova, Vijay Jagannathan, Abhas K. Jha, Roberto Jovel, Mukesh Kapila, Ioannis N. Kessides, Zahed Khan, Jolanta Kryspin-Watson, Daniel Kull, Anne T. Kuriakose, Rodney Lester, Eduardo Ley, Oeyvind Espeseth Lier, Alexander Lotsch, Mott MacDonald, Sergio Margulis, Aditya Mattoo, Michael McCracken, Deepak K. Mishra, Pradeep Mitra, Jose F. Molina, Roger Morier, Mits Motohashi, Mohinder Mudahar, Siobhan Murray, Mustopha Nabli, Ambar Narayan, Urvashi Narayan, Stephen N. Ndegwa, Ian Noble, Ilan Noy, Michael Oppenheimer, Emily Oster, Amparo Palacios Lopez, Elina Palin, Kiran Pandey, Praveen Pardeshi, Mark Pelling, Robert Pindyck, Prashant, Christoph Pusch, John Roome, Charles Scawthorn, Zmarack Shalizi, Sujai Shivakumar, Surya Shrestha, Kenneth Simler, Ravi Sinha, Nirmaljit Singh Paul, Emmanuel Skoufias, Robert Smith, Richard Somerville, Vivek Suri, Ferenc Toth, Vladimir Tsirkunov, Paula Uski, Willem van Eeghen, Marijn Verhoeven, Cesar G. Victora, Doekle Wielinga, William Wiseman, Winston Yu, Shahid Yusuf, Wael Zakout, and Ivan Zelenko.

An important component of the report was the distinguished seminar series designed to solicit inputs and ideas on selected themes. We are thankful to speakers and discussants who participated in these series and who gave their time at no cost to the World Bank or United Nations: Kenneth Arrow, Bruce Babbitt, Freeman Dyson, Daniel Kahneman, Homi Kharas, Howard Kunreuther, Wangari Maathai, Robert Mendelsohn, William Nordhaus, Edward C. Prescott, Richard Posner, Thomas Schelling, John Seo, and Martin Weitzman.

We acknowledge the financial support of the partners of the Global Facility for Disaster Reduction and Recovery. Oscar Apodaca, Fatoumata Doumbia, Max Jira, and Alisa Lertvalaikul provided excellent logistical support throughout. Judy Ka Lai assisted with resource management. Bruce Ross-Larson was the principal editor. The World Bank's Printing, Graphics, and Map Design Unit created the maps under the direction of Jeff Lecksell. The Office of the Publisher provided editorial, design, composition, and printing services under the supervision of Patricia Katayama, Nora Ridolfi, and Dina Towbin. Roger Morier and Brigitte Leoni provided support and advice on the communication strategy.

MEMORANDUM TO A
CONCERNED FINANCE MINISTER

Subject: **Natural Hazards, UnNatural Disasters:
The Economics of Effective Prevention**

This memo introduces a report that you may find useful and interesting. Focusing on preventing death and destruction from "natural" disasters, it concludes that governments can appreciably increase prevention.

The good news is that prevention is often cost-effective. It requires many actions, and some important ones are under government control. But they are not always obvious. Improving the public delivery of some services, like reliable public transport, allows people to move from unsafe areas close to work to safer locations. Reducing deforestation prevents heavy rains from washing mud, rock, and debris into populated areas. This report suggests how such measures and related spending could be identified and made effective.

Effective spending is complex, and cost-benefit analysis (underused) helps, but institutions that increase the public's involvement and oversight are vital. Large benefits result from greater transparency in all aspects of government decision making. How the public responds to such prevention measures depends on its trust in the government. Such trust flows from credible institutions, which the report persistently underscores.

Prevention pays, but you do not always have to pay more for prevention. A relatively easy and effective measure is for governments to make information about hazards and risks easily accessible (such as maps of flood plains and seismic fault lines). Allowing markets to work better also helps because much information is embedded in prices. Controls on prices, trade, and the like and excessive tax rates have harmful effects, and correcting them goes a long way in increasing prevention.

Effective prevention cannot rest on laissez-faire alone, for markets need to be complemented with appropriate government actions. Greater spending on some items is warranted: many countries are not taking advantage of the technological improvements in weather and related forecasting. Even modest increases in spending—and greater sharing of data internationally—can have enormous benefits, especially to warn people of impending hazards. Several countries, some very poor, have found large and quick gains from such spending. The gains can also spill beyond borders, enhancing regional cooperation.

Effective prevention cannot rest on a single measure or simple slogan either. Ensuring government's adequate funding of infrastructure, basic services, early warning systems, and the like will have high payoffs. But the financing of infrastructure has to be matched by adequate maintenance. Funding early warning systems is only as useful as the "last mile" of successful evacuation and response. Bangladesh shows that such a response can be effective even in poor countries, while some rich countries (such as the United States in its response to Hurricane Katrina) can stumble over this last step.

Despite adequate prevention measures, hazards will strike and funds will be required for recovery and reconstruction. So knowing disaster's effects on fiscal sustainability is important for making informed decisions. While the government can borrow, it must ultimately pay it all back from taxes or spending cuts elsewhere. And although donors provide external aid after disasters, studies show they often do so by re-labeling funds without increasing aggregate amounts. You will have to rely on the ability to tax—and spend accordingly.

Finally, one message about the future: cities will grow, especially in developing countries, increasing exposure of lives and property to disasters, but not uniformly or monotonically. Though exposure will rise, better managed cities can reduce vulnerability and risk. Although you do not run the cities, you control many aspects of their financing and can do much to reduce new risks. Damage from hazards—particularly tropical cyclones—are also likely to increase because of climate change. Your successors will have to deal with these more difficult issues, but they will benefit from the steps you take now. If you help correct the problems of the present, generations to come will welcome the future.

Overview

The adjective "UnNatural" in the title of this report conveys its key message: earthquakes, droughts, floods, and storms are *natural hazards*, but the *unnatural disasters* are deaths and damages that result from human acts of omission and commission. Every disaster is unique, but each exposes actions—by individuals and governments at different levels—that, had they been different, would have resulted in fewer deaths and less damage. Prevention is possible, and this report examines what it takes to do this cost-effectively.

The report looks at disasters primarily through an economic lens. Economists emphasize self-interest to explain how people choose the amount of prevention, insurance, and coping. But lenses can distort as well as sharpen images, so the report also draws from other disciplines: psychology to examine how people may misperceive risks, political science to understand voting patterns, and nutrition science to see how stunting in children after a disaster impairs cognitive abilities and productivity as adults much later. Peering into the future, the report shows that growing cities will increase exposure to hazards, but that vulnerability will not rise if cities are better managed. The intensities and frequencies of hazards in the coming decades will change with the climate, and the report examines this complicated and contentious subject, acknowledging all the limitations of data and science.

Four main findings

First, a disaster exposes the cumulative implications of many earlier decisions, some taken individually, others collectively, and a few by default. A deeper questioning of what happened, and why, could prevent a repetition of disasters. Several factors usually contribute to any disaster, some less obvious than others. The immediate cause of a bridge or building collapse may be a mudslide, though poor design or construction may have also contributed. But the underlying cause may be denuded hillsides that increased sediment flows (as in Haiti), or poor urban planning that put the bridge or building in harm's way. Symptoms are easily mistaken for cause: denuded hillsides may result from desperately poor people depleting the vegetation to survive or from logging concessions that encourage tree cutting but not planting. Effective prevention measures are therefore not always "obvious."

Second, prevention is often possible and cost-effective. Studies for the report examined the costs and benefits of specific prevention measures that homeowners could take in hazard-prone areas of four low- and middle-income countries. Prevention pays for assumed (but reasonable) costs and discount rates. Other prevention measures are embedded in infrastructure (such as adequate drainage ditches). The report examines government expenditures on prevention and finds that it is generally lower than relief spending, which rises after a disaster and remains high for several subsequent years. But effective prevention depends not just on the amount but on what funds are spent on. For example, Bangladesh reduced deaths from cyclones by spending modest sums on shelters, developing accurate weather forecasts, issuing warnings that people heeded, and arranging for their evacuation. All this cost less than building large-scale embankments that would have been less effective.

Third, many measures—private and public—must work well together for effective prevention. Low-lying areas around Jakarta illustrate the complexity of ensuring this: residents raise the plinth of their houses to protect against floods, but they also draw water through borewells causing the ground to subside. Even knowing this, a person has no choice if the government does not provide piped water. So, the prevention measures an individual undertakes also depend on what the government does—or fails to do—and vice versa.

That many measures do not work well together in poor countries explains why they have more disasters. The poor may know the hazard risks they face but depend more on public services that are often inadequate. They live near work on cheaper land exposed to hazards if buses are unreliable, while the rich with cars have better alternatives. The poor would willingly move to safer locations if their incomes rose or if public transport became more reliable. Many governments in poor countries struggle to provide such services, and until they do, the poor will remain vulnerable.

Fourth, the exposure to hazards will rise in cities, but greater exposure need not increase vulnerability. Large cities exposed to cyclones and earthquakes will more than double their population by 2050 (from 680 million in 2000 to 1.5 billion in 2050). The increase will differ by country and region. Vulnerability need not increase with exposure if cities are well managed, but the projected increase in exposure underscores the enormous task ahead.

Urban growth is not the only concern. Climate change has received much attention, and there are urgent calls for immediate action because the effects of climate change are cumulative and felt much later. The *2010 World Development Report* discusses the implications of climate change in detail; this report is limited to its *direct* effects on hazards. One estimate of the increase in damage associated with changed tropical cyclone activity as a result of climate change is between $28 billion and $68 billion annually by 2100. This represents an increase of between 50 and 125 percent over no climate change. There is considerable uncertainty around these long-term projections, reflecting the limits of the data and the climate models that generate them. The damage is in "expected value" terms, but averages hide extremes: a very rare and powerful cyclone could strike a highly vulnerable location causing extremely high damages. And the effects are likely to be concentrated: several small island countries in the Caribbean are particularly vulnerable.

These four findings are not actionable prescriptions. Many people must do numerous things better, but getting them to do so is the challenge. A successful policy response for effective prevention includes information, interventions, and infrastructure. Underpinning this policy response is the role of "institutions," without which any policy response would be ineffectual. Governments can do much to promote prevention—in line with the policy implications outlined next.

Four policy implications (plus one for donors)

First, governments can and should make information more easily accessible. People are often guided in their prevention decisions by information on hazards, yet the seemingly simple act of collecting and providing information is sometimes a struggle. While some countries attempt to collect and archive their hazard data, efforts are generally inconsistent or insufficient. Specifically, there are no universal standards for archiving environmental parameters for defining hazards and related data. Data exchange, hazard analysis, and hazard mapping thus become difficult. Figure 1 shows how few countries collect and archive data on hazards—even though technological advances such as the abundance of free, simple, and open source software (for example, PostGIS, Geoserver, Mapserver, the GeoNode.org project) should make collecting and sharing information easy.

And where information is collected, it is not always shared, even though sharing information on hazards involves relatively little expense because some government agencies already collect and analyze data on hazard risks. Those preparing background papers for this report had difficulties obtaining disaster and related data from various public agencies and universities, even though donors often funded the collection and automation of disaster data. Sometimes "security, commercial, and defense" reasons are invoked, but only a few are legitimate. Sometimes commercial interests take precedence over public good aspects.

So, the importance of making information about hazard risks available cannot be overemphasized. Perhaps because of this significance, the political

Figure 1 Number of countries that archive data for specific hazards

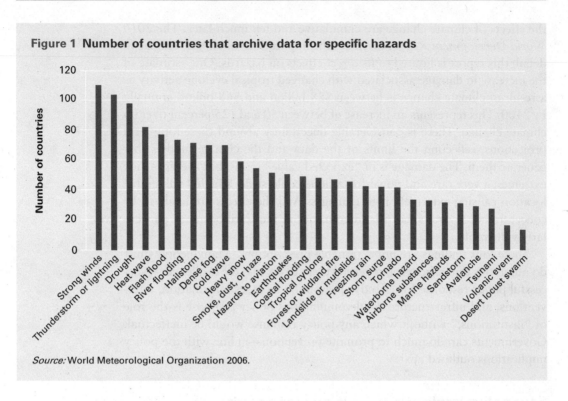

Source: World Meteorological Organization 2006.

will to not have information on rising levels of risk publicized is often strong. For example, even though the Federal Emergency Management Agency (FEMA) in the United States has updated coastal flood maps for the U.S. Gulf, it cannot get coastal communities to accept them because the information would reduce property prices. Systematic mechanisms for tracking information related to the changing nature of risk, and translating it into risk-related property valuations, would go a long way to increase the incentives for prevention. Making maps of flood plains and seismic fault lines easily accessible would make developers and property owners more aware of the risks—and more motivated to build appropriately. Collecting data on weather and climate is also integral to producing accurate forecasts.

Second, governments should permit land and housing markets to work, supplementing them with targeted interventions when necessary. When land and housing markets work, property values reflect hazard risks, guiding people's decisions on where to live and what prevention measures to take. Detailed empirical work for this report matched some 800,000 buildings in Bogota that differed in their exposure to seismic risk to a range of characteristics (such as size, construction quality, distance from the city center, and whether residential, commercial, or industrial). Because the only difference among comparable properties is their level of hazard risk, this allowed assessing whether property values are lower in riskier areas. Figure 2 shows that they are, suggesting capitalization of dis-amenities from hazard risk.

But markets, when smothered, dampen the incentives for prevention. In Mumbai, where rent controls have been pervasive, property owners have

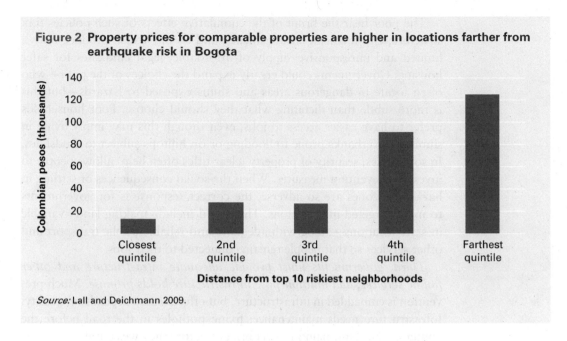

Figure 2 **Property prices for comparable properties are higher in locations farther from earthquake risk in Bogota**

Source: Lall and Deichmann 2009.

neglected maintenance for decades, so buildings crumble in heavy rains. Rent controls are not unique to Mumbai or developing countries. Rent control laws have remained in place in some form in New York City since 1943, where there are currently about a million rent-regulated and 50,000 rent-controlled apartments. As recently as 2009, legislation was passed in New York that limits the ability of landlords statewide to increase rents. Such laws are expected to return to regulation many household units previously attracting market rents. They exist in about 40 countries, including many developed countries. And rent controls are not the only market distortion. Real estate transactions in many countries incur a tax on sales, not on owning property. But taxing transactions reduces property sales and encourages undervaluation. And restrictions on cement prices and imports can create black markets and exorbitant prices, so that adulterated cement ends up weakening structures.

Getting land and rental markets to work can go a long way to inducing people to locate in appropriate areas and take preventive measures. But this will not be a straightforward task. Nor will it be easy to remove the panoply of market distortions because many benefit vested interests. And knowing what to change first is not obvious. Past policies weigh heavily on the present: many structures now standing were built earlier, and defects are difficult to detect and harder to remedy. A corollary is that correcting policies now will not result in immediate improvements, though correcting them sooner would be better than delaying. Where new construction dominates, as in developing countries' urban areas, this legacy is less of an issue, but wealthier countries also bear this burden: mispriced insurance (premia too low because of populist pressures on a regulated industry) has led to overbuilding along the hurricane-prone U.S. coastline.

The poor bear the brunt of the cumulative effects of such policies (tax structure, city financing arrangements, and so on) which produce only a limited and unresponsive supply of affordable, legal land sites for safer housing. Governments could greatly expand the choices of the poor—who often locate in dangerous areas and slums exposed to hazards—but this is more subtle than dictating what they should choose. Poor households prefer to have easier access to jobs, even though this may imply living in slums on riverbanks prone to flooding or on hilltops subject to mudslides. In some cases, security of property (clear titles often help) allows people to invest in prevention measures. When the social consequences of settling in hazardous zones are so adverse, the correct response is for governments to make targeted interventions. This could include making land available in safer locations—along with adequate and reliable public transport and other services so that people remain connected to their jobs.

Third, governments must provide adequate infrastructure and other public services, and multipurpose infrastructure holds promise. Much prevention is embedded in infrastructure, but effectiveness depends on quality. Infrastructure needs maintenance: fixing potholes in the road before the winter or the rains; painting steel bridges before they weaken through corrosion; inspecting and fixing cracks in concrete bridges. All engineers know this, but they do not always obtain budget appropriations—even in the United States, where the 2007 bridge collapse in Minneapolis drew attention to such neglect.

Spending should go down a list arranged in descending order of (economic) rates of return. But when subject to arbitrary budget spending limits and lumpiness, low-return spending often gets put ahead of postponable high-return spending. Since maintenance can be postponed, it gets deferred—repeatedly—until the asset crumbles. Drainage ditches, once built, are not adequately maintained and become clogged; so rains result in floods that drown the poor. Other less obvious public services include reliable city transport, and these require better—not always more—public spending. For example, about 30 percent of infrastructure assets of a typical African country need rehabilitation, and just $0.6 billion on road maintenance would yield $2.6 billion in annual benefits (figure 3).

Governments must ensure that new infrastructure does not introduce new risk. This is particularly important since, in many developing countries, infrastructure investment—long-lived capital stock—is likely to peak in the coming few decades. Locating infrastructure out of harm's way is one way of doing so. Where that may not be possible, another way is to execute multipurpose infrastructure projects, such as Kuala Lumpur's Stormwater Management and Road Tunnel (SMART). Floods from heavy rains are a hazard, and the 9.7 kilometers long $514 million tunnel has three levels (figure 4), the lowest for drainage and the upper two for road traffic. The drain allows large volumes of flood water to be diverted from the city's financial district to a storage reservoir, holding pond, and bypass tunnel. Combining the drain with the road has two advantages: it ensures maintenance of a

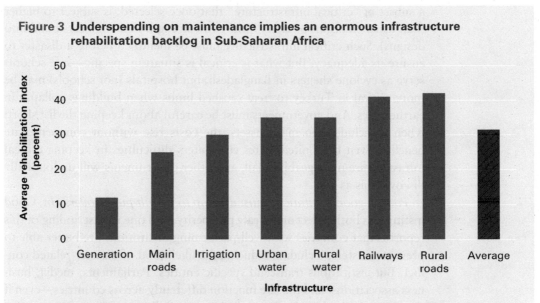

Figure 3 Underspending on maintenance implies an enormous infrastructure rehabilitation backlog in Sub-Saharan Africa

Note: The rehabilitation index shows the average percentage across countries of each type of infrastructure in poor condition and thus in need of rehabilitation.
Source: Briceño-Garmendia, Smits, and Foster 2008.

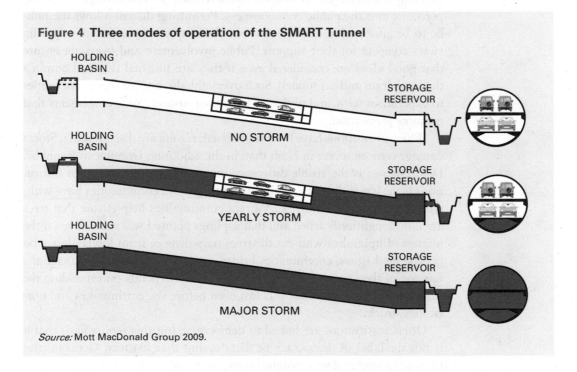

Figure 4 Three modes of operation of the SMART Tunnel

Source: Mott MacDonald Group 2009.

drain that otherwise would be used only sporadically, and it costs less than building each separately.

Infrastructure, even when well designed, constructed, and maintained, cannot always prevent disasters. Governments must, therefore, pay heed to a subset of "critical infrastructure" that once selected, is subject to higher than usual "margins of safety" (the extra strength that engineers build into designs). Such critical infrastructure must be identified before a disaster to ensure its adequacy. But what is critical is situation specific—safe schools serve as cyclone shelters in Bangladesh, but hospitals (not schools) may be more critical in Turkey to treat crushed limbs when buildings collapse in earthquakes. And governments must be careful about keeping the list short: when it includes too many assets, the costs rise without commensurate benefits. Even the United States encounters difficulties in keeping critical infrastructure manageably small, and other governments will undoubtedly discover this as well.

Fourth, good institutions must develop to permit public oversight. Good institutions both reflect and create prosperity, and one robust finding of this report is that countries with well-performing institutions are better able to prevent disasters, including reducing the likelihood of disaster-related conflict. But institutions transcend specific entities. Parliaments, media, business associations, and the like function differently across countries—even if they have similar legal authority and responsibilities.

Fostering good institutions means letting evolve a messy array of overlapping entities (the media, neighborhood associations, engineering groups) that may not all have lofty motives but nevertheless allow divergent views to percolate into the public consciousness. Permitting dissent allows the public to be informed and involved when alternative proposals and opposing views compete for their support. Public involvement and oversight ensure that good ideas are considered even if they are unusual (Kuala Lumpur's dual-use drain and car tunnel). Such oversight also encourages communities to experiment with, and to devise, their own sustainable arrangements that promote prevention.

Where institutions have been suppressed, results are discouraging. Storm damage is more severe in Haiti than in the adjoining Dominican Republic. Deforestation is the visible difference (figure 5) but the quality of institutions is the less visible one. Haiti's institutions and communities have withered from decades of misrule. Vibrant communities help ensure that trees are not thoughtlessly felled and that saplings planted will grow. Even if the interest of uplanders who cut the trees may diverge from lowlanders who get the mud flows, communities bridge these differences and manage the fair use of the commons. Prosperity ultimately depends on rebuilding the trust and social capital that was lost even before the earthquakes and hurricanes struck.

Often, institutions are linked to democracy, but this report finds that it is not the label of democracy or dictatorship that matters. Good institutions are associated with political competition more than voting alone (the conventional understanding of democracy). Across both nondemocracies and democracies, the existence of "institutionalized" political parties—parties that allow members to discipline leaders who pursue policies at odds with member interests—is significantly associated with reductions in disaster mortality. The mortality from earthquakes falls by 6 percent for an

Figure 5 The visible border between Haiti and the Dominican Republic

Source: National Geographic.

additional year of competitive elections, and by 2 percent when the average party age rises by a year. Such systems are therefore more likely to respond to citizens' needs.

Preventing disasters requires many public and private agencies to work well together, and governments could play an institutional role in this. But there is no single recipe for strengthening institutions; a wide variety of political systems can serve the purpose. But encouraging a diverse set of organizations that facilitate collective action by large groups of citizens will allow them to press more effectively for the spread of information, the availability of prevention measures and alternatives, and their cost-effectiveness.

And fifth, donors have a role in prevention as well. The report's overarching theme is that not enough is being done on prevention. Donors usually respond to disasters after they strike: about a fifth of total humanitarian aid between 2000 and 2008 was devoted to spending on disaster relief and response (figure 6).

The share of humanitarian funding going to prevention is small but increasing—from about 0.1 percent in 2001 to 0.7 percent in 2008. However, prevention activities often imply long-term development expenditures whereas the focus of humanitarian aid—already a tiny part of official development aid—is immediate relief and response. Donors concerned with prevention could earmark official development aid (rather than humanitarian aid) for prevention-related activities. And such aid, if used effectively, could

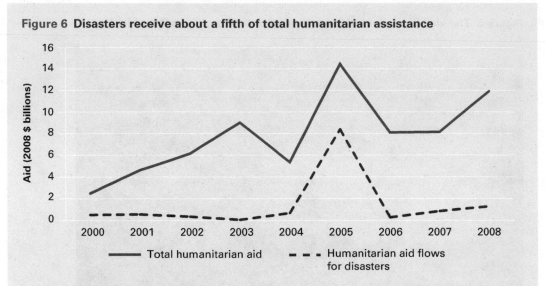

Figure 6 Disasters receive about a fifth of total humanitarian assistance

Note: Humanitarian aid is "an intervention to help people who are victims of a natural disaster or conflict meet their basic needs and rights," while official development assistance (ODA) is "money spent on development (education, health, water supply and sanitation, agriculture, and so on) and humanitarian assistance by members of the OECD Development Assistance Committee."
Source: World Bank staff based on data from the Financial Tracking System (FTS) of the UN Office for the Coordination of Humanitarian Affairs.

reduce issues arising from the Samaritan's dilemma: the inability to deny help following a disaster to those who have not taken sufficient prevention measures.

In addition to these policy implications, readers may find much of interest and use in the report, summarized in the rest of this overview.

Disaster data patterns revisited

There have been 3.3 million deaths from natural hazards since 1970, or about 82,500 a year, with large year-to-year fluctuations and no pronounced time trends. Droughts are the deadliest of the four hazard categories (earthquakes, floods, and storms are the others) and poor countries suffer disproportionately—almost 1 million people died in Africa's droughts alone. Poor countries withstand the worst of disaster deaths (map 1).

Despite the avoidable deaths, the absence of a pronounced upward trend suggests the picture is less bleak than it first appears: exposure is rising rapidly (such as poor countries' population, both total and urban) yet deaths would trend down if scaled by the relevant population. So, there has been some effective prevention.

Data on property damage are less comprehensive than those on deaths, but damage from all hazards between 1970 and 2008 totaled $2,300 billion (in 2008 dollars), or 0.23 percent of cumulative world output. Damages fluctuate with a modest but discernable upward trend even when adjusted

Map 1 Deaths shrink Asia and the Americas—but expand Africa

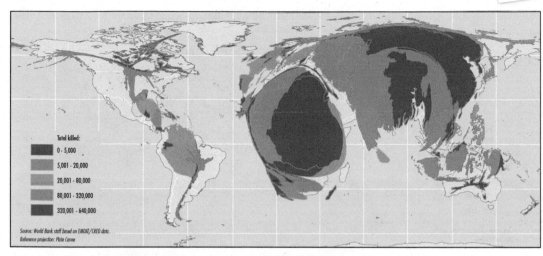

Note: Areas reflect cumulative deaths from disasters for 1970 to 2010 (February).
Source: World Bank staff based on EM-DAT/CRED.

for inflation. They vary by hazards, with earthquakes and storms causing the most damage. And they are disproportionately high in middle-income countries. Again, the data suggest some effective prevention: if damages are scaled by GDP (globally or by country), they generally trend down.

Even when scaled by output, poor countries with few assets incur little damage, and rich countries (with more capital) effectively prevent damage. Middle-income countries incur the greatest proportional damage (map 2), suggesting why absolute damage has been rising.

Institutions that prevent damage develop more slowly than assets as countries urbanize and prosper. But this is not immutable: even poor countries can undertake effective prevention, and more can rise to the challenge of doing so.

Disasters' many effects

A disaster obviously hurts those affected. It also spares many in the affected area, yet those spared may be indirectly affected. The village tinker's and tailor's businesses suffer when a cyclone spares their premises but destroys their customers' crops. And such indirect effects extend beyond the affected area, which is linked to undamaged areas through commerce. These indirect effects are often—but not always—adverse. Disentangling the effects is difficult, but clarity of concepts can help, starting with measurement.

How much output falls in the affected area, and for how long, has been controversial. Many factors (simultaneous changes in commodity prices, terms of trade, exchange rates) affect output, and studies differ on whether and how these are taken into account when measuring the effect of a disaster. A disaster may affect only a small part of a country, so it may not

Map 2 Damages shrink Africa but expand middle-income countries

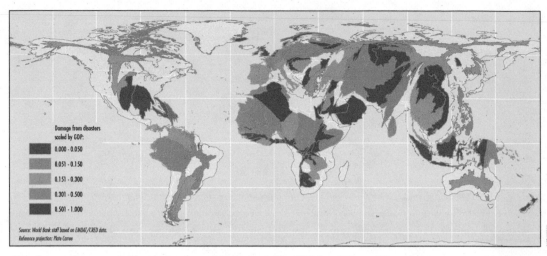

Note: Areas reflect cumulative damage from disasters scaled by GDP for 1970 to 2008.
Source: World Bank staff based on EM-DAT/CRED.

reduce national output to the same extent as in the affected area. Studies for this report find that national output always falls after a severe disaster, but (depending on the hazard) sometimes rises after a mild one. An earthquake reduces output, but subsequent reconstruction increases economic activity—though people are obviously worse off. Economic growth is output's rate of change, so even if output recovers only to its former level after falling, growth (for a brief period) would be higher than pre-disaster rates.

Output does not measure peoples' well-being, especially following a disaster. And not everyone is affected equally—even in the affected area. Farmers who have not lost their crops get higher prices if overall harvest were lower. So the indirect effects—especially in the area outside the disaster zone—are not all adverse.

Governments often assess the damage after a disaster, and such assessments differ in scope, purpose, and technique. The report discusses the conceptual and practical issues in measuring damage and the direct and indirect effects from a disaster. Measuring damage is tricky, prone to both overestimation (for example, double counting) and underestimation (it is difficult to value loss of life, or damage to the environment). Biases also affect the accuracy of estimates, especially when the prospect of aid affects incentives.

Accurate measurement is more likely when its purpose is clear, though some items of interest cannot be measured. Damage assessments have multiple and often overlapping purposes. They could guide government relief (such as how much to spend on alleviating the victims' suffering, knowing that other spending must be cut or taxes raised). They could show how to hasten economic recovery or identify specific measures to improve prevention. This report examines the conceptual and practical feasibility of meeting each purpose.

People do not wait for help to begin repairing their homes and rebuilding their lives, but the poor, with nothing to fall back on, may require help. The government often provides transfers in cash and kind, but "compensation" is a misnomer because the amounts (typically less than twice per capita GDP) are usually less than what people have lost. The government's fiscal situation limits these transfers because even if it could borrow, the debts must be later serviced. So, knowing the disaster's medium-term fiscal implications would be more useful than measuring the damage to private property. If relief and recovery spending displace maintenance of infrastructure, as they often do, the deaths and damage from future disasters would rise.

Recovery requires that commerce resume, and this involves restoring the affected area's links with the rest of the economy. It is in the self-interest of people and private firms up and down the supply chain to repair these links (banking, trucking)—but physical infrastructure (roads, bridges, railways) is often the government's responsibility. Assessing damage to public infrastructure is urgent, and governments must quickly decide what, where, and whether to rebuild. This decision will in turn affect individual decisions to rebuild. Who in government decides depends on the country's administrative structure, and the people affected are best placed to guide the choice of which road or bridge to repair first.

A disaster's effect on an economy's output, or on the government's budget, is not the same as its effect on people's health and well-being. A disaster undoubtedly reduces the well-being of those affected—and even if survivors recover and consume at their earlier levels, they will have suffered in the immediate aftermath.

Many studies have examined how disasters affect people in the short run, and this report complements those studies with others that find longer lasting adverse effects on schooling, cognitive abilities, and mental health. Some survivors are pushed over the edge and never completely recover: widespread droughts in Africa result in stunted and malnourished children, with permanent adverse effects. An effective safety net can reduce these consequences, but not every safety net is effective.

The literature has long noted that disasters and conflicts are connected. Hazards, particularly earthquakes and droughts, tend to prolong conflicts, but good institutions reduce the likelihood of their erupting. Such institutions are typically associated with democracy and good governance—factors also associated with prosperity. This report finds that the link is through political competition rather than voting alone. Do disasters increase scarcity and thus conflict? Or do they create an opportunity for peace, as in Aceh? Either is possible, and good institutions make the better outcome more likely.

Prevention by individuals

The analytical framework of prevention, insurance, and coping has proved useful in many settings, and the report is structured around these concepts, distinguishing individual choices and collective decisions (at different levels

Figure 7 Private preventive measures pay

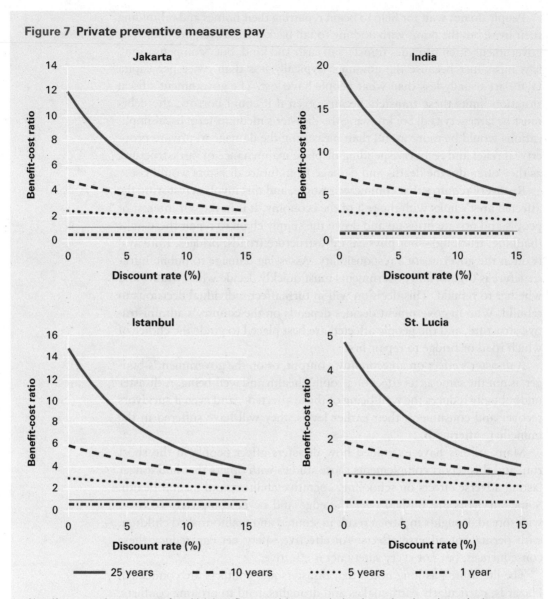

Note: Key prevention measures for which benefit-cost ratios were calculated are: elevating a house by 1 meter to reduce damage from floods (Jakarta); protecting windows and doors and upgrading roofs to prevent hurricane damage (Canaries and Patience, St. Lucia); retrofitting buildings to increase quake resiliency (Istanbul); and flood-proofing a brick house (Rohini River Basin, Uttar Pradesh, India).
Source: IIASA/RMS/Wharton 2009.

of government). People choose how much prevention to undertake (consciously or by default), how much insurance to purchase, and how much residual risk to bear through coping. Is individual prevention adequate and effective?

People undertake prevention to the point where expected benefits (avoiding losses) exceed the costs—subject to their budget constraint (figure 7).

But people differ and everyone chooses differently. Such differences do not necessarily imply that some choose badly, but it is reassuring when large numbers take prevention measures that seem well justified. Rates of returns for several commonly-used prevention measures—such as raising the plinth in flood-prone Jakarta, or protecting windows and doors against wind and rain damage in the Canary Islands—show that some measures are warranted but not all.

One person's choice may puzzle another: many live in exposed areas known to be hazardous—whether in poverty in Bangladesh or in affluence along the Florida coast. Recent theories and experimental findings show that people sometimes misperceive risks and may not always act in their own best interests. But there also are more prosaic explanations involving tradeoffs such as proximity to work and access to such conveniences as public transport, given limited budgets.

Living in riskier locations is cheaper for the individual and allows spending on other necessities (food, children's schooling), so the poor face difficult choices. Safer structures could be built in risky areas (on hill slopes, in seismic areas) with sufficient knowledge, care and expense. But when a person's ownership of property is not secure, the possibility of eviction or demolition erodes the incentive to invest in safe structures. A study of 1.2 million land titles distributed in 1996 in Peru finds that land titling is associated with a 68 percent increase in housing renovation within four years.

Insecurity of land holdings is not the only disincentive to build well: rent controls or other similar regulations erode a landlord's incentive to maintain buildings. The situation in Mumbai, India, where neglected buildings collapse in severe storms, killing occupants, is described in some detail. Mumbai has had rent controls and distorting taxes whose adverse effects have accumulated over decades. Buildings were restricted to being only a few stories tall, hindering agglomeration, and decaying industries occupy land that could be put to better use. Such policies also contribute to the dearth of good housing and to the poor living in unsafe shanty towns that mushroom in and around prospering cities. They have also starved cities of tax revenues, so the needed infrastructure is not built, or is built badly.

Structures are also shoddy because people do not always know the hazards they face or what it takes to build well. Detailed accounts from Italy, Pakistan, and Sri Lanka illustrate the challenge of improving building practices, the importance of information (about hazards and how to build better), and the limited role of building codes.

Calls for stronger building codes reverberate after a disaster, and stricter enforcement becomes the siren call. But there are few improvements if private owners and builders view these codes as yet another hurdle to overcome, or if officials are corrupt or complacent. Like any regulation, codes are also susceptible to capture by vested interests (California's first building code of 1933 sought to prevent the use of steel to protect the jobs of bricklayers, even though unreinforced brick structures are highly vulnerable in seismic areas). Codes work through "institutions," and are one cog in a complex system of inculcating better building practices. They are most effective when they contain accurate and accessible information about hazard risks and the properties of newer building materials, and when there are incentives to build sound structures (for example, private owners having clear title). Good building practices can be fostered even without a code, as the rebuilding after the 2005 earthquake in the remote and mountainous region of Pakistan shows.

Prevention through governments

Governments can help in effective prevention, but struggle to do so. It is difficult to measure *how much* governments spend on prevention because this is not a specific budget item. Detailed analysis in Colombia, Indonesia, Mexico, and Nepal found that prevention spending was less than post-disaster spending except in Colombia (figure 8). But this does not imply that it was "too little," for it is hard to isolate what constitutes prevention and even harder to determine adequate spending.

Effective prevention measures are often embedded in other spending (in such infrastructure as an embankment), and there are indications that reversing the past neglect of maintenance (painting bridges to reduce corrosion and subsequent failure) and investing in intangibles (tallying decrepit structures) has large benefits. So, why does it not happen, and who determines government spending? Some assert that politicians are short-sighted, but competition in the market for votes, like other competition, would generally provide what the public wants. In the United States, voters favor relief spending over prevention, leading some to conclude that voters (not politicians) either are myopic or misperceive hazard risks. The findings are equally consistent with far-sighted voters being skeptical (perhaps justifiably) of politicians' ability to organize prevention effectively.

The challenge for governments is to translate spending into effective prevention, and cost-benefit analysis is a useful tool—but one that must be used with care. The benefits of prevention are understated if human lives are not valued, but attaching a value to life has enormous moral and ethical implications. Most government spending, especially on prevention, has distributional implications: a dam protects one group but may increase the flood risk of another. Cost-benefit analysis attaches implicit weights—and while these could be explicitly changed, officials lack the moral authority to decide unilaterally. Such decisions require a political consensus that countries with good institutions possess.

Cost-benefit analysis is a filter that can rank alternatives, not a scoop that can generate options. Prosperous countries have better prevention because they also have good institutions that oversee government decisions. Such oversight cannot be only through legislative bodies. And broader involvement requires the government to fully disclose what it knows and does—transparency not just about a decision but the entire process—and to encourage (not just grudgingly tolerate) dissenting views.

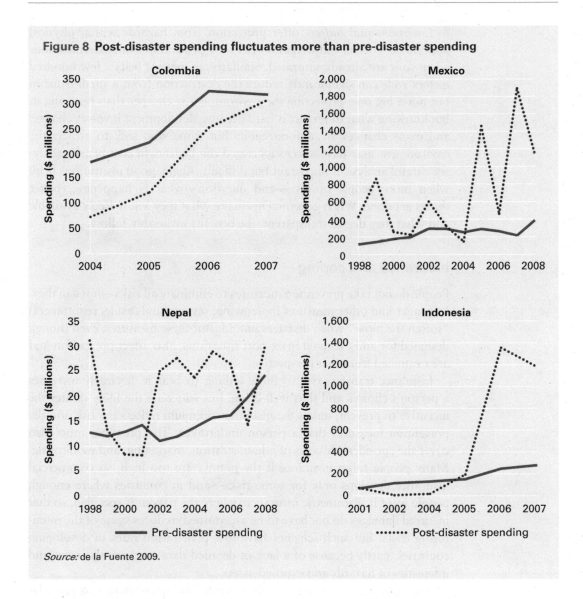

Figure 8 Post-disaster spending fluctuates more than pre-disaster spending

Colombia

Mexico

Nepal

Indonesia

——— Pre-disaster spending   •••••••• Post-disaster spending

Source: de la Fuente 2009.

The report identifies three specific spending items desirable for prevention. *An early warning system* can save lives and property. There have been many advances in weather prediction technologies, but few countries have taken full advantage of that. The report outlines these technological developments and how a modest but well allocated increase in spending—and sharing real-time data internationally—would benefit countries.

Critical infrastructure that functions during and after a disaster reduces the loss of life and property. While all infrastructure must be well designed, constructed, and maintained, designating a subset as "critical" allows the government to pay special attention to it. What is critical depends on the situation and the hazard. Critical is not synonymous with the importance of some infrastructure in normal times: the choice requires informed judgment.

Environmental buffers offer protection from hazards within physical limitations. Forests and wetlands offer little protection from extreme floods when soils are already saturated. Similarly, mangrove belts a few hundred meters wide can significantly reduce the destruction from a small tsunami but not a big one. Protecting the environment is cheaper than restoring it, but knowing what to protect is hard because development involves change, and many changes are unforeseeable. But some who seek to protect the environment may have also exaggerated the benefits in cost-benefit analysis: careful analysis is important but difficult. Again, good institutions help: when more people observe—and question—what is happening, better things get done. When governments make what they know freely available and what they decide transparent, the benefits invariably follow.

Insurance and coping

People do not take prevention measures to eliminate all risks—nor can they. Insurance and other measures (borrowing, setting funds aside, remittances) "soften the blow" when disasters unfold. But these measures, even though designed for and executed in ex-post situations, also affect prevention and are examined from that perspective.

Insurance transfers risk to those willing to bear it. It clearly increases a person's choices and thus well-being, but softening the blow dilutes the incentive to prevent, unless the insurance premium reflects the risk and the prevention measures that a person undertakes. The premium must also cover the considerable costs of administration, marketing, and monitoring. Many people forgo insurance if the premia are too high, so commercial insurance develops only for some risks—and in countries where enough people want it. Parametric insurance (where the payout is specified, so that incurred damages do not have to be ascertained) reduces some of the monitoring costs. But such schemes have low penetration rates in developing countries, partly because of a lack of detailed data on the frequencies and intensities of hazards and exposed assets.

Insurance invariably draws in the government—as regulator, as provider (in many countries), or as reinsurer—inevitably adding a political dimension. This often results in attempts to lower the premia through subsidies (as with flood insurance in the United States), or, conversely, to favor insurers by keeping premia high or keeping out competition. An inappropriate premium has adverse effects that are difficult to rectify later: too low a premium encourages construction in hazard-prone areas (vacation homes in Florida).

Whether governments should buy insurance against disasters is not as clear-cut as it may seem: the alternatives are to set funds aside in reserve or to borrow so that they have funds to spend after a disaster. Many governments are already indebted, and even those with low debts may find it difficult to borrow when they most need to. While individuals are risk-averse, there are good reasons for some governments acting on their behalf to be risk-neutral. A risk-neutral entity would buy insurance only if the premium were lower than the probability times the expected loss (which leaves nothing to cover the insurer's costs). This argues against governments buying commercial insurance. But a disaster that is large relative to their economy's size (as in the Caribbean, where the main unknown is the island that gets hit) may make some governments risk-averse, and insurance could be beneficial.

The Caribbean Catastrophe Risk Insurance Facility, which pools disaster risks regionally, helps countries in such circumstances purchase insurance less expensively than otherwise. Prices that insurance firms offer may differ from prices in capital markets, and such price comparisons can produce large savings, as Mexico found when issuing catastrophe bonds. The World Bank's Catastrophe Risk Deferred Drawdown Option is a loan that disburses quickly, to provide immediate liquidity if and when the borrowing government declares an emergency.

What cannot be prevented or insured against must be borne, and a variety of coping mechanisms ("informal insurance," as distinct from market insurance) have developed over the centuries, many embedded in tradition and custom. Private individuals and groups abroad send remittances directly to those they know, and such remittances surge after a disaster, even when there is no media coverage. The funds arrive quickly to help people cope.

While remittances are routinely spent on consumer durables, some improve the quality of housing. Houses made sturdier could be considered a prevention measure, though the situation varies. In Turkey, 13 years after the 1970 Gediz earthquake, the reconstructed area was peppered with improperly reinforced concrete houses—mostly paid for by the earnings of family members in Germany. Better building practices are needed to ensure safe buildings. But not all who need help receive remittances, and there are sometimes impediments to such flows that the government could remove (controls on capital flows, dual exchange rates). Private remittances also help develop banking and money transfer facilities that strengthen an area's commercial ties with other parts of the country and the world.

Aid also has a role in prevention, but it can be double-edged: while some aid is warranted, it can also give rise to the Samaritan's dilemma. Some observers have noted the disincentives donor programs can create—they can, for example, erase a country's incentive to provide its own safety nets. Nicaragua declined to pursue a weather indexing program after it had been priced in the global reinsurance market: it cited international assistance following Hurricane Mitch in 1998 as an indication of dependable alternatives. Some new but not very strong evidence suggests that post-disaster aid reduces prevention. It may be unfair, though, to blame only countries for neglecting prevention: Mozambique, anticipating major floods in 2002, asked donors for $2.7 million to prepare and got only half the amount, but $100 million were received in emergency assistance following the floods, with another $450 million pledged for rehabilitation and reconstruction.

Vibrant communities, however, use aid well. The main lesson for donors is to be aware of the potentially adverse effects of their actions. Governments in recipient countries can do much to prevent waste that may result from a sudden flow of uncoordinated aid or from inappropriate aid in kind.

Game-changers? Burgeoning cities, climate change, and climate-related catastrophes

That urban areas and population will grow is certain; but which cities will grow, and how fast, is less predictable. Most growing cities are in developing countries, and growth increases exposure to hazards (map 3).

The growing density of people and economic activity will change the economics of effective prevention. But greater exposure need not increase vulnerability if cities are well managed.

Climate change complicates this further. The scientific models to forecast weather do not allow confident projections at the local level, but the intensity, frequency, and distribution of hazards will change with the climate. The expected annual damage from climate-change induced tropical cyclones alone could be in the $28 billion to $68 billion range. These estimates, sensitive to various parameters and assumptions about the future, are in "expected value" terms per year. But the damages are not expected to come in a steady stream. Climate change is expected to skew the damage distribution of tropical cyclones and is likely to cause rare—but very powerful—tropical cyclones to become more common. This report finds that for the United States, destructive storms that would come every 38

Map 3 Exposure to cyclones and earthquakes in large cities may rise from 680 million people in 2000 to 1.5 billion people by 2050

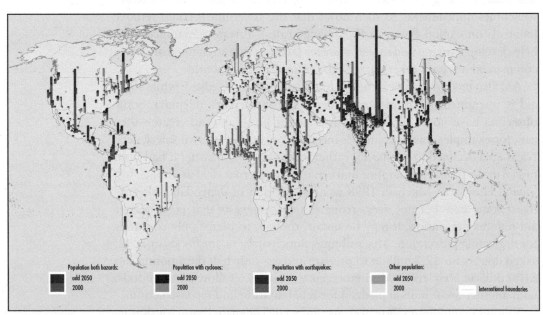

Source: Brecht and others 2010.

Figure 9 Climate change shortens the return period of large storms

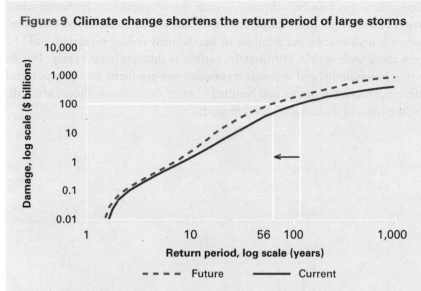

Note: The figure shows the return period for tropical cyclones of different intensity in the United States for one specific climate model (MIROC). A $100 billion storm is estimated to happen once in a 100 years in the United States given the current climate. With a future warmed climate, it is expected to happen once in about 56 years.
Source: Mendelsohn, Emanuel, and Chonabayashi 2010a.

to 480 years given the current climate, would come every 18 to 89 years with future climate change. Climate change "fattens the tail" of the tropical cyclone damage distribution (figure 9). Even though very rare and damaging storms are part of today's climate, they will become more frequent in a warmer climate.

Scientists have identified several catastrophes that a changing climate might trigger: drastic sea level rise, disruption of ocean currents, large-scale disruptions to the global ecosystem, and accelerated climate change, for example, from large releases of methane now trapped by permafrost. Catastrophic risks and costs need to be weighed differently than less severe events. Prudence in responding to catastrophic threats calls for a portfolio of measures that emphasizes learning and mid-course corrections. A broad portfolio is desirable because the potential effectiveness of individual measures is uncertain.

Cities, climate, and pending catastrophes are altering the disaster prevention landscape. While hazards will always be with us, disasters show that something has failed. But determining what has failed and deciding on the corrective measures are not always obvious. And arguing whether Hurricane Katrina or Cyclone Nargis occurred as a result of climate change detracts attention from policies that continue to misprice risk, subsidize exposure, reduce individuals' incentives to reduce risk, and promote risky behavior in the long run.

People rise out of poverty through better technology, greater market access, and more investment in activities that spill benefits from one set of economic actors to others through greater interdependence, higher productivity, and stronger institutions. Living in cities facing serious risks of inundation is undesirable, but a failure to significantly reduce poverty would be even more undesirable. Fortunately, neither is inherently necessary. People acting individually and through responsive governments can prosper and survive. Progress requires and results in better institutions: those, after all, are the basis of sustainable development.

CHAPTER 1

Fluctuating Deaths, Rising Damages—the Numbers

Earthquakes, storms, and other hazards killed about 3.3 million people between 1970 and 2010, an annual average of 82,500 deaths worldwide in a typical year, a small fraction of the roughly 60 million who die every year and of the 1.27 million killed in traffic accidents alone (WHO 2009). Disasters kill many simultaneously and affect many more but evoke more attention than the numbers warrant. For example, for every person who dies in an earthquake, more than 19,000 people must die of food shortage to receive the same expected media coverage, all else equal (Eisensee and Strömberg 2007). That the attention comes from sensational media coverage ("sell newspapers") is a circular explanation. Psychologists, sociologists, anthropologists, and others offer different explanations for our emotions: how one dies matters, and our reactions differ whether a person drowns while fishing for a living, surfing for fun, or in a flood that washes a home away.

Our emotional reaction may be accentuated by a perceived lack of control over the event (Acts of God). But natural disasters, despite the adjective, are not "natural." Although no single person or action may be to blame, death and destruction result from human acts of omission—not tying down the rafters allows a hurricane to blow away the roof—and commission—building in flood-prone areas. Those acts could be prevented, often at little additional expense.

This report is about prevention—measures that reduce the risk of death, injury, and damage from disasters—and how to ensure it cost-effectively. Post-mortems of disasters often find that much of the death and destruction could have been averted fairly inexpensively, but this is misleading. Consider $2 billion in damage from a disaster that could have been prevented by measures costing "only" $20 million annually. If the hazard occurs only once in 200 years, the expected annual loss is $10 million (= $2,000,000,000 ×

Box 1.1 The framework for the report

Disasters occur when households and assets are both exposed and vulnerable to natural hazards. Preventing disasters thus means undertaking measures that reduce exposure and vulnerability to contain deaths and damages. Not all disasters can be prevented however, and impacts depend on how individuals and governments react and cope.

Box figure 1.1. The framework for the report

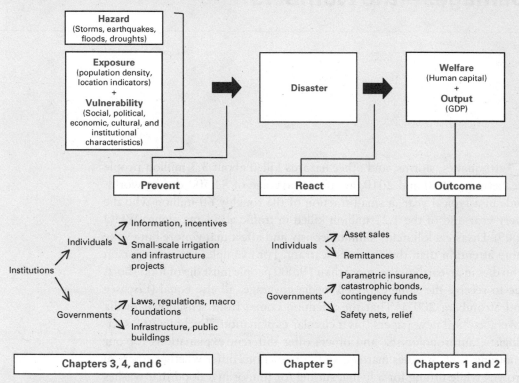

Chapter 1 describes the distribution of damages and deaths from natural disasters by type of hazard and countries, and what this may imply. Chapter 2 looks at the effects of disasters on welfare, and on economic aggregate output and government finances, and how these are measured. Chapter 3 presents a simple framework to understand how individuals manage risk. Chapter 4 starts with a discussion of disaster spending priorities and who determines them. Various collective preventive measures are then discussed (early warning systems, protecting critical infrastructure, and environmental buffers). But people cope, and how they do and the role of insurance and aid flows are covered in chapter 5. Exposure, vulnerability, and hazard patterns change over time, and chapter 6 provides some perspective on the future in the context of urbanizing cities and a changing climate.

Source: World Bank staff.

1/200), and the $20 million on prevention could be better spent elsewhere. Prevention is economical in this numerical example only if the event were more frequent, the damage greater, or the prevention cheaper.

Prevention measures differ in cost and effectiveness. A person can undertake some unilaterally, such as building a house on a higher plinth—and others collectively, such as building an embankment. Some individual measures

Box 1.2 Understanding the terms in the report

The terms in this report are used differently across disciplines.

Hazard is a natural process or phenomenon (floods, storms, droughts, earthquakes) with adverse effects on life, limb, or property. Hazards differ in severity, scale, and frequency and are often classified by cause (such as hydro-meteorological or geological).

Exposure is the people and property subject to the hazard.

Vulnerability is a characteristic that influences damage: some communities absorb and recover more readily than others because of *physical assets* (building design and strength), *social capital* (community structure, trust, and family networks), and *political access* (ability to get government help and affect policies and decisions). Measures to reduce vulnerability include *mitigation* (which reduces the hazard's likelihood, as in reforesting the slopes to prevent rapid runoff and floods or reducing greenhouse gas emissions to reduce the frequency and intensity of extreme weather events), *prevention* (measures to reduce damage, as with higher plinths for floods), *preparedness* (evacuation plans), and *relief* (help after a disaster).

Disaster is the hazard's effect on society as a result of the combination of *exposure* and *vulnerability*. So strictly, disasters, not hazards, cause deaths and damage.

Disaster risk is often calculated as a multiplicative function of *hazard*, *exposure*, and *vulnerability*. It is multiplicative because for disaster risk to exist, all three—hazard, exposure, and vulnerability—have to be present.

Deaths are readily counted, but *injuries* require some judgment about their seriousness. Those with broken limbs are included, but what about those with mere scratches—or major mental depression—that go untreated? Differences in criteria, and how data are gathered in practice, make comparisons across countries (and time) difficult. The numbers of *affected persons* (injured, homeless, and in need of immediate assistance) often measure the scale of the disaster; but adding the homeless to those whose farmland was temporarily flooded implicitly accords each equal importance.

Note: For formal definitions, please see http://www.unisdr.org/eng/terminology/terminology-2009-eng.html.
Source: World Bank staff.

substitute for the collective (a house on stilts instead of flood embankments) and others are complements (cholera may increase during floods, but installing a septic tank is pointless if others do not). What people do affects others: those behind an embankment, for example, are protected from floods, but the redirected waters could increase damage elsewhere. And even those behind the embankment would incur greater damage if there were a breach; so embankments lower the risk of modest damage and increase the (low) risk of severe damage. These complexities are examined in later chapters. This chapter simply presents the related data and patterns (box 1.1).

Some reports on disasters have noted a rising toll that has set off alarms with calls for action. While some actions may be appropriate, it is important to know how the numbers are collected and analyzed and what they may imply. (Box 1.2 explains the terminology and box 1.3 discusses the various data this report uses.)

Box 1.3 Global natural hazard databases: Varied purposes, varying details

The three main global sources for data are EM-DAT, NatCat, and Sigma. EM-DAT is the acronym for data that the Center for Research on the Epidemiology of Disasters (CRED) has been collecting by country since 1988 (going back to 1900). CRED collects data on deaths, injuries, and damage from news accounts and other (unspecified) sources for earthquakes, hurricanes, floods, and other disasters that killed 10 or more people, affected at least 100, or resulted in a "state of emergency" or a call for international assistance. Other databases are by event, not country, with different inclusion criteria (and so are not strictly comparable). Munich Reinsurance Company maintains NatCat, and Swiss Reinsurance Company (Zürich Re) maintains Sigma (fewer events but includes both insured and uninsured damages).

For 1988–2002, EM-DAT reports 756 million people affected, NatCat reports 277 million, and Sigma 19 million (Guha-Sapir 2002). All these databases have differing levels of detail and have their own strengths and weaknesses.[1]

Larger numbers do not necessarily attest to more comprehensive data because there are, sometimes, exaggerated reports of mortality; and insurers ignore countries with few commercial prospects. An example cited in box 2.3 of the UN 2009 Global Assessment Report on Disaster Risk Reduction is the 1999 landslides in Venezuela. World Bank reports put fatalities at 50,000; EM-DAT at 30,000; but Universidad Central de Venezuela anthropologist Rogelio Altez, who carefully examined detailed death records in each state, concluded that fewer than 700 died (Altez 2007).

CRED's data (EM-DAT) is the only publicly available global disaster database. It is used to portray trends in this chapter, and for some cross-country empirical analyses in other parts of the report.

EM-DAT records disasters (a disaster triggers the inclusion into the hazard category; for example, earthquakes in uninhabited areas are not recorded), and trends related to these records are analyzed and shown further in this chapter for the 40 years between 1970 and 2010. For presentational purposes, disasters are divided into five hazard categories: droughts, earthquakes (which also include tsunamis, volcanoes and dry mass landslides), extreme temperatures (heat and cold waves), floods (which include wet mass landslides caused by rains), and storms (including cyclones and typhoons).

Source: World Bank staff.

3.3 million deaths in the 40 years to 2010

Some 3.3 million people died between 1970 and 2010, and the deaths fluctuate considerably: some years with many deaths punctuate several years with few deaths (figure 1.1). Some short spans suggest a trend (1973 to 1975, or 1993 to 2005), but statistical tests attach a low confidence level for an overall upward trend.[2] The absence of a pronounced upward trend in mortality when population and exposure (those living in the hazard prone areas) have risen dramatically suggests that some prevention measures have likely been effective.

More people were affected in the two recent decades than earlier. This increase may reflect greater exposure to hazards, or better reporting in recent years, or both. Half the world's people now live in cities up from 30 percent in 1950, and most large and rapidly growing cities in poor countries struggle to provide public services, including disaster prevention. Individuals build shacks in the flood plain or on steep hillsides vulnerable to hazards, an issue examined in greater depth in chapter 3.

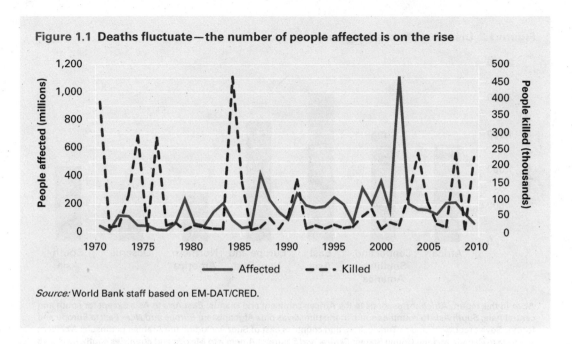

Figure 1.1 Deaths fluctuate—the number of people affected is on the rise

Source: World Bank staff based on EM-DAT/CRED.

Disasters can strike anywhere

Disasters affect all regions (figure 1.2). Floods and storms are the most common, while droughts much less so (except in Africa) (figure 1.3).[3] Deaths are more concentrated: droughts in Africa are the deadliest; storms in East and South Asia also take many lives (figure 1.4).

Differences across countries suggest that some countries prevent disasters better than others. The contrast in the death toll in Haiti and the Dominican Republic, sharing the same island and storms, underscores the point that disasters are manmade, not natural. We are capable of reducing the death toll even in poor countries: moving food averts a famine despite droughts; early warning systems reduce deaths caused by storms and floods. Clearly, more can be done to reduce deaths, but property cannot flee from an imminent hazard, so we turn to damage.

Damages are rising

The annual global damage from disasters between 1970 and 2010—adjusted for inflation—fluctuates like deaths but is also rising in spurts.[4] Damage in the recent two decades is significantly greater than in the earlier decades (figure 1.5). This could reflect greater exposure, or better reporting, or both. Most of the damage is from storms, earthquakes, and floods—in that order.

More so in rich countries, less in poor

Rich countries (North America, Europe, and increasingly Asia) incur greater absolute damage (though not relative to GDP). The damage is least in Africa,

Figure 1.2 Disasters affect all regions

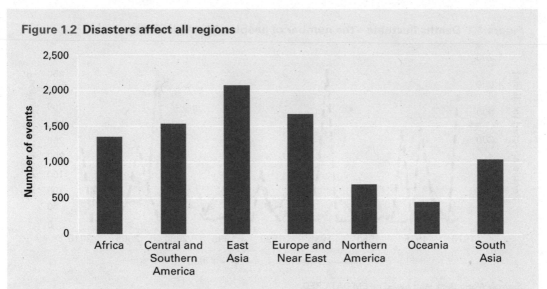

Note: In this report, *Africa* corresponds to the African continent and islands; *East Asia* to Asia except for south and central Asia; *South Asia* to countries south of the Himalayas plus Afghanistan; *Europe and Near East* to Europe and former Soviet republics, and to Turkey, Iran, and countries east of Suez, including the Arabian peninsula; *Northern America* to Canada and the United States; *Central and Southern America* to Mexico and countries south, including the Caribbean; and *Oceania* to Australia, New Zealand, and the Pacific islands. Countries are grouped by continent and shared seismic characteristics and other common hazard characteristics. Number of events by region, 1970–2010 (February).
Source: World Bank staff based on EM-DAT/CRED.

Figure 1.3 Disasters almost everywhere (1970–2010)

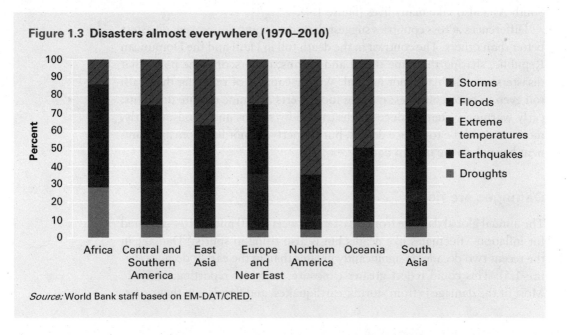

Source: World Bank staff based on EM-DAT/CRED.

where the poor possess little (figure 1.6). Earthquakes and storms are the most destructive, again not surprising because they affect valuable structures, often in richer countries.[5]

Figure 1.4 Droughts deadliest in Africa, earthquakes elsewhere

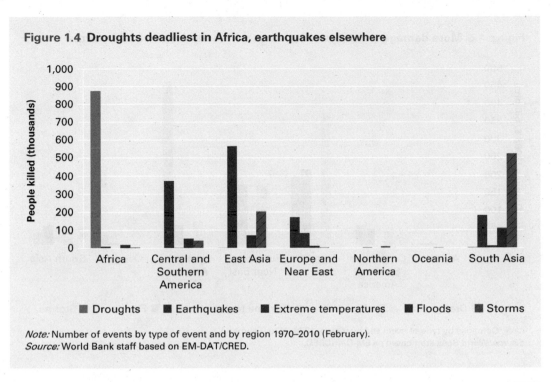

Note: Number of events by type of event and by region 1970–2010 (February).
Source: World Bank staff based on EM-DAT/CRED.

Figure 1.5 Damage on the rise in the last two decades (global damage from hazards, 1970–2010)

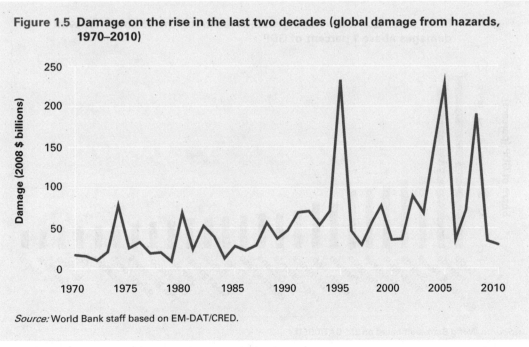

Source: World Bank staff based on EM-DAT/CRED.

Small island economies are hit hard

Because absolute damage is larger in rich countries (with more assets), the numbers are often scaled by GDP (a flow, though damage is of the asset stock) to allow comparisons among countries. That disasters have a higher

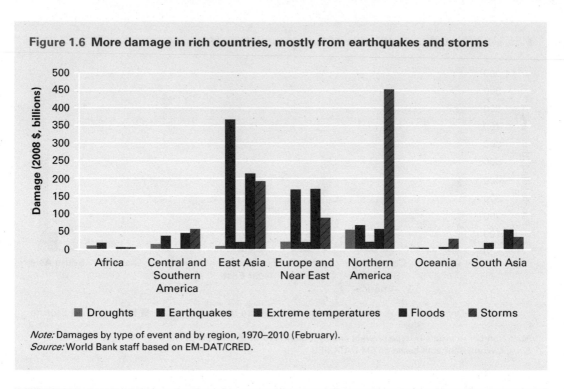

Figure 1.6 More damage in rich countries, mostly from earthquakes and storms

Note: Damages by type of event and by region, 1970–2010 (February).
Source: World Bank staff based on EM-DAT/CRED.

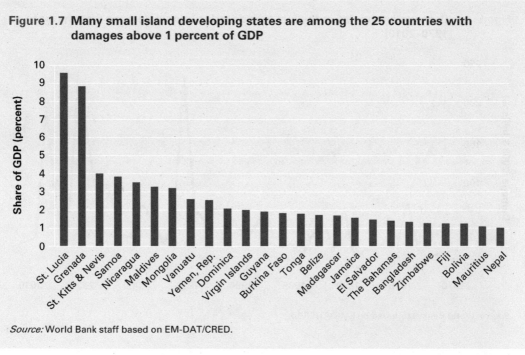

Figure 1.7 Many small island developing states are among the 25 countries with damages above 1 percent of GDP

Source: World Bank staff based on EM-DAT/CRED.

cumulative impact on small economies is already known, but this exercise quantifies that impact more accurately.[6] Many of the 25 countries with damages more than 1 percent of GDP (in a sample of 175 countries) are small island economies (figure 1.7). Even a single event can adversely affect the economy of a small, vulnerable country. And even though damage is less than 1 percent of GDP for 86 percent of countries, a country's GDP is irrelevant to the victims who may lose all they possess. A high ratio of cumulative damage to GDP suggests when help from international donors could be useful, but most are "repeaters" that need prevention more than relief.

Deaths expand Africa—damages shrink it

Some countries are barely recognizable when a map's areas reflect deaths (map 1.1). Africa looms as large as Asia, and the Americas shrink (the north to almost nothing). And when those areas reflect damages, Africa shrinks and middle-income countries expand (map 1.2).

Map 1.1 Deaths shrink Asia and the Americas—but expand Africa

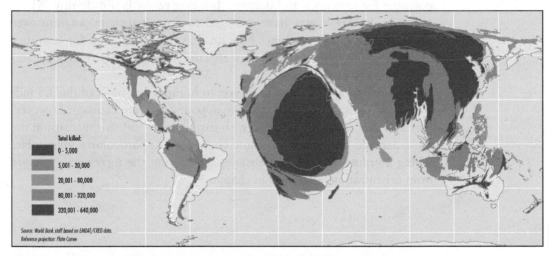

Note: Areas reflect cumulative deaths from disasters for 1970 to 2010 (February).
Source: World Bank staff based on EM-DAT/CRED.

Map 1.2 Damages shrink Africa but expand middle-income countries

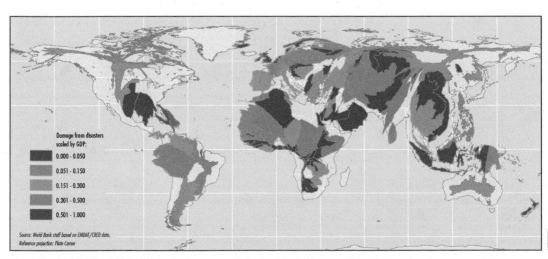

Note: Areas reflect cumulative damage from disasters scaled by GDP for 1970 to 2008.
Source: World Bank staff based on EM-DAT/CRED.

Multiple hazards, clustering in different ways

Each hazard afflicts countries differently, but many countries are subject to multiple hazards, though the importance of each differs. Earthquakes and volcanoes (geophysical hazards) tend to cluster along fault boundaries characterized by mountainous terrain. Floods, cyclones, and landslides (hydrometeorological hazards) affect the eastern coastal regions of the major continents as well as some interior regions of North and South America, Europe, and Asia. Drought is more widely dispersed across the semiarid tropics.

Areas subject to hazards fall primarily in East and South Asia and in Central America and western South America (map 1.3). Many of them are also more densely populated and developed than average, leading to high potential for casualties and damage. But geography is not destiny. Many countries in harm's way have managed to protect their population over time, and this report examines how this has happened. And for countries that have not dealt with disasters effectively, this report asks why and explores ways for doing so.

Rich and poor countries are subject to hazards, but most of the 3.3 million deaths over the last 40 years were in poor countries. Damage, however, may be rising in absolute terms, with earthquakes and storms causing the most damage. And middle-income countries are particularly vulnerable. Rising absolute damage is plausible, considering the increased exposure from urbanization (examined in chapter 6).

Map 1.3 Where hazards have struck

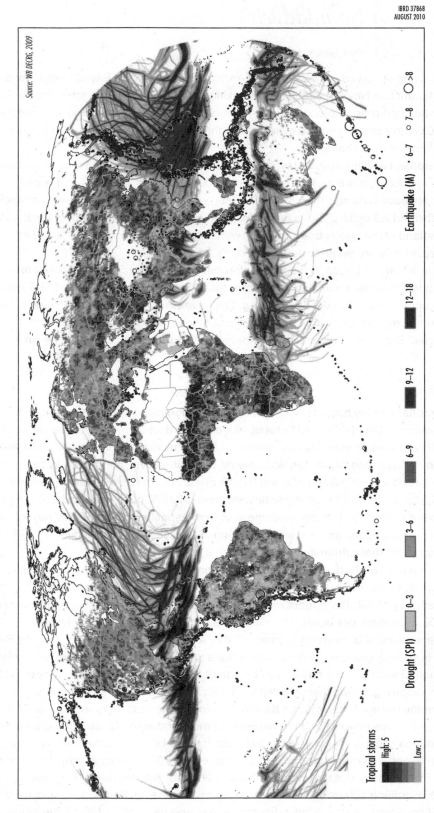

Source: WB DECRG, 2009

IBRD 37868
AUGUST 2010

Tropical storms
High: 5
Low: 1

Drought (SPI)
0–3   3–6   6–9   9–12   12–18

Earthquake (M)
· 6–7   ○ 7–8   ○ >8

Source: World Bank staff. Earthquakes above magnitude 6 on the Richter scale for 1950 to February 2010 (from Northern California Earthquake Data Center, www.ncedc.org); tropical storm tracks for 1975–2007; droughts based on standardized precipitation index (SPI, larger values indicate a higher probability of precipitation deficits) compiled for the Global Assessment Report 2009 (from www.preventionweb.net/english/hyogo/gar).

Spotlight 1 on Bangladesh

The Antecedents of Lives Saved

Cyclone Sidr was first observed southwest of the Andaman Islands in the Bay of Bengal six days before it made landfall on November 15, 2007. Tracking its path and growing strength, the Bangladesh authorities had time to prepare a well-rehearsed response: they issued warnings and activated 44,000 volunteers who helped evacuate roughly 3 million people from their homes and accommodate 1.5 million in shelters.

Few were surprised and unprotected when Sidr hit, but its immense force was devastating. The category 4 cyclone (5 is the most severe) with a 1,000 kilometer diameter and winds up to 240 kilometers an hour whipped up 5.5 to 6.0 meter waves that surged over embankments designed to withstand 2.5 meters. Sidr's forces were moderated when passing over the Sundarbans, a large wetland of mangrove trees, but such wetlands have diminished over the years, and vast unprotected areas were severely damaged.

Rescue and relief efforts began immediately after the cyclone abated. The 12 worst affected districts, though less densely populated and poorer than the national average, had 18.7 million people: 55,000 injured, and 4,400 dead or missing. The government estimated that assets worth $1.16 billion were damaged, almost all in housing and other infrastructure. Losses of $517 million were expected. But it could have been far worse if the country had not learned from earlier tragedies.

Endemic hazards

Bangladesh is prone to many hazards (spotlight map 1). Cyclones are frequent and occur before and after the monsoons (April–May and October–November are when most cyclones occur): 508 formed in the Bay of Bengal over the past century, 17 percent making landfall in Bangladesh, others in adjoining India and Myanmar, and several dissipated over the ocean. In November 1970, a cyclone killed over 300,000 people and fed the discontent that led to Bangladesh's separating from Pakistan in 1971. The parliamentary elections of 1970 gave East Pakistan's Awami League an absolute majority, but the outcome was not respected. The political turmoil and street protests complicated the government's handling of the cyclone, and the disaster added to the growing discontent that culminated in Bangladesh's independence.

Cyclones are not the only hazard: there are also frequent floods, infrequent earthquakes, occasional droughts (19 between 1960 and 1991 and a severe one in July 1983 that affected 20 million), and tornados (in April, the hottest month, and *kal-baishakhi* pre-monsoon storms, with winds up to 100 kilometers per hour). The Himalayas are rising and seismically active as the Indian subcontinental plate is thrust under that of Tibet. A major earthquake (over 7 on the Richter scale) is a 1 in 50 year event in Bangladesh; but there is little awareness and few precautions. The 1947 partition of India and the further subdivision of Pakistan in 1971 left Bangladesh with a single seismic monitoring station that detected the 4.2 Richter scale tremors in February 2001 but could not determine the epicenter without data from neighboring India to help triangulate it.

Spotlight map 1 shows where the three hazards are most prevalent. Most of Bangladesh is a flood plain, and high ground is scarce in the flat delta formed by three heavily silt-laden rivers (Ganges, Meghna, and Brahmaputra) that split into more than 700 waterways emptying into the Bay of Bengal. Eighty percent of the waters arrive in a few months: the rivers' combined catchment area of 1.76 million square kilometers is 12 times the size of Bangladesh and includes much of the subcontinent (northern India, Bhutan, Nepal, and parts of China). Of the inflow, 95

Spotlight map 1 Bangladesh is prone to disasters

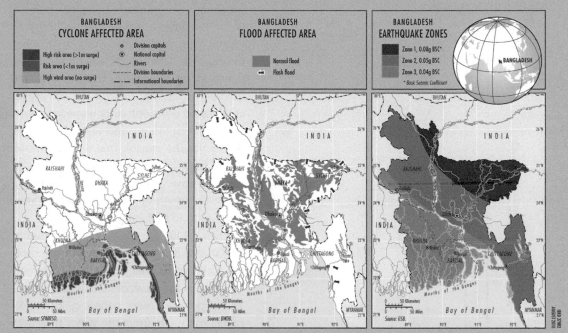

Source: Bangladesh Space Research and Remote Sensing Organization, Bangladesh Water Development Board, Geological Survey of Bangladesh.

percent (844 billion cubic meters) is between May and October, and more than 80 percent of the rain falls between June and September. Unlike violent cyclones, flood waters rise slowly but inexorably and turn deadly only when everything is submerged. Even if people survive by clinging to trees and rooftops, they may later starve if their livestock drown; so men often stay back with their cattle and evacuate reluctantly. This habit serves people poorly in coastal districts where sudden storm surges wash away those who do not heed the warnings to evacuate.

Traditional adaptation

Why has this hazard-prone delta been populated for centuries? Because the settling silt makes the land very fertile. People grew rice and jute, accommodating the river's seasonal rhythm. Long-stalked rice varieties that survive the post-monsoon floods beginning in June constitute the aman crop. The aus crop is planted in the premonsoon months of March and April and harvested during July and August. And the boro crop is planted in the dry season and harvested in March-April (later for high-yielding varieties).

Farmers choose rice varieties best suited to their local area's rainfall and flood patterns, and build their houses (plinth heights) as safely as their budgets and technology permit. The 1947 partition put some jute mills in India, and the movement of goods and people across the border largely stopped: jute's importance continued to decline as synthetic fibers replaced it, and rice remains the main crop.

Prevention: Expensive embankments . . .

The 1970s and 1980s were deadly (spotlight figure 1). Various flood abatement schemes were proposed: the Master Plan of 1964 called for massive embankments preferred by the engineers

Spotlight figure 1 Mortality from floods and storms in Bangladesh

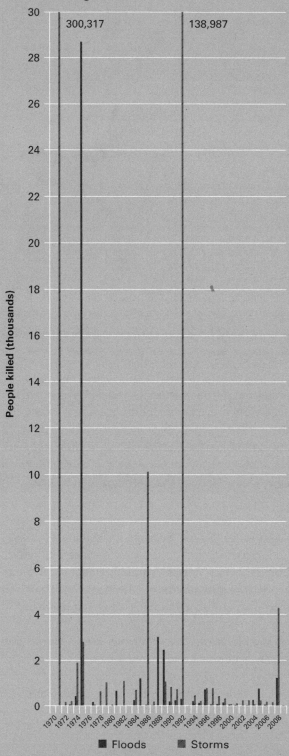

Floods   Storms

Source: World Bank staff.

in the Water Development Board. The proposals languished because donors (who became important after Bangladesh's independence) were split over their choice. The World Bank financed the construction of some embankments, but its 1971 Land and Water Study urged small scale developments, especially low lift pumps to tap ground water for irrigation in the dry season that allowed more of the high-yielding short-stem rice varieties to grow. The government restricted the use of tube wells when the water table was found to be falling.

Over 5,700 kilometers of embankments (3,400 in coastal areas), 1,700 flood control/regulating structures, and 4,300 kilometers of drainage canals were built over 30 years. The experience was sobering. Embankments merely redirect the water flow and are effective only when they are well located, designed, constructed, and maintained—but many were not. The resulting breaches rendered the entire embankment ineffective, and some farmers, seeking to protect their crops and fields, also created some breaches intentionally. The farmers often were neither consulted when the embankments were built nor compensated when their more vulnerable fields flooded. Embankments act as dams impeding the flood waters from draining rapidly, and protracted immersion increases damage to standing crops.

Local authorities had also built some embankments, ignoring the larger delta's hydrology. But rivers change course, often with little warning, as silt scours their banks. During the 1966 flood season, the river moved 1,500 meters (almost 1 mile) laterally downstream from Faridpur, digging a new 30-meter-deep channel. This shifting river course confounds land ownership and increases fatalities from floods when farmers stay put to preserve their land claims.

The 1988 floods were not particularly deadly—although they claimed 2,440 lives that year—but they affected Dhaka, the capital, galvanizing the government (and donors) into action. The 1989 Flood Action Plan dusted off the 1964 proposals for embankments along the entire length of the river, but donors balked at the staggering cost, prompting additional studies. Millions living between the river and the planned embankments would remain exposed. Resettlement was impossible: many were fishermen needing ready access to the river, and these unprotected farmers and fishermen found advocates at home and abroad to voice their concerns.

. . . to cost-effective measures

As doubts over the embankments' merits grew, there was a thoughtful search for better alternatives that took account of the delta's complex hydrology and agronomy. The World Bank 1971 study's benefits of underground aquifers for drinking (reduced water-borne diseases) and irrigation began to be appreciated.

The 1987 National Water Plan had estimated underground aquifers' capacity at 69 billion cubic meters, but a more careful estimate in 1991 raised it to 78 billion. The declining water table was found to be localized around Dhaka, which drew water from wells for its growing city population; so restrictions on drilling for irrigation were lifted elsewhere. Tube wells proliferated, especially after private agricultural investment was deregulated and import tariffs (on pumps and the like) were lowered.

Agriculture was transformed: low-yielding varieties in the *aus* and *aman* cultivation gave way to high-yielding (irrigated) varieties that rose from 14 percent higher yield in 1973 to 54 percent higher yield by 1993. But there were also unexpected setbacks. In some areas, tubewells led to arsenic poisoning when the substrate's naturally occurring minerals leached into the water. A remedial program to test and treat potable water was begun. But the merits of groundwater use and agriculture's reduced vulnerability were apparent after the severe 1998 floods: rice harvests that were expected to fall by 11 percent actually rose by 5.6 percent.

After the 1970 cyclone and independence, and building on the early cyclone shelter construction that started in the late 1960s, the government, in partnership with the Bangladesh Red Crescent Society, established the Cyclone Preparedness Program in 1972. Working with local communities, a system appropriate to the area was developed to transmit hazard warnings—radio broadcasts complemented by flags of various colors, hoisted for all to see. People were taught what they signified, and what to do. Cyclone shelters began to go up in the late 1960s, and the livestock refuges in the early 1970s. But after 138,000 people died in the April 1991 eastern coastal zone cyclone, the Multipurpose Cyclone Shelter Project began to increase the number of shelters. Each district's deputy commissioner chaired a disaster management committee that included local representatives, both elected and from nongovernmental organizations (NGOs).

The May 1997 cyclone, of similar magnitude, claimed 111 lives—far fewer than the cyclone in 1970. But a cyclone's severity is not the only determinant of fatalities, just as lives saved are not automatically the result of shelters built. Other factors matter. In 1970, large numbers of migrant workers were in the area for the harvest, and the 1997 cyclone struck the less densely populated hilly districts of Chittagong. How many people are exposed depends on the place, the season, and even the time of day.

Better preparedness has helped, and cyclone shelters have reduced cyclone risks for millions. More remains to be done: shelters have space for about 2.8 million people, or 7 percent of the coastal area's population, but many shelters are not functional. The government has built 2,133 shelters and 200 livestock refuges in 15 of the 19 coastal districts, but the estimates of those functioning vary between 1,639 (Centre for Environmental and Geographic Information Services 2004) and 1,868 (Local Government Engineering Department). Almost a thousand schools were constructed to double as shelters, but many are not suitable; because their location and livestock facilities are inadequate.

Continuing complexities

While more shelters would help, they will not be enough. Rivers continue to bring down silt and the effects of upstream neglect: increased flows from glacier melt (reflecting deforestation and climate change), and poor effluent treatment (sewage and toxic waste). Development is also changing Bangladesh's vulnerability. The growing share of manufacturing in output increases exposure in rapidly growing cities: Dhaka with 8 percent of the country's population accounts for 15 percent of the GDP, and the port of Chittagong is a world "hotspot." Well-engineered embankments around densely populated towns may be cost-effective, but the settling silt raises the ground level, putting the town at a lower level and increasing the likelihood of—and damage from—an embankment breach. So while the country may be less susceptible to minor floods, it is more exposed to major storms, floods, and earthquakes.

Tackling these new challenges requires greater cooperation with neighbors. The delta's complex hydrology requires having and sharing data on river flows and hydro-met conditions—in real time, if people are to be warned of imminent danger. Without upstream water level data, Bangladesh could not forecast floods with sufficient accuracy and lead times until recently. Now satellite data based on global weather models allow 10-day forecasts. A proposal to link the Brahmaputra with its huge water flows with the Ganges languishes because each country is suspicious of the other's data and motives and because the engineering, ecological implications, and economics remain unexamined.

Such differences go back to when Bangladesh was the eastern province of a hostile Pakistan. India signed a treaty in 1960 to share the Indus waters with Pakistan, dividing the eastern and western waters, which could then be harnessed by each country separately. But Pakistan's role in and after India's 1962 conflict with China prevented a similar agreement over the Ganges. In the late 1960s, India began building a barrage at Farakka (completed in 1974) to keep the port of Calcutta (India) open and the Hooghly River navigable by diverting water during the dry season. Following a short-lived agreement after Bangladesh's independence, disputes over the barrage's effects on (Bangladesh) Khulna's agriculture and on other northwestern districts continue, underscoring the complexities of the legal and hydrological issues.

The water dispute extends to other issues and complicates disaster prevention. Talks have begun in early 2010 between Bangladesh and India to attempt to resolve outstanding issues relating to water sharing and protecting banks of common rivers. Bangladesh's population continues to grow (though its rate of increase has slowed), and some 35 million people, a quarter of the country, now inhabit coastal areas exposed to cyclones. The mangroves of the Sundarbans (which reduced Sidr's destructive force) have shrunk in half over the last 50 years.

Cities and manufacturing normally attract the growing numbers, but Bangladesh's cities are not in safe locations, and an international border cordons off the low-lying delta. Migration is a thorny issue, especially when India's central government struggles with the grievances of border hill tribes and Myanmar remains closed. How many more can the crowded Gangetic delta safely accommodate before prevention becomes prohibitively expensive?

These are not questions for Bangladesh alone. Governments that created the borders could make them more permeable. Should donors nudge them to do so, much as they did with cyclone-proof shelters? Donors with funds and good intentions also make faulty suggestions, and decision-making was unlocked only after a disaster outraged people. Better institutions that enable sound and timely decisions come with development, so disasters are a barometer of development. While this message echoes through this report, Bangladesh shows how even poor countries can prevent disasters, thereby nourishing such institutions.

CHAPTER 2

Measuring Disasters' Many Effects

John Stuart Mill, the English philosopher and economist, wrote "what has so often excited wonder, the great rapidity with which countries recover from a state of devastation; the disappearance, in a short time, of all traces of the mischiefs done by earthquakes, floods, hurricanes, and the ravages of war" (Mill 1872). Is what Mill wrote in 1872 still applicable in today's context? And even if he was correct in asserting the "great rapidity with which countries recover"—subsequently consuming at their earlier levels—what about the welfare of those affected?

Economists typically use individuals' incomes or a nation's output to measure prosperity. Income—or output—is surely an important but imperfect determinant of welfare. Indeed, if output were a perfect measure of welfare, one would rejoice the birth of a farm animal and bemoan that of a child (Bauer 1990).[1]

In the context of disasters, measuring changes in output is an imperfect measure of changes in consumption,[2] and it cannot fully capture the pain and suffering inflicted by personal injury, the injury or death of loved ones, or the anxiety engendered by dislocation and uncertainty about the future. Even so, given the frequency of calculating and using output measures of disasters' effects, it is important to understand the approaches and pitfalls.

This chapter first attempts to assess disasters' effects on aspects of well-being measured by health, nutrition, education, and mental state of mind. It then examines assessments of disaster's local and economy-wide effects on output (gross domestic product, or GDP). Certain findings confirm and validate what we know and might expect, but others could be surprising.

Most studies of disasters' effects focus on the immediate aftermath. The chapter begins by complementing such studies with others that find longer lasting effects on various aspects of well-being such as schooling, cognitive abilities, and mental health. Disasters, even if short-lived, can have long-term consequences: some survivors are pushed over the edge and never completely recover. Droughts, particularly widespread in Africa, result in stunted and malnourished children with permanent adverse effects. The chapter discusses the association between disasters and conflicts. Do disasters increase scarcity and thus conflict, or do they create an opportunity for peace, as in Aceh?

The chapter then turns to disasters' effects on economic output, growth, and a government's budget. If and how much output falls, and how long it takes to recover from a disaster, are controversial issues because some distinctions (such as affected versus unaffected areas; those directly affected versus others) are not always clear. Physical damage and disruption reduce output in the affected area, and because the area usually is linked to undamaged areas through commerce, people elsewhere would also be affected. These indirect effects are often, though not always, adverse: those relying on the affected area for supplies or markets may be hurt, but others who offer alternative supplies may be able to increase output. So, national output may not fall as much as that in the affected area.

Studies also differ over whether and how they correct for the effects on commodity prices, terms of trade, and exchange rates, which also affect output. New studies that correct for such factors find that national output always falls after a severe disaster but sometimes rises after a mild one. This may surprise those who think of output as the sole measure of people's well-being, because people are obviously worse off. The seeming disparity arises because output and welfare are not the same. Repairs and rebuilding add to economic activity. And economic growth is output's rate of change, so growth could exceed pre-disaster rates as output catches up to its pre-disaster levels. These outcomes in measures of material economic activity are thus consistent with potentially severe losses in overall well-being.

Governments often assess damage after disasters, and such assessments typically have different and multiple purposes. Keep in mind the intended purpose(s) of assessments, particularly since accurately measuring a disaster's effects is tricky: making informed decisions requires reliable estimates of the *relevant* measurement concepts of damage and loss. Moreover, biases such as double counting could sneak in unless one is careful. The accuracy of damage estimates is also affected by biases in measurement, especially with the prospect of aid. But what is valuable is not always valued, such as the effect of disasters on intangibles.

What could make damage assessments more accurate and helpful? While people do not wait for help to repair their homes and rebuild their lives, the recovery is faster with appropriate and timely help from others (family, suppliers, customers, nongovernmental organizations [NGOs]) and from the government. Commercial ties with other individuals and firms help the recovery. But businesses and individuals also rely on public infrastructure (roads, bridges, railways). The government must therefore quickly decide on the sequence of repairs and on whether to change the location and resilience of structures. These decisions will affect what firms and people do. So, assessing the damage to public infrastructure, and the costs of repairs and rebuilding is urgent, to efficiently implement public measures for recovery. And this requires quickly assessing the impact of a disaster on a government's fiscal position.

But repairs to public infrastructure cannot be instantaneous—the costs are spread over time. Governments in developing countries struggle to raise taxes for the 10 to 20 percent of GDP they typically spend, so even if costs of repairing public infrastructure are spread over time (or financed through borrowing), damage assessments should examine the disaster's fiscal implications for the public sector and the ability to finance recovery—keeping in mind that fiscal revenues depend on national output, which will not fall as much as that in the affected area.

A frequent purpose of damage assessment is compensation: with much of the damage to private property, governments may wish to compensate at least the poorest for the damage they incurred. Whether it is useful to try to comprehensively value damage to private property is questionable. Setting aside the complexities of measurement and biases, compensation is seldom linked to damage. While it may be desirable to limit such transfers to those who are both poor and have incurred damage (a subset of those in the affected area), distinguishing between the chronically and the temporarily poor is difficult. And it would be unfortunate if such spending displaced that on adequate infrastructure and its maintenance—especially since their neglect increases vulnerability to future disasters. Not everything needs to be measured or valued in a desire to be comprehensive for governments to help people directly. Indeed, damage assessments could be more useful if they were simpler.

Finally, damage assessments are often conducted as a prelude to foreign aid. However, if donors seek instead to help a country achieve more than a recovery to the *status quo ante,* then damage estimates, especially if based on pre-disaster measures of output and asset values, may not be that informative. Recognizing the limits of damage assessments would also enhance their value.

Individuals over the edge

Studies on the short- to medium- term effects of a disaster on poverty abound.[3] Many survivors of disasters, rich and poor, recover fully, but a few do not. Healthy people survive temporary deprivation, but elder people and women are particularly vulnerable. Even temporary malnourishment could permanently stunt growth and lower cognitive abilities among children younger than three. While much has been written on short-run effects, panel data to examine the longer term effects on human welfare, some more subtle than others, are scant; but the absence of data does not mean the absence of a problem. Some new studies explore the sufferings of survivors, particularly children.

Declines in schooling and health

Enrollment rates for children aged 7–15 fell by about 20 percent in parts of Côte d'Ivoire with extreme rainfall changes between 1986 and 1987 relative to unaffected regions (Jensen 2000). Earthquakes had similar effects: school attendance fell by almost 7 percent among households heaviest hit by the two strong earthquakes that affected El Salvador in 2001 (Santos 2007). Children in households most affected were about three times more likely to work than attend school.

Temporary withdrawal from school sometimes becomes permanent: children withdrawn from schools during droughts in Central Mexico between 1998 and 2000 were about 30 percent less likely to resume their studies (de Janvry and others 2006). Boys in Tanzania worked longer hours after a drought: a 5.7 hour increase in work reduces their schooling by a year, observed 10 years later (Beegle, Dehejia, and Gatti 2006).

Complementing these country studies in a background paper for the report, Cuaresma (2009) conducts a cross-country analysis of the link between disasters and human capital accumulation (measured by secondary school enrollment). The findings are that those more exposed to earthquakes between 1980 and 2000 have lower secondary school enrollment rates: 1.65 percentage points lower for a country with mean occurrence of quakes compared with a country with no quakes.[4] Another study finds that households with a higher probability of experiencing floods in Bangladesh are more likely to "hold" extra years of schooling relative to land (Yamauchi, Yohannes, and Quisumbing 2009a, 2009b). In Ethiopia and Malawi, exposure to highly frequent droughts in some cases reduced schooling investment. And asset holdings prior to disasters, especially household human capital stock, help maintain schooling investments.

Disasters reduce school enrollment: parents want education for their children but may pull them out temporarily after a disaster to help with more pressing tasks, or because schools have been disrupted. Resuming education requires effort, and a permanent loss or decline may be because many children (or parents) give up or because teaching remains disrupted. In either case, something must be done; what, depends on the details. Moreover, cognitive and analytical abilities—only imperfectly related to schooling—could be affected even without reductions in school enrollment.

Visits to the doctor decline after a disaster, but with little effect on health. After Hurricane Mitch in 1998, sick children in affected areas were 30 percent less likely to be taken to clinics but with no significant difference in the prevalence of illness. The larger point: outputs, like cognition or health, are harder to measure than declines in school enrollment or doctor visits.[5]

Increased stunting . . .

Malnourishment has adverse effects, especially on young children, and this occurs during extended droughts, especially in Africa. Children who lose weight may catch up later (Foster 1995), but while "wasting" (low weight-

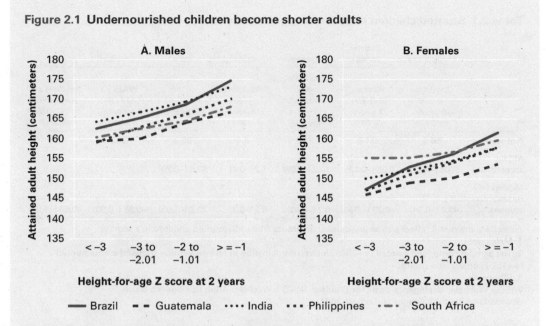

Figure 2.1 Undernourished children become shorter adults

Note: Z-scores (standard deviation scores) are a system by which a child or a group of children can be compared to the reference population. For population-based assessment—including surveys and nutritional surveillance—the z-score is widely recognized as the best system for analysis and presentation of anthropometric data. (WHO, http://www.who.int/nutgrowthdb/about/introduction/en/index4.html)
Source: Victora and others 2008.

to-height ratio) is reversible, "stunting" (low height-to-age ratio) is almost always permanent (figure 2.1).

In a group of 400 rural households, children aged 12 to 24 months at the time of the 1982–84 droughts in Zimbabwe were 2.3 centimeters shorter in late adolescence (Alderman and others 2006). In the Kagera region of Tanzania, children younger than 5 years exposed to a drought in 1991–94 were roughly 1 percent shorter than the population's median height 10 years after (Alderman and others 2009). In Ethiopia, children either in uterus or younger than 36 months affected by the 1984 famine were 3 centimeters shorter than other comparable children 10 years later (Porter 2008). In China, rural adults who were children in the 1959 and 1962 famines were 3.03 centimeters shorter (Chen and Zhou 2007). And in Indonesia, females born in a year with 20 percent higher rainfall are 0.14 centimeters taller (Maccini and Yang 2008).

. . . and diminished cognitive abilities

Malnutrition that causes stunting also diminishes cognitive skills by inhibiting learning (reducing schooling) and productivity. In rural Zimbabwe and rural Tanzania, malnutrition reduces the years of schooling completed. In both cases, after finding that droughts reduce children's height, their

Table 2.1 Stunted children have lower cognitive scores

	Philippines	South Africa	Indonesia	Brazil[1]	Peru	Jamaica[2]	
	Cognitive score (8 years, $n = 2489$)	Ravens Matrices (7 years, $n = 603$)[3]	Reasoning and arithmetic (9 years, $n = 368$)	Attained grades (18 years, $n = 2041$)	WISC IQ (9 years, $n = 72$)	WAIS IQ (17–18 years, $n = 165$)[3]	Reading and arithmetic (17–18 years)[3]
Not stunted	56.4	0.17	11.2	8.1	92.3	0.38	0.4
Mildly stunted	53.8 (–0.21)	0.05 (–0.12)	10.3 (–0.26)	7.2 (–0.4)	89.8 (–0.20)		
Moderately or severely stunted	49.6 (–0.54)	–0.23 (–.040)	9.7 (–0.43)	6.5 (–0.7)	79.2 (–1.05)	–0.55 (–0.93)	–0.60 (–1.00)

Note: Data are mean (effect size as unadjusted difference from non-stunted children in z scores).
1. Males only.
2. The sample comprised stunted (< –2SD) children participating in an intervention trial and a non-stunted (> –1SD) comparison group.
3. SD scores.
WISC = Wechsler Intelligence Scale for Children. WAIS = Wechsler Adult Intelligence Scale.
Source: Grantham-McGregor and others 2007.

educational achievements as adolescents were regressed on their height when they were younger. In Zimbabwe, the 12- and 24-month stunted children during the 1982–84 droughts had delayed school enrollment (3.7 months) and lowered grade completion (0.4 grades) 13 to 16 years later. And in Tanzania, schooling at adolescence in 2004 was nearly a year more for a boy in the 95th percentile of height distribution than for another in the 80th percentile, when they were under 5 and exposed to the 1991–94 drought.

Children between 12 and 36 months who are moderately or severely stunted compared with not stunted (height-for-age greater than one negative standard deviation) have reduced cognitive skills (measured through IQ tests) in later childhood (Grantham-McGregor and others 2007).[6] For example, in the Philippines, reading and math test scores for children at age 8 who were stunted during childhood were 0.75 standard deviations below that of children not stunted (table 2.1).

Malnourished children become less productive adults: their lower body mass makes manual labor less productive, and their lower cognitive skills make skilled work more difficult.[7]

. . . reduce subsequent earnings

Children malnourished during the 1982–84 drought in Zimbabwe had a 7 percent loss in (extrapolated) lifetime earnings (Alderman and others 2006). The 1991–94 drought in the Kagera region of Tanzania also reduced lifetime earnings by about 1 percent, a smaller but still significant effect because the sample included older children who were less vulnerable. Similarly, the 1959–61 birth cohort (malnourished in famine) earned less as adults: the 1959 cohort in areas where the death rate is higher by 1 in 1,000 earns 2 percent less per capita (Chen and Zhou 2007).[8]

This effect of nutrition on earnings may act through cognitive skills. Poor nutrition in Guatemala lowered cognitive skills and reduced earnings (Hoddinott and others 2008). For two groups with 25–42 year olds, those who got nutritional supplements as 0 to 3 year old children had higher wages.

Mental health falls—but can recover

Income, consumption, and health are poor proxies of welfare, and Amartya Sen suggests measuring welfare by functionings and capabilities—what people accomplish with income, health, and education (Sen 1987). Physical or psychological trauma diminishes welfare even if earnings do not fall.

There is justified concern with the psychological effects of disasters. Norris (2005) reviews 225 studies in developing and developed countries and finds that many suffer from post-disaster psychological disorders. But most of these studies address small samples (150 people on average) and very few studies have systematically followed larger samples of affected people over several years. A background paper for this report, using household data employing a baseline collected ten months prior to the 2004 Aceh tsunami, examines the mental health of its adult survivors (Frankenberg and others 2009). Annual follow up surveys in the subsequent four years provided a "before and after" indication of mental wellbeing. For 9,000 adult survivors of the 2004 tsunami in Aceh, post-traumatic stress reaction (PTSR) scores for each respondent in affected areas were high in heavily affected areas as much as 6 to 14 months after the tsunami. But even without treatment, these scores declined with time (figure 2.2).

This analysis also addressed the association between disaster-induced PTSR and key socioeconomic outcomes such as physical health, demographics

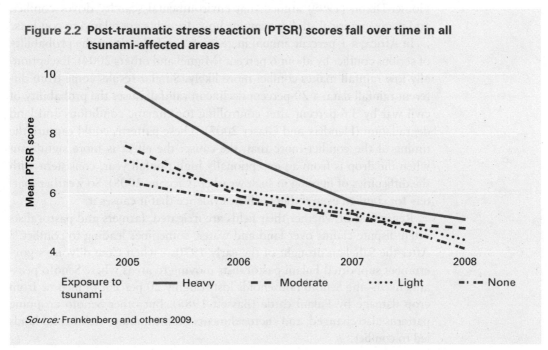

Figure 2.2 Post-traumatic stress reaction (PTSR) scores fall over time in all tsunami-affected areas

Source: Frankenberg and others 2009.

(widowhood), work, income, and household wealth. It controlled for community-fixed effects and damage area as well as the age, gender, and education of each respondent, finding little influence of initial PTSR on most outcomes.[9]

It may not be possible to generalize the Aceh findings, especially because mental health issues are culture and condition sensitive. But if these findings hold in other contexts, they have important policy implications. And though mental health counseling was relatively unavailable in the aftermath of Aceh, much PTSR faded over time and no long-term socioeconomic effects were reported. This suggests that it may be better to channel scarce resources in a disaster's immediate aftermath toward traditional relief activities as opposed to early-stage mental health interventions. The enduring response, however, may say otherwise. As reconstruction begins, PTSR declines, but new cases of adverse behavior may emerge among some people. And these people may benefit from targeted mental health interventions. Clearly though, more work is needed to explore the links between mental health and disasters. Future research should consider the composition of this more vulnerable group and how to help them lead better lives after a disaster.

Conflicts: Cause or consequence?

Some claim that disasters lead to conflict,[10] particularly in Africa with its droughts and earthquakes (Wisner and others 2004). Earthquakes occur much more in countries where there is civil war (Brancati 2007). This association prompted plausible theories that invoke greater scarcity of resources: Homer-Dixon (1999) argued that environmental scarcity drives conflict, and many empirical studies examine how droughts are related to conflicts.

In Africa, a 1-percent annual increase in rainfall reduces the probability of serious conflict by about 6 percent (Miguel and others 2004). Exceptionally low rainfall makes conflict more likely. Similar results come from different rainfall data: a 20-percent decline in rainfall raises the probability of civil war by 3.6 percent after controlling for climatic conditions and land degradation (Hendrix and Glaser 2007). These patterns could capture the timing of the conflict more than the cause: the effect is more significant when the drop is from an exceptionally high rainfall year, consistent with the difficulties of fighting in such weather (Ciccone 2008). So weather matters for conflict, even if there is little evidence that it causes it.

Regardless of whether their fields are irrigated, farmers and pastoralists often dispute claims over land and water, sometimes leading to conflict.[11] After the Sahelian drought of the early 1970s—when Côte d'Ivoire's government supported Fulani pastoralists moving to areas where Senofo peasants lived—the Senofo households lost roughly 20 percent of income from crop damage by Fulani cattle (Bassett 1988). But other Senofo cropping patterns also changed, and encroachments on the manure-rich Fulani lands led to conflict.

Similarly, of 800 households interviewed in the Sahel region of northern Nigeria, 200 experienced conflicts, more than half related to resource access; 60 percent occurred in the dry season, and the most violent ones were in the fertile flood plains (Nyong and Fiki 2005). Pastoralists claim that farmers cultivate along cattle paths during droughts, while farmers said pastoralists watered their cattle at their wells and allowed them to graze on their crops. Qualitative studies show that drought in Afghanistan and volcanic eruptions in eastern Congo exacerbated conflict in 2002 (Wisner and others 2004).

Conflicts are not only strongly correlated with earthquakes—but also last longer when earthquakes occur (Brancati 2007). Countries in conflict experience earthquakes roughly six times as often (every four years while those without civil war had one every 25 years).[12] And the duration of the 44 conflicts where there were no earthquakes was 8.8 years, a little more than half the 15.4 year duration of the 19 conflicts where there was at least one earthquake.[13] The analysis ensured that this relationship is not simply the spurious result of longer wars increasing the temporal window for earthquakes to occur.

The probability of an earthquake in a conflict year (0.25) is greater than when countries are at peace or where there is no conflict. Civil wars obviously do not cause earthquakes, nor earthquakes civil wars. Instead, earthquakes prolong conflicts, perhaps reducing the advantage of the stronger power, the government. Take the 1999 earthquake in Colombia: 1,000 died, thousands were injured, and 35,000 lost their homes. Coffee production suffered, and survivors, frustrated at the government's slow disaster response, clashed with the police and looted establishments. This diverted government security forces, and the rebels took advantage of the situation to renege on an agreement to withdraw from the demilitarized zone, increasing attacks and prolonging fighting.

Relief

Relief (which foreign donors also provide) is often another weapon in the conflict, and those who control its distribution provide it to victims who support them, victims who could be won over to their side, or those expected to remain neutral (victims or non-victims). It all depends on how the war is fought.

In Sri Lanka, the 2004 tsunami pummeled the contested areas of Ampara and Batticaloa. How was relief for housing reconstruction allocated across districts?[14] Of the 5,300 Muslim and 5,260 Tamil homes destroyed in Ampara, 2,080 homes were rebuilt, and about 2,560 of the 8,600 Tamil homes destroyed had been rebuilt in Batticaloa (Kuhn forthcoming). In contrast, in the largely Sinhalese districts of Galle, Matara, and Hambantota, about 9,120 of the 9,350 homes destroyed were rebuilt. These findings suggest that the government assists only its committed supporters when assisting potential supporters in contested areas is difficult. Political considerations are important even in areas under government control, which is not surprising. There is evidence of political bias in the distribution of disaster aid in the United States and elsewhere (Keefer and others 2009).

The same 2004 tsunami devastated Aceh, where the conciliation and peace that followed is a refreshing contrast. Aceh, the stronghold of the GAM rebels, was largely outside the control of the Indonesian government that administered the assistance that followed in the tsunami's wake. But some of the assistance was used to re-integrate the GAM insurgents into peaceful civilian life.

Elsewhere, combatants use disaster relief to gain a military advantage. A 1976 earthquake in Guatemala killed at least 20,000 people outright and many more from illness and injury. The government allowed international assistance, including religious groups and other NGOs and bilaterals, unfettered access to the damaged area. But the western highlands, where the quake struck, were not yet embroiled in the fighting. The government used quake relief to gather intelligence and squelch any incipient rebellion (Hinshaw 2006). Aid was part of the effort to prevent the earthquake from becoming a recruiting tool for insurgents.

Spotlight 4 describes Ethiopia's use of food aid as another weapon in its long drawn out civil war and nearby Sudan's similar response to the same drought. The fighting disrupted aid delivery, the government made little effort to assist the three southern provinces in 1984, and theft (including that by government forces) hobbled logistics at Port Sudan (Burr and Collins 1995). As the drought persisted and aid finally trickled in, the insurgent Sudan People's Liberation Army (SPLA) blocked aid until the villages they controlled (not necessarily the most drought ravaged) also received aid. Only after disease (visceral leishmaniasis and meningitis) broke out in the south and spread to Khartoum in 1987, did food aid flow. But only for a short time.

Insurgent success facilitated relief flows to areas that supported them: by April 17, 1989, the SPLA had taken 11 government garrisons and three district capitals, and donors delivered more aid between January and February 1989 than they had in the five years between 1983 and 1988. Both economic and military assistance to the Sudan government dropped, the defense and finance ministers resigned, inflation in Sudan approached 80 percent, and bread shortages emerged in Khartoum. The SPLA wouldn't cooperate on land transportation, and foreign donors moved 40 percent of relief by air at a huge cost of $700 a ton. Even these restricted flows ended, and the war between the government and SPLA continued.

Breaking the cycle of conflict

Could Aceh be the example, not the exception? Could disasters break the conflict cycle? Pakistan and India have fought long and hard over Kashmir. But they cooperated to provide assistance even in disputed areas after the 2005 earthquake, though each feared that aid could provide an advantage to the other and that it restricted the use and staffing of relief aircraft (Renner and Chafe 2007).

Table 2.2 Civil war, rainfall, and the rule of law

Dependent variable: Probability of civil war	Not controlling for rule of law	Controlling for rule of law
Rainfall growth from last period (t–1) to current period (t)	–0.11	–0.05
	(0.04)	(0.34)
Rainfall growth, (t–2) to (t–1)	–0.08	–0.03
	(0.07)	(0.5)
Rule of law (t–1)		–0.17
		(0.001)
Rule of law (t–2)		0.1
		(0.03)
Number of observations, countries	451,32	451,32
R^2	0.08	0.14

Note: Ordinary least squares with clustered standard errors are used because rainfall is not significant controlling for country-specific fixed and year effects, with or without controls for the rule of law. Nearly all variation in rule of law is cross-country. Other control variables are initial income per capita, ethnic fractionalization, religious fractionalization, whether a country is an oil exporter, how mountainous the country is, and the log of population. *P-values* are in parentheses.
Source: Keefer and others 2009.

Such cooperation may be of interest to both countries: while the Kashmir conflict is militarized, both Pakistan and India want to win the Kashmiris' hearts and minds. The governments competed while cooperating with aid logistics, but they did not address territorial claims. Goodwill is short-lived, so disasters spur incipient dispute resolution efforts but rarely stop conflicts. Kelman notes how Cuba and the United States lost four opportunities to thaw frosty relations through post-hurricane aid: Hurricane Michelle in 2001 and Hurricanes Dennis, Katrina, and Wilma in 2005 prompted one country to offer aid that the other rejected (Kelman 2007). Weak though such glimmers of hope may be, they should not be missed.

The empirical association between disasters and conflicts, and the episodes just outlined, suggest that both may result from something else—the missing variable of "institutions of good governance."[15] When proxies for such institutions are included in regressions, they are statistically significant. The effects of rainfall shocks on income are strongest in Africa (Fiala 2009). And in Sub-Saharan Africa, rainfall declines can trigger conflict (Miguel and others 2004). This result is strong, and the effects of rainfall on growth appear to be entirely conditional on the rule of law.

Rainfall does not significantly affect the chance of war when a proxy is included (table 2.2). The two law proxies have opposite signs because they summarize two effects: the improvements in the rule of law, and the high rule of law. If the rule of law were unchanged, the law proxy reduces the probability of civil war; if the rule of law improves, the probability of civil war falls even more.[16]

The likelihood that disputes turn into conflicts after a disaster depends on what the government does. Governments that do not take measures to prevent disasters do not protect their peoples' rights to property or protect their people against insurgency. So a disaster could ignite conflict. The quality of governance and institutions matter in two ways: private investment in recovery does not take place, and people scramble to seize what is not theirs. Collier and Goderis (2007) note that this also happens in what they call the "natural resource curse."

The analysis of conflicts produces three points. First, disasters have an adverse effect on conflict only in places where the rule of law is already weak, so a disaster could ignite conflict. Second, there is a strong incentive to divert disaster relief during conflicts. And third, disasters can occasionally break the conflict cycle, as shown in Aceh after the tsunami, but such goodwill is short-lived.

Disasters undoubtedly reduce the well-being of victims and their surviving families. But their effect on victims is not synonymous with their effect on an economy's output or output growth.

Welfare falls, but what are the effects on output? And for how long?

A disaster could reduce output (certainly in the affected area and possibly nationally) both because of physical damage and because of a disruption in normal economic activities (figure 2.3).

There are two related questions. How long will it take before output recovers, if it does? And what, if anything, can the government do to hasten

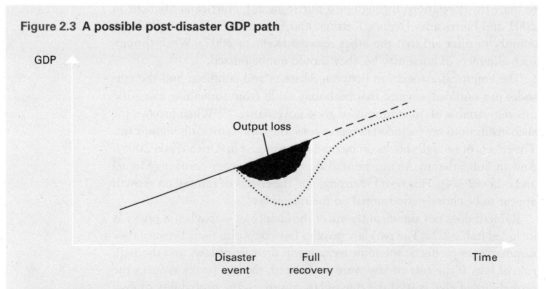

Figure 2.3 A possible post-disaster GDP path

Note: Other paths are also possible. For example, output could also rise above pre-disaster levels, but this can be an artifact of a reconstruction boom, as discussed later in the chapter.
Source: World Bank staff based on Hochrainer 2006.

the recovery? The answers have generated much discussion, in large part because studies come to different conclusions. Many find that disasters have adverse longer term effects, but some find little or no effect, and a few even find that national output increases—a result that does not contradict a drop in welfare (box 2.1).

Box 2.1 Previous studies find a medley of effects of output and growth

Previous studies find ambiguous effects of disasters on national output. There are many reasons for this, but the underlying one is that it is particularly difficult to identify causal effects of disasters on output. Differing findings suggest that models may be misspecified, often because relevant variables are omitted. It is also difficult to include all relevant factors, especially when some (like the network of links between affected and unaffected areas) cannot be measured. Results also vary because studies differ in the period they examine and the techniques they use.

Otero and Marti (1995) found that disasters decrease national income and tax revenues, raising the fiscal and the trade deficits (exports fall and imports rise) in the short run. In the longer run, post-disaster spending increased debt service payments, reducing development and creating persistent external and fiscal imbalances.

Benson (1997a, b, c) and Benson and Clay (1998, 2000, 2001) examined the short-term effects of several disasters in Dominica, Fiji, Vietnam, and the Philippines. Agriculture was most strongly and adversely affected, and poverty and inequality rose, but the effects of the disaster could not be isolated from other adverse developments (such as terms of trade).

Murlidharan and Shah (2001), in examining the effect of disasters on medium-term economic growth, found that growth was reduced. Disasters were also associated with growing external debts, budget deficits, and inflation.

Hochrainer (2006) examined 85 disasters in 45 countries and found that GDP fell in the disaster year and that growth subsequently did not rise to more than compensate (a fall in cumulative GDP).

Noy (2009) found that the country's ability to mobilize resources for reconstruction and global financial conditions helps explain disasters' effects on GDP growth. Cuaresma and others (2008), in one of the few longer term studies, found that disaster risks reduce knowledge spillovers from developed to developing countries. One plausible reason behind this finding is the importance of institutions in a nation's absorptive capacity for foreign technologies: disasters tend to affect technology absorption positively only in countries with relatively high levels of GDP per capita.

Not all studies found adverse effects. Albala-Bertrand (1993) looked for, but did not find, significant longer term effects of disasters in developed countries. And the effects in developing countries faded away after two years, though some adverse effects on income distribution persisted. He concluded that disasters are "a problem *of* development, but essentially not a problem *for* development" (p. 202).

Albala-Bertrand questioned many of the assumptions and estimating techniques used in the literature. Attributing all the change in output and economic growth to the disaster would be misleading because other factors also influence growth: studies that do, find effects to be small and to differ in sign. This suggests that economies and disasters differ so much that any effect on growth and output depends on the details: some are adverse, others not; some are ephemeral, others long lasting.

Caselli and Malhotra (2004) found that disasters did not reduce GDP, fiscal deficits, or inflation in either the short or medium term. Fatalities and damage appear to depend on the stage of a country's development, not the disasters *per se*. Caselli and Malhotra also concluded that the loss of capital and

(continued)

Aggregate and sectoral effects on economic output and growth in the long term

Debates over disasters' effects arise because, as box 2.1 shows, the findings vary: studies use different data and estimation techniques, and include different disasters. Several background papers were commissioned for this report to build on these studies to look past the immediate effects of a disaster (always adverse). These new studies correct for other factors to isolate the effect of disasters; each technique has its advantages and limitations that are briefly discussed along with its findings. Despite statistical care, the limitations of cross-country regressions in some of the studies reported here must be emphasized, and the conclusions here reflect those caveats.

Hochrainer (2009) considers 225 large disasters between 1960 and 2005, and compares the country's post-disaster GDP with what he projects (had the event not occurred).[17] GDP is on average 2 percent lower even five years later (however, with large deviations around the mean), and a nonparametric test including detailed uncertainty analyses finds this difference to be statistically significant. But the GDP is measured against projections based on recent growth without correcting for the many other factors that influence the economy (the difference between observed and projected output is explained using two techniques).[18]

Two background papers examine the issue from another perspective by adjusting for the effect of the many factors that also influence output in the medium term (5 years) and the short (1 to 3 years).[19] Loayza and others (2009) estimate the medium-term effects of different hazards simultaneously on economic growth using a model with three main sectors (agriculture, industry, and services) and with the whole economy, correcting for two sets of variables that also affect growth.[20] The first set comprises structural and institutional variables such as education, financial development, monetary and fiscal policy, and trade openness. The second, external conditions such as terms of trade and period-specific dummy variables. They calculate rates of growth (not levels of output to make the series stationary that econometric techniques require) in discrete five-year periods using data for 94 countries (68 developing) over 45 years (1961–2005); so each country has at most nine observations (table 2.3).[21]

Table 2.3 Growth effect of a "typical" (median) disaster

		Effect on:			
		GDP growth	Agricultural growth	Industrial growth	Service growth
Median intensity of:	Droughts	−0.6%***	−1.1%***	−1.0%**	−0.1%
	Floods	1.0%***	0.8%***	0.9%***	0.9%***
	Earthquakes	−0.1%	0.1%	0.9%*	−0.1%
	Storms	−0.1%	−0.6%***	0.8%*	−0.2%

Note: The effects on GDP growth rates—the rate of change of output—and not on output levels. So, a typical drought could reduce overall GDP growth by 0.6 percent; agriculture growth by 1.1 percent, and so on. *significant at 10%; **significant at 5%; ***significant at 1%.
Source: Loayza and others 2009.

Five-year non-overlapping rates of growth do not capture short-run effects (hence the parallel study summarized in sequence). The main findings are that medium-run economic growth is generally lower after a disaster. But the effect depends on the type of hazards and is not always statistically significant or uniform.

- Overall growth falls by 0.6 percent after a *drought* of typical (or median) intensity, with the most adverse effect on agricultural and industrial growth.
- Overall growth barely falls after a typical *earthquake,* but industrial growth rises, perhaps because of reconstruction.
- Agricultural growth falls by 0.6 percent after a typical *storm,* but industrial growth rises, again perhaps because of reconstruction.
- Interestingly, overall growth rises by a statistically significant 1 percent after a *flood* of typical intensity. This is plausible because although floods disrupt farming and other activities, they may also deposit nutrient-rich silt and may increase hydroelectric power, which boosts industrial growth. For example, in Norway, an unexpected glacial lake outburst flow in 2001 allowed the Norwegian utility Sisovatnet to produce an additional year of hydropower.[22] Capturing such gains depends partly on having the right infrastructure in the first place (here, a reservoir capable of holding excessive water).

But severe disasters (limited to only 10 percent of all disasters) have adverse effects regardless of type. The adverse effect on agricultural growth doubles for severe droughts; the rise in growth after severe floods becomes statistically insignificant; and severe storms are more damaging, particularly for industrial growth. Table 2.4 shows the results.

In the second parallel background paper, Fomby and others (2009) trace the annual growth in the year of and the year following the events to examine the adjustment path in the shorter run (1 to 3 years). The model pools the experiences of various countries over time to arrive at mean responses of growth to disasters of different intensities. While losing country specificity,

Table 2.4 Growth effect of a "typical" (median) severe disaster

		Effect on:			
		GDP growth	Agricultural growth	Industrial growth	Service growth
From median intensity of severe:	Droughts	–1.0%***	–2.2%***	–1.0%*	0.3%
	Floods	0.3%	0.6%	0.1%	0.4%
	Earthquakes	–0.0%	–0.1%	0.3%	0.0%
	Storms	–0.9%**	–0.8%**	–0.9%	–0.9%

*significant at 10%; **significant at 5%; ***significant at 1%.
Source: Loayza and others 2009.

the model detects the time pattern of the recovery reasonably and robustly. The full sample has 87 countries, with some from every region, and covers 48 years from 1960 to 2007. The full sample and a developing countries subset (70 percent of the full sample) are analyzed, adjusting for the severity of disasters.

They find that moderate and severe disasters affect growth more in developing countries than in rich countries; but this may reflect their size and diversity rather than their income. Growth typically does not rise after severe disasters, especially in developing countries. But the effects on output still depend on the hazard and the structure of the economy (similar to Dumas and Hallegatte model, which emphasizes the elasticity of substitution in production). This may be why earlier studies that did not adjust for the effects of other (nondisaster) factors found growth effects that differ depending on the period.

Particular cases would of course differ from the "average" findings: not every flood raises agricultural growth (flash floods wash away sediment, but annual floods in Bangladesh deposit rich silt). And the effect is on national output: the affected area may differ, and as the previous section showed, some survivors suffer even long after the national economy recovers. These studies, unlike many earlier ones, have accounted for the many nonhazard factors that influence output (structural and institutional variables, terms of trade). But our understanding of economic growth is incomplete, so not every relevant factor may have been included. Even so, two conclusions are warranted. First, a disaster has a smaller effect on the national economy, especially if the affected area is small in relation to the rest of the country and there are substitute producers and markets in the affected area. Second, the area's commercial links with the rest of the country (and world) would moderate the effect.

Two additional background papers look at disasters' effects on output from a different perspective. In a paper commissioned for this report, Lopez (2009) develops a general equilibrium model and shows that while disasters can have dramatic negative effects on the level of per capita income, they may propel a formerly stagnating economy into a virtuous path of continuing growth. Under certain conditions (if disasters reduce the tangible to intangible asset ratio in an economy, and if governments do not repeat past policy biases against intangibles), the rate of per capita income growth could increase over the long run.

In another background paper prepared for this report, Dercon and Outes (2009) examine 240 households in six villages in the Indian states of Andhra Pradesh and Maharashtra over 30 years (1975–2005, with gaps in 1983 and 2001) to empirically test the impact of disasters on income levels in these villages. They predict income over time and find it to be lower than what they project by regressing current income (available for nine waves) on the earlier year's income using as instruments annual village rainfall (alone and interacted with land area and the number of children per household). Much depends on the accuracy of their projected incomes and the importance of omitted factors like the prices of the commodities the farmers grow. They find that droughts cause some households' incomes to plummet and not recover, especially in households with lower education and landholdings in the 1970s. They interpret this as a permanent loss.

To summarize, even short-lived impacts of disasters on health and education can have long-term effects on income and well-being. Disasters always reduce well-being of those affected, but may or may not have a negative impact on output growth in the medium term (5 years), which depends, in part, on the severity and type of hazard and level of economic development. Storms and droughts seem to have systematic negative impacts on medium-term growth; not so for floods and earthquakes. But severe disasters (10 percent of all disasters) have adverse effects regardless of their type.

Measuring the damage: Twice over and half under?

Measuring damage twice over

Many estimators, reporters, and aid agencies add damages (to stocks) and losses (of flows) together—which may result in double counting, as noted above.[23] Consider the collapse of a building with rented apartments: when rents and building values are observed, one finds that the collapsed building's value ("damage") is the present value of lost rental stream (future flow "losses," adjusting for maintenance and other costs).[24] Buildings may not change hands frequently, and space may not always be rented out. But even if prices and rents are not readily observed, conceptually, the lost asset value from physical damage equals the present value of the lost income flow from the affected assets.

While this relationship is clear with privately owned assets, valuing damage to public infrastructure is more complicated. Why? Because these assets do not have market-based valuations. Valuing the flow of lost economic benefits is harder; and the economic rate of return on the public asset may be far greater than the rate of return on private capital (especially in countries where infrastructure is insufficient to begin with).[25] Even so, a damaged asset generates a smaller income flow, and the economic value of the physical damage is the present value of this reduced flow, which may not equate to the capital loss or to the cost of repair and reconstruction. This implies that adding measures of the lost social benefits from damage to a public hospital (due to reduced access to care), and the cost of reconstruction (as a crude proxy for the lost value of the asset), would double count the output losses.

The discussion applies to lost output from affected physical capital. But output could also fall without damage to physical assets—for two very different reasons.[26] Take droughts: without water (an input), harvests decline, reducing aggregate output in agricultural economies, although the long-term value of the land may not be affected. The effect is not limited solely to agriculture. And it is not just agricultural growth that is affected: droughts, again through a direct effect on input (water), could reduce industrial output—as in Kenya—through reduced hydroelectric power generation.[27]

Disruption is the second reason for a decline in output without damage to physical capital. SARS in East Asia disrupted travel and the supply chain that spanned countries reducing output—though there was no physical damage to assets and very few died from the disease (Brahmbhatt and Dutta 2008). So output could fall without physical damage. But a disaster often results in both physical damage and disruption, and keeping the two conceptually separate avoids error in measurement such as double counting.

Lost rentals of a destroyed building (either explicitly observed or implicit) are the direct effects, but may be indirect effects as well. Displaced people may travel longer distances to work and food grains for consumption and cement for repairs may be costlier because roads have been washed away. To measure all the indirect effects, however, indirect benefits should also be estimated. Tourism to the affected area may decline, but output elsewhere would rise when the tourists travel to other destinations.[28] These effects, perhaps significant, are more difficult to measure—and this is not done systematically and consistently, perhaps because they accrue to non-victims and are diffused over a wider area. The loss estimates therefore rarely measure reduced national output. Even within the affected area, overall loss measures mask the fact that not everyone is adversely affected (those with undamaged fields and silos benefit from higher prices of grain).

Damage measurement is highly sensitive to the measurement concept. Consider estimating the value of physical damage when Cyclone Sidr knocks down a thatched hut in Bangladesh (for which there is neither a rental nor a property market). Is the damage what the farmer had spent in materials with or without the (forgone) value of his time in building it? This "acquisition cost" (what it cost the farmer) could differ substantially from "replacement cost" (what it would now cost to rebuild the hut) or from the conceptual asset value of the structure (what the lost structure could have fetched in exchange).[29]

These are different concepts, but there is no record of many of these measures, so the estimator makes an educated guess that depends on the purpose at hand. Donors (domestic and foreign) may want to know, "What do *I* have to spend to replace the farmer's hut?" Foreigners would consider the landed price of imported materials (such as sheet iron and steel), adding the local labor costs (at "fair" wage rates) if they intend to build the structure before giving it to the farmer. The local NGOs may consider the prices of the locally available bamboo, and consider the prevailing wage rates to arrive at a lower number—and the two may differ by much more than the transport cost—because the "law of one price" does not hold internationally (Isard 1997). For the victims, few of whom wait for governments or donors to rebuild their house or provide the materials, the relevant measure of damage is, "what is the cheapest way for *me* to get it working/habitable again?"

If the Bangladeshi farmer could recover some of the scattered material and rebuild while waiting for his flooded fields to dry (when his time may be worth little because there are no competing farming demands), the expense incurred (the replacement value of the "damage") would be far less than what enumerators estimate.[30] And this amount cannot be ascertained by asking victims (usually through translators with local officials also present) because the prospect of aid may influence their answer. Questioning these claims would add insult to victims' injuries; and estimators, being human, are moved by the very visible deprivation of the victims.[31]

Reported estimates mix many concepts. Moreover, such estimates from earlier assessments are not compared with subsequent output declines. To make this comparison correctly, one must also take account of other factors that affect output (as summarized earlier). Nor do the loss estimates measure the decline in victims' well-being. Sometimes what the government provides is added (in cash or in kind, as with food or tents). But this fiscal cost is only a transfer (from taxpayers to the beneficiaries) and not an output loss. The fiscal cost may be relevant when requesting aid; but the effect on output should not be confused with its effect on the budget. The point is that accurate estimates are more likely when the purpose of measurement is clear.

Measuring damage half under

Biases in measurement can also go the other way, leading to underestimates of damages. Although the dead are counted, damage estimates ignore the value of lives lost (the difficult conceptual and ethical issues of valuing consequences of risks to life are discussed in chapter 4). The destruction of "the commons"—environmental buffers, forests—is rarely included because they are difficult to value and have no well-defined claimants. Such effects could be substantial: Markandya and Pedroso-Galinato (2009) find that disasters (earthquakes, storms, and floods) destroy natural capital (cropland, pastureland, and protected areas) and that the destruction is greater when disasters last longer.[32] The effect on natural capital is further complicated because it is not possible to distinguish disasters that have positive side-effects (floods that increase fertility or forest fires that sustain forests) from those that do not. Clearly, what is valuable is not always valued.

Recognizing that GDP is not a perfect metric of welfare, another background paper goes beyond the effect of disasters on output to estimate the effect on "genuine savings," (Mechler 2009).[33] This is an alternative welfare indicator based on concepts developed for green national income and wealth accounting (see Hamilton and Atkinson 2006). Genuine savings aims at better measuring the "true" national savings by adding investments in human capital and subtracting the consumption of capital stock, the depletion of natural resources, and the adverse effects of air pollution. Disasters, by reducing genuine savings, could affect medium to longer term welfare (as measured by changes in consumption expenditure over 5 to 33 years). The findings, though tentative, suggest that including all disaster asset losses may better explain variations in post-disaster welfare, and these findings are most pronounced for low-income countries, perhaps because of their greater dependence on natural capital. This is likely to be an underestimate because of the limited number of observations, mainly because of a lack of genuine savings data for some highly vulnerable countries, such as for many disaster-prone Caribbean countries.

Improving measurement, clarifying purposes

An assessment can have several purposes. But clarity is needed about who makes what decision and which estimate is most relevant for accurate measurement. This section makes three points. First, comprehensive damage assessment of public infrastructure is useful, especially if decisions on repairs and priorities are made centrally. Second, decisions for the sequence of repairs and the funds require estimating a disaster's fiscal effects, which is different from estimating property damage. Third, whether it is useful to try and value damage to private property in an attempt to be comprehensive is questionable, especially if compensation is not linked to damage: it is unclear what decision requires it, and if possible biases could be avoided. If the reason is to determine where and whether the government should rebuild, gauging the extent of damage (as opposed to valuing it) may be a better option. Likewise, the merit of estimating output declines by *sector* is unclear because of high sectoral interdependence. Projecting sectoral output correctly is highly complex and useful only in a few situations, and market prices may be sufficient signals of shortages.[34]

One purpose of post-disaster efforts is to promote a quick recovery. Supply chains and services (such as banking) are often disrupted, and it is in peoples' self-interests to restore these services by drawing on established family and commercial ties. In a background paper for this report, de Mel and others (2008) examine the post-tsunami recovery in Sri Lanka and find that despite the lack of insurance and low aid flows, affected households drew on their own savings and that of relatives and friends to replace 60 percent of lost assets (microenterprise owners two-thirds) by the summer of 2007; three quarters of microenterprise owners had replaced all their damaged housing by April 2008.[35] Not everyone recovered as rapidly, but many did recover. People rebuild their lives and livelihoods more quickly and easily when their commercial links with the rest of the country (food,

Box 2.2 Revenues and expenditures: Disasters' fiscal consequences

Lis and Nickel (2009) examine the budgetary effect of large weather disasters (droughts, heat and cold waves, floods, storms, and wildfires) in 138 countries between 1985 and 2007. They adjust for the effects of other variables on the deficit such as business and political cycles (parties in power). Large disasters are defined as those affecting 100,000 people or more. Such disasters raise the budget deficit in developing countries by between 0.23 and 1.1 percent of the GDP but they rarely do so in rich (OECD and EU) countries.

In a three-year study, Benson and Clay (2004) examine country studies of disasters to assess their economic effects including those on government finance. They find that accounting systems do not track spending in ways that allow a thorough analysis (as chapter 3 also observes), but they have some interesting insights.

The three elements of government finance examined are revenue, expenditure, and external assistance (typically from international donors). The effect on revenues was most difficult to estimate: the structure of taxes changed in Bangladesh after trade tariffs fell starting in the 1980s, so econometric estimates from past data would be a poor guide. Countries differ substantially in their sources of tax revenues: Montserrat relies more on consumption taxes, and personal incomes and consumption fell after the volcanic eruption in the 1990s.

Disasters increase government expenditures almost immediately. Budgets are reallocated and relief spending rises after a disaster. This happens almost every year in some countries like Bangladesh. Benson and Clay find evidence that such reallocations come at the expense of maintenance in Dominica. Capital spending, largely discretionary, falls. But in some countries (the Philippines), budget headings are too broad to tell what is happening.

Disasters' long-term effects on government spending are also difficult to estimate: budget categories change, and disaster management spending is not a separate category. Moreover, multiple agencies and public enterprises keep different accounts and do so differently (firms are on accrual, budget is on cash basis), and several state-owned enterprises (including banks as in Bangladesh) also provide relief.

Benson and Clay find that although donors frequently provide aid after disasters, they do so by re-labeling the funds without increasing the aggregate amounts. Disasters have had little effect on aid trends in Bangladesh, Dominica, and Malawi, which all received substantial aid even before disasters. This suggests that post-disaster aid may not augment what governments have to spend, so they may ultimately have to rely on their ability to tax their people and spend accordingly.

Source: World Bank staff.

building supplies, telephone, and banking services) and within the region are restored, including public infrastructure (roads, bridges).[36]

The government must repair damage to public infrastructure to restore severed links. This requires decisions on the sequence of repairs and on the government's wealth. Estimating a disaster's fiscal effects therefore takes on some urgency. Forecasting tax revenues (to pay for rebuilding) may be the harder task, and even when revenues fall by a small fraction of national output, the fiscal sustainability of many developing countries may be jeopardized. A wider budget deficit in poorer countries following a disaster underscores the importance of careful spending (box 2.2).

While the better off find the resources to rebuild, many are left destitute. Governments sometimes build temporary shelters and provide relief, but those who have lost everything (say, if what land they had is deemed unsafe) have nowhere to go and may need direct government assistance. It would be a misnomer to call such transfers from the government (land to resettle, or payments in cash and kind) "compensation" because the amounts are typically small (generally less than two times per capita GDP, and the relatively better off get little even if they lost more assets).

It may be useful to limit such transfers to those who are both poor and who have incurred damage (a subset of those in the affected area), though distinguishing between the chronically and temporarily poor is difficult. The difficulties are compounded especially when the help is needed quickly.

Morris and Wodon (2003) examine the allocation of relief after the 1998 Hurricane Mitch in Honduras and argue that "the nature of emergency aid often makes it difficult to allocate aid in a differentiated pattern among beneficiaries." Examining data from a household survey conducted six to nine months after the hurricane, they find that the chance of receiving relief was related to assets lost but inversely related to wealth (i.e., the rich are less likely to get help); but if one controlled for whether their dwelling was damaged, the amount of relief was neither related to pre-Mitch wealth nor assets lost. Put simply, what a person got in kind (food aid) after a house was damaged was not related to the value of what was lost or owned before. Mauritius, a small country with few people, distributed transfers in a public meeting based on simple observable criteria of house damage (so any deception is deterred by public disclosure). Pakistan, recognizing the challenges after the earthquake (described in chapter 3), gave each person or family fixed amounts for relief and to help rebuild their destroyed houses.

If the transfer amounts, whether for relief or rebuilding homes, are far lower than the damage incurred, why measure damage to private property? Aid could be given to all in heavily damaged districts or counties (as in Pakistan or Mauritius), and these districts could be identified through aerial photographs or satellite imagery. All Africa Global Media (December 3, 2009) reports that the Kenya-based International Livestock Research Institute will analyze freely available satellite data from the National Oceanic Atmospheric Administration that could distinguish live from dead vegetation in northern Kenya. This data could tell insurers whether to pay claims, thereby reducing the costs of verifying the distinction by a visit. Haiti provides a more recent example, where Operation GEO-CAN—Global Earth Observation Catastrophe Assessment Network—estimated and classified building damage based on high-resolution aerial imagery in areas severely affected by the earthquake. The first set of damage maps for the city of Port-au-Prince was produced within 48 hours of the project's commencing.[37] Such assessments would be easier than *valuing* the damaged assets, which is highly susceptible to incentive and other measurement issues. Providing aid based on assets damaged in such cases would obviate the time and effort to measure and value everything.

It is important to understand the limits of damage assessments when using them. Much of the discussion here applies to disasters that cause destruction on a scale relatively small compared to the rest of the economy, with the economy expected to recover (ultimately) to its former state. But attempts to measure and value damage for such tragedies as the January 2010 Haiti earthquake—where the scale of destruction is such that it rewrites the future landscape—may be misplaced. If a disaster fundamentally altered a whole economy, neither flow nor stock estimates before the crisis would reflect the new long-term equilibrium after it. In such cases, estimating the value of damage matters less than identifying the prevention measures.

Measures to move from the depths of the disaster to a new and different post-disaster resilient state will depend on what that state is envisaged to be. On preventing future disasters, later chapters explain why no single or simple measure exists: effective prevention requires cooperative measures. And the underlying cause of a disaster (and thus the effective prevention measure) is less obvious than its proximate cause. The assessment following the 2009 cyclone in the Lao Democratic People's Republic found that people were not adequately warned of the impending flood, although such predictions were possible from upstream flows and rainfall measured over the previous several days. Better weather and hazard forecasting (chapter 4) would clearly have helped, but would dams upstream have been more cost-effective? Such searching questions are difficult for a damage assessment to answer.

Spotlight 2 on Turkey

Where civilizations and tectonic plates meet

The Marmara earthquakes struck İzmit, an industrial city some 90 kilometers east of Istanbul, with a 7.4 magnitude early on August 17, 1999, before most people awoke, and struck Düzce, with an epicenter about 100 kilometers east of the İzmit earthquake, with a 7.2 magnitude on November 12 of the same year.

In İzmit alone, building collapses killed 17,000, injured another 40,000, and made about 200,000 homeless. Total damage, estimated at $5 billion, could have been worse. The fire that raged for days when a 90-meter-high reinforced concrete heater stack collapsed at the İzmit refinery did not spread to the adjacent oil storage tanks. In Düzce, close to 700 lives were lost.

After caring for the dead and injured, the government considered how to prevent similar disasters. Seismic fault lines crisscross the country, and many cities are on fault lines, with new faults discovered as detection technology improves. The 1999 Marmara quakes followed a well recorded westward movement of earthquakes along the 1,500-kilometer North Anatolian fault line (spotlight map 1). Scientists think it very likely that between 73,000 and 120,000 people will be injured if a major quake shakes Istanbul, home to 12 million.[1] The Turkish government tried three things to preclude further disasters: increase insurance coverage; improve buildings' quality; and better prepare itself. Following is a discussion of each.

Spotlight map 1 Turkey is at the meeting of three tectonic plates

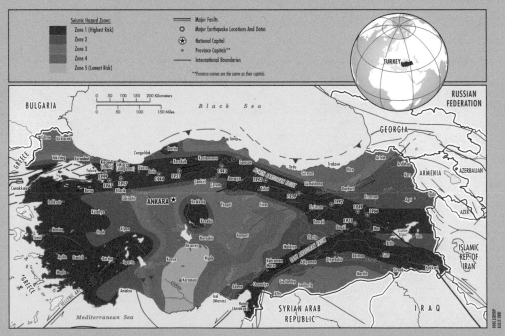

Source: World Bank staff.

Reducing government liability—promoting insurance

The government was financially responsible for rebuilding even privately owned structures that collapse in an earthquake. The 1959 law that stipulated this (no.7269) eroded public finances (it is impossible to pay claims with insufficient tax revenues, especially taking into account that Turkey's macroeconomic stability is recent). It also eroded the owners' incentive to construct sound structures.

Almost immediately after the 1999 earthquake, the government sought to amend the law and established a quasi-governmental Turkish Catastrophe Insurance Pool (TCIP under Decree 587) to cover earthquake damage both direct and indirect (e.g. fires, explosions, and landslides that follow). Turkey had many private insurance firms, but the small insurers were distrusted and few homes were insured. The insurance was compulsory for all residential buildings within a municipality (and to qualify for cheap loans under existing schemes) and voluntary for industrial and commercial buildings and for private homes outside the municipality (such as unincorporated villages).

Only time will tell if the government's explicit refusal to cover uninsured losses would hold in the political aftermath of a disaster, but the attempt is laudable. Chapter 5 discusses the role of insurance in preventing disasters, and commendable efforts were made in Turkey to encourage insurance on commercial terms (premia reflect some risks and prevention measures).[2] But the government's role remains large, and it is TCIP's insurer of last resort: it explicitly undertook to pay claims that exceeded TCIP's funds in an exceptionally large catastrophe.

Despite insurance being compulsory and TCIP setting affordable insurance premia, only 22.3 percent of registered urban dwellings countrywide (slightly over 3 million dwellings) were insured as of June 2009. That was similar to the nonmandatory coverage in California, but far lower than the 30 percent market penetration predicted for 2001 and 60 percent for 2006. Poor enforcement is often blamed, but low penetration reflects deeper difficulties. Only legally built buildings with proper permits may be insured when, as in many developing countries, construction without permits is widespread. Squatter communities—*gecekondu,* literally "overnight settlers"—spring up in areas unsafe for construction.

But the difficulties do not stem from absence of clear title alone: many with clear title to land do not always secure a permit before starting or extending their buildings. Such structures are liable to be demolished; but the threat may also exacerbate the construction of unsafe structures. Those with insecure rights lack the *incentive* to build safe structures. There is no evidence that those with permits build better structures than those built "illegally," though the construction inspection process in place for the "legal" buildings should ensure the compliance with the current technical standards. But lack of *information* on the hazards, such as precise location of fault lines and how to build safer structures, also contributes to poor building *practices*. Overall, the improvement of building practices—discussed in chapter 3 and briefly mentioned here—is paramount for a disaster-prone country like Turkey.

Improving building quality

The collapse of housing, typically four to eight stories high with many tenants, accounted for most of the deaths and injuries in the Marmara quakes. Many structures that collapsed were on or too near the fault lines. But clearly some structures are better designed and built than others often of the same vintage. The photograph in spotlight figure 1 shows a collapsed building while the adjacent one does not. Spotlight figure 2 shows a collapsed bridge with undamaged but displaced spans; so the fault may not lie only with private owners who flouted a building code.

Spotlight figure 1 **Damages to dwellings**

Source: Archives of the Turkish Photo Reporters' Association.

With much of Turkey earthquake-prone, less damage and fewer lives lost require better structures. About 30 percent of publicly owned buildings (3,600 of 12,000) in Istanbul are vulnerable to earthquakes. But a major effort to retrofit and reconstruct important public structures is now under way. A World Bank project (The Istanbul Risk Mitigation and Emergency Preparedness Project, ISMEP approved in 2006) has sought to make Istanbul a more seismic-resilient city by helping its provincial administration develop thumb rules to help choose between retrofitting and rebuilding as well as to fix about 840 public buildings initially. Even though this is less than a quarter of all public buildings and a third of the 2,400 buildings deemed critical, the number of buildings retrofitted is likely to be higher given the additional resources attracted. The unprecedented scale of this retrofitting is improving engineering practices, but only careful evaluation after the project's completion can tell how successful it has been.

In addition to publicly owned buildings, some 35 to 38 percent of private buildings are thought to be unsafe, and 70 percent to be below the higher current seismic standards (JICA 2002). Retrofitting is expensive, but more worrying is that with poor records and unlicensed construction, it is unclear how much new construction is safer. And there is every reason to be concerned. Because retrofitting and urban transformation go hand in hand, much attention has been given to improving Turkey's building code and its enforcement.

The role of a code, more than its contents

Turkey has tried to learn from the experience of others, particularly from California's and the EU's experiences. Turkey's seismic code, originally drawn in 1975, was updated in 1998 and

Spotlight figure 2 Damage to infrastructure

Source: Arifiye Bridge (by Suleyman Arat from Hurriyet 2009).

2007. Together with a 1985 development law that defined urbanization principles and other relevant aspects related to structures, the code provided the basis for safer structures and better urban planning. But compliance is poor, despite a new edict on building inspection that parliament enacted in 2000 to improve it. Chapter 3 explains why flouting the code is also not always an enforcement issue, but a symptom of a different sickness: the unfortunate combination of lack of information and incentives.

Much effort went into adapting the content of California's quake-resistant norms into Turkey's seismic code, but greater understanding of the role of a code in a country's institutional setting would have also helped. Municipalities, including Istanbul, have underfunded municipal engineering and staffed planning departments with unaccredited engineers. In such situations, building codes become mere hurdles to overcome, opening the door to corruption: in 2006, 40 municipal officials in three towns in Turkey were arrested for taking bribes in return for allowing unlicensed construction (Escaleras, Anbarci, and Register 2007).

Clearly, the role of a code depends on the situation and that differs across countries and changes over time. It is unfortunate when attention to building codes (regardless of how appropriate or necessary) distracts from what can be done to improve building practices. Owners need both the incentive and information to build well, and chapter 3 shows that the government can do much to correct the former and supply the latter. It is difficult to say how many fewer lives would have been lost in 1999 had all Turkish buildings complied with the code. But even if all new buildings are well constructed, many people will remain vulnerable because of the large existing stock of buildings of dubious quality. Retrofitting will take time even if it is worth doing. So improving preparedness is urgent.

Improving preparedness

Greater Istanbul and the Istanbul Governorate have sought to reduce the city's vulnerability by increasing emergency preparedness (skills and technical capacities of response units, but also public awareness and training). A World Bank project is helping build and equip new Disaster Management Centers with modern emergency management information and communication equipment. Containers with first aid equipment and supplies are in several localities, and civic organizations know what to do (spotlight figure 3). Forty-six neighborhoods in Istanbul and 73 in the Marmara region have been equipped with materials for first responders, and the District Disaster Support Project (Mahalle Afet Destek Projesi) has trained 3,136 volunteers.

Each of the three pieces—advancing insurance, inculcating safer building practices, and improving preparedness—is a necessary ingredient for a safer Turkey. The government can complement these initiatives by making access to better information easier and restoring owners' incentives sooner. No two disasters unfold the same way, however, and only when the next one strikes will the adequacy of these arrangements be known.

Spotlight figure 3 Container for emergency medical relief and the cover of the Handbook for Local Disaster Preparedness

Source: Istanbul Provincial Disaster and Emergency Directorate.

CHAPTER 3

Prevention by Individuals

This chapter examines how people choose prevention measures individually, and the next chapter, collectively. It begins with a simple analytical framework to understand how much prevention individuals choose to undertake, how much insurance to purchase, and how much residual risk to bear. It then concentrates on whether individuals undertake enough prevention.

People are guided by information—much of it embedded in prices—and limited by their budgets: they undertake prevention up to the point when the expected benefits (avoiding losses) exceed the measures' costs. Yet people differ, and their choices are not identical even when confronted with similar budget constraints. Some choices reflect distorted prices and others inadequate knowledge of the hazards or newer technologies of prevention. Individuals also differ in their risk aversion. Many live in exposed areas known to be hazardous—whether in poverty in Bangladesh or in affluence along the Florida coast. Observing this, some conclude that people are fatalistic or myopic. Recent findings that people misperceive risks lend credence to the view that people do not always act in their own interests, but there are also more prosaic explanations.

A detailed empirical study finds that property values in Bogota, Colombia, reflect hazard risks after correcting for proximity to work and access to such conveniences as public transport. This is consistent with risk being perceived correctly and suggests people make informed choices—even if some seem harsh when people live in riskier locations. But structures that are safe could, with sufficient care and expense, be built in risky areas (on hillslopes, in seismic areas). But when a person's ownership of property is not secure, the possibility of eviction or demolition erodes the incentive to invest in safe structures. Of 1.2 million land titles distributed in 1996 Peru, land titling is associated with a 68 percent increase in housing renovation within four years (Field 2005).

Insecurity of land holdings is not the only thing that erodes incentives to build well: rent controls or other similar regulations diminish a landlord's incentive to maintain buildings. Neglected buildings collapse in earthquakes and severe storms kill occupants. The harmful effects of such controls and distorting taxes (such as stamp duties on transactions) accumulate over decades. They have led to poor land use and building size and location (decaying industries on land that could be put to better use). They have also contributed to a housing shortage, leaving the poor to live in unsafe shanty towns that mushroom in and around prospering cities. And they have starved cities of tax revenues, so the needed infrastructure is not built, or is built on the cheap.

Prevention, insurance, and coping: A simple framework

Ehrlich and Becker (1972) explain how a person chooses how much risk to bear and how to reduce it given the choices they have (De Ferranti and others 2000; Gill, Packard, and Yermo 2005; Baeza and Packard 2006). The person (or family) can take prevention measures ("self-protection" in their paper) that reduce the loss from a hazard (living on an upper floor or building on a higher plinth to avoid losses from a flood), and buy insurance that compensates for losses when they occur. They also distinguish self-insurance, when the person hopes to be able to absorb a loss, from market insurance, which pays a specified sum when the event occurs. Prevention entails measures that have a cost, and insurance entails a premium, and a person chooses the level and combination that best moderates consumption fluctuations.

Everyone makes such choices every day in many settings, and each person may choose differently. Some buy a costlier car built to reduce the risk of a fatal accident, others a cheaper flimsy car—and insurance. Similarly, some farmers self-insure by planting different crops in dispersed plots, sacrificing some yield by doing so. Informal arrangements (reciprocity with neighbors) reduce the losses from a broken leg or the death of an ox, but they cannot fully handle the risk of a disaster that simultaneously affects the entire local community. Market insurance helps in such cases because it extends beyond the local community. When prevention is "excessively" costly, insurance allows people to make transfers in specified "states of the world" (e.g. if an earthquake occurs).

Put differently, people generally choose the desired amount of prevention given their income—but a few may spend excessively to avoid all risks, and others too little. Taking risks implies that they will occasionally have adverse outcomes and must "cope" with them. Table 3.1 summarizes how people prevent, insure, and cope as individuals, communities, and through governments (coping collectively is "relief and recovery").

Table 3.1 Individuals and governments prevent, insure, and cope with disasters

Measure	Individuals/household	Community	Government and international organizations
Prevention	• Owning multiple assets and with many sources of income; • Investments to protect and maintain assets (timely repairs); • Permanent migration.	• Relocating to safer areas as a group; • Community-training programs; • Local public goods and services (community-based Information systems, small-scale irrigation and infrastructure projects).	• Good analysis and a system to convey information about risk (disaster risk profiles, raising public aware-ness, early warning systems); • Public works; • Well specified and enforced property rights and, by extension, predictable policies and political systems.
Self-insurance	• Owning both financial and nonfinancial assets (livestock, stored grain, durables).	• Local borrowing and savings schemes; • Rotating access to common property resources.	• Facilitating markets for different assets, including household goods; • Ready access to prevailing market prices; • Adequate physical and social infrastructure.
Market insurance	• Property and catastrophe insurance; • Agricultural insurance.	• Microfinance (semi-formal); • Savings and credit associations; • Cereal and grain banks.	• Sovereign budget insurance and catastrophe bonds.
Coping (relief and recovery)	• Temporal migration intensification or expansion of household labour; • Draw on stocks of social capital (credit, food, charity/begging); • Running down stocks of human and physical capital; • Reducing or minimiz-ing household expenditures.	• Rotating savings and credit associations (ROSCAs); • Inter-household transfers and private remittances; • Public employment guarantee schemes.	• Safety nets (cash transfers and public works); • Social investment projects (social funds); • Disaster aid funds or food donor assistance (contingent loans).

Source: World Bank staff, based on Gill and Ilahi 2000.

Prevention: Do individuals do enough?

This section takes two approaches, both limited, to attempt to answer the question. The first examines the financial merits of specific prevention measures, and whether they are "widely" undertaken. The second approach examines whether observed market prices reflect known risks: if they do, one is more confident that people act appropriately in their self-interest.

A study commissioned for the report examined the costs and benefits of specific retrofitting measures that homeowners could take against different natural disasters in hazard-prone areas of four low- and middle-income countries (box 3.1) (IIASA/RMS/Wharton 2009).

Figure 3.1 shows benefit-cost ratios for the four examples using assumed (but reasonably typical) costs: elevating a house with mixed wall, concrete floor, and asbestos roof by one meter in Jakarta; protecting windows and doors in a wood frame house in Canaries, St. Lucia; retrofitting a five-story building to increase quake resiliency in Istanbul; and flood-proofing a brick house by building with new brick on a raised plinth in the Rohini Basin, Uttar Pradesh, India. The benefit-cost ratio is shown for a range of assumed discount rates (0–15 percent) and different expected durations of the structure (1, 5, 10, and 25 years). Prevention seems cost-effective for the above measures in all four cases if the structure lasts 10 years or more.[1] For shorter time periods, cost effectiveness depends on the discount rate (for high discount rates, the benefit-cost ratio is less than one for some of these measures, implying that prevention is not financially viable).

Are people undertaking such prevention? Some do, others do not. A survey of 254 adults from five locales in Istanbul after Turkey's 1999 earthquake on risk perceptions and attitudes towards prevention found that while people were aware of the risk, only a fifth of respondents said they had taken some preventive action: 13 percent inside the home and 9 percent for the building (Fişek and others 2002). Only about half those who had taken no action invoked high costs (a possible proxy for a tight budget constraint) as a reason for inaction.[2] Such seemingly inconsistent behavior warrants an explanation, and many are turning to the recent findings of behavioral economics.

A walk on the behavioral side

Traditional economists explain peoples' choices invoking prices and incomes, rarely questioning whether people choose wisely. A growing body of work in cognitive psychology lends credence to these doubts. These disciplines have come together as behavioral economics, and its findings have important implications for how we view risk.

Kahneman and Tversky (1979) pioneered this field, and the biases that they and others have since found go by different labels. Rabin (1998, 2002) surveys this vast and growing literature and lists several systematic biases. People have a loss aversion bias: they care more about the costs of undertaking some action (could be retrofitting or buying insurance) than about its gains, even if these are equal-sized. Ricciardi (2007) surveys the

Box 3.1   Evaluating the costs and benefits of structural mitigation measures

The commonly used metric for measuring the hazard risk of an asset or portfolio of assets is the exceedance probability (EP) curve. An EP curve indicates the probability that a given loss will occur in a given year. Most risk models involve four main modules:

- A *hazard* module characterizes the hazard in a probabilistic manner. Often the events that can impact the risk are described—estimating location, magnitude, and associated annual probability among other characteristics.
- An *exposure* module describes a structure or multiple structures that may be damaged. Key characteristics that describe a structure's susceptibility to damage are defined.
- A *vulnerability* module estimates the damage to the exposure at risk, given the magnitude of the hazard.
- A *financial loss* module draws on these first three modules to create loss estimates that have a given probability of exceedance.

Based on these modules, an EP curve can be constructed as depicted in the figure below, where the likelihood that losses will exceed L_i is given by P_i. The x-axis shows the magnitude of the loss (for example, in dollars) and the y-axis shows the probability that annual losses will exceed this level (Grossi and Kunreuther 2005, Hochrainer 2006).

Box figure 3.1. Example of an exceedance probability (EP) curve

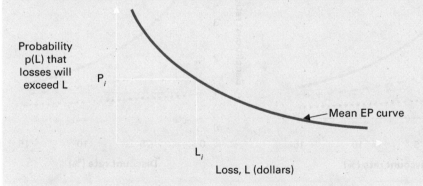

For each case study, relevant measures were selected for reducing losses from the disaster. EP curves were constructed for a representative house or houses with and without the preventive measure in place. Benefits were quantified through reductions in the gross average annual loss (area under the EP curve) after preventive measures are applied to a structure and discounted over the relevant time horizon. Cost estimates of each preventive measure were derived from various sources. Combining these estimates, benefit-cost ratios were calculated.[3] Measures are effective when the benefit-cost ratios exceed one.

Source: IIASA/RMS/Wharton 2009.

behavioral finance literature, which finds the average investor perceives the pain of a loss twice as much as the pleasure from an equivalent gain. This loss aversion bias is related to the status quo bias: people prefer things as they are to changes that involve losses of some goods, even if these losses

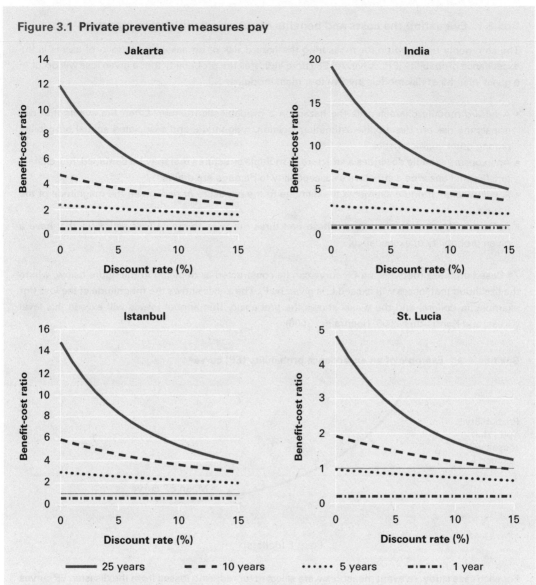

Figure 3.1 Private preventive measures pay

Note: The figure refers to the following examples: elevating a house with mixed wall, concrete floor, and asbestos roof by one meter in Jakarta; protecting windows and doors in a wood frame house in Canaries, St. Lucia; retrofitting a five-story building to increase quake resiliency in Istanbul; and flood-proofing a brick house by building with new brick on a raised plinth in India.
Source: IIASA/RMS/Wharton 2009.

are more than fully compensated. It is less clear how such biases translate into prevention measures. Is paying for prevention the immediate loss (in which case there may be insufficient prevention), or is the expected damage the loss that weighs on people (in which case prevention measures would be undertaken)?

Experiments also find that people attach greater value to something they already own ("endowment effect") than they did before having it—even when selling or buying involves no transaction cost. Kahneman, Knetsch, and Thaler (1990) gave mugs worth $5 each to a group of students, and offered to buy them back. Students exchanged their mugs for almost twice what another (statistically identical) group not given the mugs bid for them ($7 vs. $3.50). People seem to prefer what they already possess, and this endowment effect appears in many settings. It suggests inertia or the psychological cost of change: new efforts at prevention are less likely than protective measures already in place, but it does not say whether existing measures are sufficient.

Kahneman and Tversky have also exposed systematic misperceptions of probabilities and risks: people overestimate low probability events and underestimate large probability events. This would imply that Turks may overestimate earthquake risks and, if these translate into action, would overprotect their properties while Bangladeshis would underestimate the risk of floods and under protect their homes and assets.

But the biases are not consistently related to the frequency of events: people underestimate the risks they have not experienced and overestimate those that they have. Those who have driven without incident have a lower perception of the risk of an automobile accident than those who had a recent accident. Similarly, the perceptions of risk rise after an earthquake, an infrequent event, and people take more precautions (Jackson 1981). The perceived risk of an airplane crash or a terrorist attack is especially high *after* one has occurred, and hearing about an event raises risk perceptions less than experiencing it. Hung, Shaw, and Kobayashi (2007) found that those living outside the river dyke in Hanoi who experienced the catastrophic floods of 1971 expected future floods more than others.

People are misled by how questions are phrased in a survey or how information is presented, so "framing" matters. In the classic "Asian disease" experiment, people were asked to choose between two undesirable options to counteract a disease threatening 600 people. Tversky and Kahneman (1981) showed how people chose different alternatives, even though the choices had the same consequences, depending on how the outcomes were described (saving people or people dying). Yamagishi (1997) found that people generally think a disease to be less dangerous when fatalities are conveyed as percentage probabilities (12.86 percent) than as proportions or fractions (1,286 out of 10,000). Keller, Siegrist, and Gutscher (2006) found that psychology students in the University of Zurich perceived a higher threat of flood when flood was presented as a 40-year risk (with 33 percent probability of flood) as opposed to an annual risk (with 1 percent probability of flood).

A survey conducted in the United States in 2006 finds that most respondents assess their risks as "below average" (Viscusi and Zeckhauser 2006). Those in riskier areas who experienced disasters estimate their risks to be higher, but not as high as they should statistically. Put differently, these people appeared to underestimate their risks even though the survey was conducted when the World Trade Center attacks and Hurricane Katrina were neither fresh nor forgotten.

More prosaic explanations

Behavioral economics is interesting, especially the research under way. But should policies change when we know that answers to a survey depend on how the question is phrased and how behavior in experimental settings is inconsistent? Behavioral economics finds biases in both directions. Did Istanbul's current residents experience the 1999 Marmara earthquake (in which case they overestimate the likelihood of an earthquake) or hear about it (in which case they underestimate the odds)? And if any bias depends on distance, would perceptions cross international boundaries into neighboring Greece?

There are at least three more prosaic explanations for why people may take fewer prevention measures than others think they should. First, people without security of ownership (this includes renters) will be reluctant to incur the expense of prevention—even if they know the benefits—because they would not benefit if evicted. Insecure ownership is widespread, and the country spotlight on Turkey illustrates the prevalence of buildings without permits, often on land to which they do not have clear title. Similarly, landlords would not incur the expense if rents were controlled or rent increases were restricted (as with laws that limit rent escalation in a lease).

Second, if retrofitting capacity were limited, perhaps because only a few have the resources, skills, or special equipment necessary, it would take several years to retrofit the existing stock of buildings—even if retrofitting were cost-effective. A survey like that of post-quake Istanbul cited earlier would find that only a fraction of the buildings were retrofitted. But it is difficult to infer myopia from a snapshot, and subsequent surveys may find an increase in retrofitted buildings.

Third, even if retrofitting were cost-effective now, there is an "option value" to waiting if retrofitting technology itself changes rapidly and costs are expected to decline. Even if the financial returns to retrofitting were high, the returns from postponing the retrofit may be greater still because lower cost technology may soon be available. Under these circumstances, owners who do not retrofit are being far-sighted, not myopic (though tenants would live with the risk of postponing the retrofit).

It would be inappropriate to make "policy recommendations" based on such ambiguous evidence: more searching studies are needed to know whether people systematically ignore risks and why people appear to neglect prevention.

Prices reflect hazard risks when land and real estate markets work

If property values reflect hazard risks correctly, people can make informed choices based on prices that guide their decisions on where to live and what prevention measures to undertake. To examine empirically whether property values indeed reflect such risks, one must correct for other desirable qualities (location, view, and other amenities) that also influence property prices. Moreover, unlike stocks (equities) that trade frequently on a centralized exchange, every house and building is unique and trades infrequently. Even when property changes hands, the recorded price may not be accurate if there are taxes or other adverse consequences. And even if prices were recorded accurately, houses that trade in consecutive periods may differ considerably in size, quality, and location. So it is difficult to construct price indices without making some assumptions. Consequently, the price indices may *appear* to change sluggishly even if the prices (bid and ask) respond quickly to information and to changing market conditions, and econometric techniques must respect these limits of the data. Even so, many studies find that property prices reflect the risk of hazards.

Istanbul property values in 2000 were lower near the fault lines in the Sea of Marmara than those farther away (Onder, Dokmeci, and Keskin 2004). In contrast, proximity to the fault line did not matter for 1995 property value data. The 1999 earthquake may have made people aware of earthquake risks, so more recent property prices reflect this. But as the Turkey Spotlight shows, there have been many quakes through history, and a more likely explanation is that after the 1999 earthquake, many fault lines were newly identified and publicized.

Similarly in the United States, flood zone disclosure is mandatory in some areas of North Carolina, so buyers are aware of flood risk before buying a property. Using a hedonic property price model, Bin, Landry, and Meyer (2009) find that the property market reflects geographic differentials in flood risk, reducing property values on average by 7.3 percent. The market capitalizes risk as flood insurance premia equal the discount in property values. Bin and Polasky (2004) examine the effect of Hurricane Floyd on property values in North Carolina (September 1999, affecting 2 million people and causing $6 billion in property damage). Few properties were insured before the hurricane, and the prices of houses in the floodplain fell between 4 and 12 percent. This decline was more than the capitalized insurance premia, suggesting that home owners bore costs that exceeded the insured value. (The reduction of the property values on average was $7,460 and the increase in premia for flood insurance was $6,880.)

A background paper for this report examines whether property prices reflect seismic risks in Bogota, Colombia (Lall and Deichmann 2009). Hedonic models allow measurement of the extent to which land and house prices capitalize the attractions like size, views, and amenities (Lancaster 1966; Rosen 1974), and this technique could also capture the effect of disaster risks. Some 800,000 buildings in Bogota that differed in their exposure to seismic risk were matched on a range of characteristics (such as size, construction quality, distance from the city center, and whether residential, commercial, or industrial).[4] This technique implies that the only difference among comparable properties is their level of hazard risk. This allows us to assess whether property values are lower in riskier areas, and if they are, that suggests capitalizing dis-amenities from hazard risk.

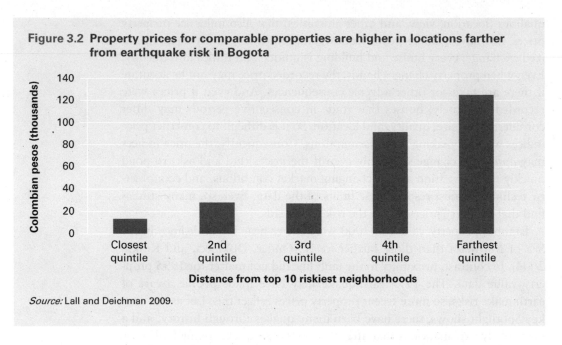

Figure 3.2 Property prices for comparable properties are higher in locations farther from earthquake risk in Bogota

Source: Lall and Deichman 2009.

Property values per unit of construction were compared in the 10 most seismically risky neighborhoods, grouped by distance from the riskiest area (figure 3.2). Properties in areas adjoining the riskiest neighborhoods are valued 13,434 pesos higher than in the riskiest area, with the price difference increasing with distance: 28,265 pesos for the second quintile and 124,533 pesos for the farthest quintile of neighborhoods.

So, land and property values reflect seismic risks in a poor country, a remarkable finding that casts doubt over assertions that people are myopic and ignore hazard risks.

Office rents also reflect hazard risks. Gomez-Ibañez and Ruiz Nuñez (2007) gathered data on office rents in the central business district of 155 cities around the world in 2005, along with information that could affect rentals such as construction wage rates, steel and cement prices, metropolitan populations, and incomes. These data were linked to that on disasters hotspots to see whether office rents are sensitive to disaster risks.

Rents are lower (by 30 percent) in earthquake-prone cities, but not in cities prone to floods and cyclones.

The results suggest that, where markets function, prices tend to reflect hazard risk. But what these studies do not distinguish is whether prices reflect risk stemming from exposure (in a hazardous site) or vulnerability (building characteristics that influence damage). This may well be an artificial distinction since technological advances make it increasingly possible to build safe buildings in hazardous areas. There is suggestive evidence, however, that prices reflect even vulnerability—at least when information about vulnerability (building characteristics) is readily available. Nakagawa and others (2007) use a 1998 hazard map of the Tokyo Metropolitan Area to examine the extent to which rents reflect earthquake risk and seismic-resistant construction. The Building Standard Law amended in 1981 to improve buildings' seismic resistance applied only to new construction. Rents on older buildings (likely less safe) were lower in the risky areas. In Tehran, Willis and Asgary (1997) found by interviewing real estate agents that earthquake-resistant houses in all city districts are significantly more expensive than others.

This evidence suggests that vulnerability-reducing measures also tend to be capitalized into property values—at least when they are revealed through hazard-location maps or data on building quality: expenditures in such measures are likely to be recovered through increases in property prices. And such investments are likely to increase with economic density because people have more to lose with disruptions from natural hazards.

Just as we should be careful about inferring too much about aggregate behavior from individual—and often idiosyncratic—behavior, we ought to be cautious about deducing individual behavior from aggregate analyses. Still, the discussion here underscores the role of markets in capitalizing hazard risk into property prices, and the role of prices and information in helping individuals perceive risks and make informed choices. Tokyo is a city where rental and land markets operate reasonably well. When such markets are stifled—as in many developing countries—that reduces the incentives for individuals to undertake such risk reduction measures.

Smothered markets dampen prevention incentives

Prices incorporate a lot of information—even about hazard risk, as just shown—and people make better decisions when markets are allowed to function. So, the importance of making hazard risk information available cannot be overemphasized. Perhaps because of this significance, the political will to not have information on rising levels of risk publicized is often strong. For example, even though FEMA in the United States has updated coastal flood maps for the U.S. Gulf, it cannot get coastal communities to accept them because the information would reduce property prices. Systematic mechanisms for tracking information related to the changing nature of risk, and translating it into risk-related property valuations, would go a long way to increase the incentives for prevention.[5]

The markets relevant for safe buildings are those not only for land but also for related goods and services: if cement prices are controlled, a black market emerges where prices exceed what they would otherwise be. And if cement were allocated to selected villages or people (deemed deserving or vulnerable), many would surreptitiously sell and not use it because of the high prevailing prices. Although people know that their mud huts may wash away for want of cement, they make the difficult tradeoff if the proceeds could be better used to feed a starving family or buy medicine for a sick child.

Important markets have been smothered in many countries, sometimes inadvertently. For example, price and rent controls imposed by the British Empire during World War II remain in some cities (such as Cairo and

Mumbai).[6] Mumbai's building predicament shows how vested interests became deeply entrenched long after that war ended and countries became independent. Buildings in Mumbai collapse during the heavy monsoon downpours because they have deteriorated for decades and because of feeble attempts to improve the situation.

Rent controls in Mumbai may have initially benefited tenants at the expense of landlords, but over time everyone suffers. Rent controls cause landlords to forgo maintenance and neglect their properties, and tenants not only live in dilapidated buildings but die when they collapse in heavy rains. Even if tenants are willing to either pay higher rents or to maintain the building, each tries to not pay his share of the expense (free riding), especially if appropriate retrofitting involves structural changes to the entire residential structure and not to individual apartments. Tenants also may lack the legal authority to make changes to their building's structure. And even when tenants overcome free riding (and the tenants of the entire building agree), they may lack the title to obtain a mortgage. Tenants with funds soon move to newer and safer buildings, and those who remain are often poor with few alternatives. Tenants in rent-controlled apartments often sublet without the landlord's agreement, but they would demand the present value of the lower rent in return ("key money" in New York; "pugree" in Mumbai). Their legal right to do so varies, and in Mumbai the sums are so large and the tax rates are so high that this "black money" is rarely declared.

Rent controls are not unique to Mumbai or developing countries (Seligman 1989). They exist in about 40 countries, including many developed countries (Global Property Guide 2009). Rent control laws have remained in place in one form or the other in New York City since 1943, where there are about a million rent-regulated and 50,000 rent-controlled apartments (Council of the City of New York 2009). As recently as 2009, legislation was passed in New York that limits the ability of landlords statewide to increase rents. Such legislation is expected to return to regulation many household units previously attracting market rent (Peters 2009).

Rent controls are not the only market distortion. Real estate transactions in many countries incur a stamp tax—the same that spurred American colonies to rebel in the 1770s.[7] The ad valorem is on sales (at a punitive 20 percent rate until quite recently), not on owning property. But taxing transactions reduces property sales and encourages undervaluation when new owners register their claim in the city office, where registrars often do not dispute it, perhaps in exchange for a bribe. So, true market prices are difficult to discern. The revenues are not large, but they do not accrue to the city that provides the infrastructure and services (water supply, garbage collection). Worse, real estate is often transferred or bequeathed without being recorded, making the land register out of date. So, borrowing against property is difficult. More pernicious than low revenues accruing to a part of government that does not provide city services is the poor land use that results—a particular problem in rapidly transforming cities. Decrepit "sick" industries that barely operate (such as once-profitable textile mills) remain on large land tracts in prime locations with easy access to old roads and railway lines while new industries locate where workers cannot easily commute.

A city cannot provide services without revenue, and Indian cities depend on what the state or central government transfers. And when the city's residents do not pay taxes directly to the city administration, officials are not always responsive to their needs. To prevent excessive demands on existing and ancient infrastructure, the city of Mumbai restricts a structure's floor-area ratio or "FAR" (a building's total floor area divided by the lot size) to 2.0 for a four-story building, preventing the construction of tall buildings. Mumbai planners went against the grain of markets: floor-area ratios were 4.5 when introduced in 1964 and instead of allowing denser development to accommodate urban growth, they were reduced to 1.3 in 1991. Mumbai's buildings have fewer floors than other major cities: a third that of Shanghai and less than a fifth that of Moscow. The potential gains from denser development are so large that some developers have offered to pay for infrastructure in exchange for being allowed to construct taller buildings. But such deals can easily spawn more corruption. Besides, tackling infrastructure in an ad hoc rather than a well-planned way would result in more difficulties down the road. So land use is dismal: growth is accommodated outward not upward, putting greater demands on transport.

These difficulties are not unique to Mumbai. Bertaud and Brueckner examine the welfare costs in Bangalore, an even faster growing Indian city where traffic congestion threatens continuing prosperity (Bertaud and Brueckner 2004). Other cities have attempted to regulate development densities, reducing housing supply on suitable land. In 1979, the federal government in Brazil established the basic legislation at the national level for developing, approving, and registering urban land subdivisions. Among these parameters: a minimum lot size of 125 square meters, with minimum frontage of 5 meters, and a compulsory donation of 35 percent of development area for public uses and open spaces. This effectively zoned many poor people out of the formal land and housing market (Lall, Wang, and Da Mata 2007).

Disparities, discount rates, and the poor

Poor people face disproportionately high hazard risks: the aggregate statistics in chapter 1 show this, and the developments in Mumbai illustrate why. Evidence from Bogota shows that the poor tend to cluster in more hazardous areas. Map 3.1 shows areas of differing seismic risk. Map 3.2 shows that the poor live in the most earthquake prone-areas: on average, twice as risky.

What can one infer from this? Property prices reflect seismic risks, so risky property is cheaper to rent or buy. Not surprisingly, the poor live in these areas—not just in Bogota but elsewhere. As property prices in the worst affected areas fell after Hurricane Andrew in 1992, more low-income households moved to these locations (Smith and others 2006). This is a

Map 3.1 An earthquake risk index for Bogota

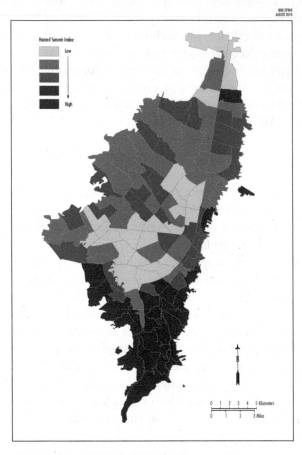

Source: Lall and Deichmann 2009.

pattern repeated around the world: the poor often live in dangerous areas and slums are often at risk for disasters.

It is sometimes asserted that the poor are (besides being cash constrained) myopic and have a higher discount rate than the rich. Yet those who have carefully examined how the poor live find they save an impressive proportion of their meager incomes (Collins and others 2009). Using 250 detailed, yearlong "financial diaries," they show that villagers and slum dwellers in Bangladesh, India, and South Africa maintained that even those living on less than a dollar a day save large proportions of their meager incomes. Such savings are entrusted to friends and relatives and do not directly find their way to banks or other formal financial intermediaries. The poor routinely make huge sacrifices for future gains—moving far from their rural families to squalid urban settings to earn money to send home and provide their children with more food and better education. Scrounging through the rubbish bins as rag-pickers is still working, and living in the drainage ditches may not be an intertemporal choice but a location decision that combines cheap land and housing with proximity to employment centers. The poor's

Map 3.2 Poor people live closer to hazard-prone areas in Bogota

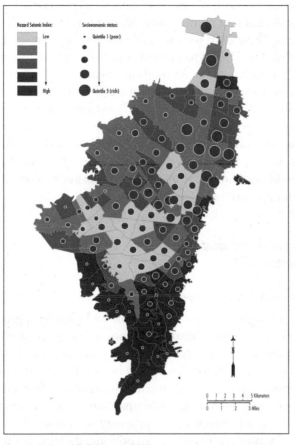

Source: Lall and Deichmann 2009.

choices are limited by the absence of adequate public goods, such as public infrastructure: most cities in poor countries lack reliable buses, and many regulations deter collective taxi and mini bus services.

A study of informal settlements in Jakarta before, during, and after the February 2007 floods found that people know the risks they face (Texier 2008). Some 68 percent of respondents knew the high risk of flooding, but more than 40 percent preferred to stay despite the dangers, not to move and risk losing their jobs. Similar evidence from Pune, India, shows that poor households prefer to have easier access to jobs, even though many of the slums are on riverbanks prone to flooding or on hilltops subject to mud-slides. Some 45 percent of houses in Santo Domingo's largest slum are on a river flood plain and vulnerable when it rains (Fay and others 2003). Poor families on steeply sloped land in Caracas and Rio de Janeiro are vulnerable to landslides.

The poor bear the brunt of the cumulative effects of such policies (tax structure, city financing arrangements, and so on). In a city like Mumbai, they typically live in slums that mushroom on vacant land, much of it owned by the state and central government (directly or indirectly, such as the sewage authority or railways). Worse, the slum's garbage is dumped in adjoining drainage ditches that become clogged; so rains result in floods that the poor drown in. These lands were set aside for good reasons (drainage, flood overflows), but it is difficult to prevent squatters and almost impossible to evict them. The Indian Slum Areas (Improvement and Clearance) Act of 1954 is a central government law that the city and state have no stomach to enforce. Slum dwellers pay thugs "rent" or "protection money," and the thugs buy off the local constables with a bribe, deliver electoral votes to grateful politicians, and intimidate rival candidates seeking change. Under these circumstances, suggestions to strengthen or enforce the building code to prevent buildings from collapsing during the heavy monsoon rains would likely hurt those it is trying to help.

Improving individuals' decisions: What can governments do?

Get land and real estate markets to work

This can go a long way to inducing people to locate in appropriate areas and undertake prevention. Markets cannot work when transactions are taxed at prohibitive rates. A city should raise revenue with a low tax rate on a wide base; but its administration should be simple. And although a tax on property values has much merit, ascertaining appropriate values requires a functioning property market, and perhaps even changes to central government taxation. An ad valorem tax on property value not only raises revenue without misallocating resources but also provides the incentive to put land to its best use. The most appropriate economic density of urban development would then follow. Taiwan, China; Hong Kong SAR, China; and Singapore became major commercial centers in large part because much of their fiscal revenues are from taxing land values (World Bank 2008). Hong Kong SAR, China, therefore did not tax trade and commerce heavily, and other cities such as Johannesburg and Sydney tax real estate only through land values. Some cities in Pennsylvania have a two-rate system, with land values taxed at a higher rate than improvements (buildings). Property taxes account for up to 30 percent of local revenues in many European countries.

It will not be easy to remove the panoply of distortions, because many now benefit vested interests. Nor is knowing what to change first obvious. Such issues are outside the scope of this report; but even if such changes were made and people responded promptly (a fear of reversal may slow the response, especially because the politician's successor is not bound), a measureable improvement in building quality can take years. New construction is a small fraction of the existing building stock in established cities, and if a building lasted 50 years, only 2 percent would be replaced in any year.

Better policies will show their benefits more quickly in the newer developments, such as "infill" redevelopment where decayed industries stand and in peri-urban areas (Pelling 2003).[8]

For the poor, the government could greatly expand their choices, and this is more subtle than dictating what people should choose. Security of property (clear titles often help) allows people to invest in prevention measures, but this does not imply giving title to flood plains on which people have encroached. Indeed, in the United States, where property generally has clear title and well defined rights, FEMA purchased privately owned land in the flood plains to move people to safer locations. Land in safer locations must be made available—along with adequate and reliable public transport and other services. But locations cannot be easily categorized as "dangerous" or "safe": with the right design and construction, safe structures can be built on hillsides; but appropriate choices are likely only when many markets (including that for construction materials) are allowed to function.

Make hazard risk information more easily available

The government must map flood plains and fault lines, disclose them, and consult the public to decide which areas are unsuited for buildings (chapter 4 discusses what it takes to collect and analyze hazard information). Some government entities routinely collect information and data on hazards (flood plains, seismic fault lines) and properties (city records), but most are inaccessible to the public. This is even though technological advances—such as the abundance of free, simple, and open source software (for example, PostGIS, Geoserver, Mapserver, the GeoNode.org project)—make collecting and sharing information easy.

Prospective dwellers must be made aware of the risks of living in buildings close to active fault lines and on vulnerable soils. This requires investment in geological surveys and hazard monitoring stations, and dissemination of the resulting information as a public good. Providing information to landlords can also boost the chances of retrofitting, if landlords revise their cost-benefit calculations based on more precise probabilities of earthquake risk. And even if the revised (accurate) probability does not change the calculation, the public disclosure of the fact that building owners decide to build in high-risk areas or that they do not retrofit buildings in those areas appropriately, could spur public shaming. This could boost the probability of adopting appropriate disaster prevention measures (World Bank 2000).[9]

However, the seemingly simple act of collecting and providing information is not easy. Background papers for this report found obtaining disaster and related data from various public agencies in cities difficult, even though donors often funded the collection and automation of such data. Sometimes "security, commercial, and privacy" reasons are invoked, but only a few security interests are legitimate. Taking photographs from airplanes and at airports is illegal in India (a World War I measure), while far better and more sensitive images are routinely available from satellite imagery and accessible

Box 3.2 Assessing risk in Central America

Many Central American countries are on seismic fault lines and in the path of hurricanes. Determining their exposure and vulnerability is the first step in prevention and for insurance markets to develop. Much of the data and techniques to analyze risks are common to all of them; so sharing these data and what governments learn as they proceed would benefit all involved.

The Central American Probabilistic Risk Assessment (CAPRA) is a set of evaluation techniques and a communication platform to help governments make decisions. It begins with a catalogue of past events and resulting losses along with an inventory of assets (such as population, housing, and infrastructure) that are exposed to various hazards. The frequency of hurricanes, earthquakes, volcanoes, floods, tsunamis, and landslides are in the database, and probabilistic risk assessment models permit calculating loss exceedance curves or risk maps by hazard, sector, and period. A National Risk Atlas can illustrate the various hazards and risks, and the risk can be communicated and managed.

The platform's architecture has been developed by regional experts to be open, free, and modular, so a user could adjust it to each country's circumstances. It allows existing initiatives to be incorporated and avoids duplicating efforts. The Center for the Prevention of Natural Disasters in Central America led the efforts, supported by the United Nations' International Strategy for Disaster Reduction and the World Bank (through the Global Facility for Disaster Reduction and Recovery).

The first phase, begun in February 2008 with Costa Rica and Nicaragua, is being extended to other Central American countries.

Source: World Bank staff.

through the Internet. Sometimes commercial interests take precedence over public good aspects. Some countries have begun the long but important process of mapping hazards, vulnerability, and modeling risk (box 3.2).

Implement better building practices

Many die when buildings and infrastructure collapse during earthquakes, severe storms, and mudslides. Hazards reveal the weakness of buildings and other structures like bridges that, constructed differently, would have sustained less damage. A common emotional reaction is to blame private landlords, but many owner-occupied and government-owned buildings and structures also collapse. Corruption and builders are also blamed and public outrage and cries for the government to "do something" often result in such "stroke of the pen" measures as stronger building codes that are less effective than they sound.

This section discusses the role of building codes, examining what it takes to have better buildings and structures, not easy even in developed countries, such as Italy (box 3.3). Building well is not necessarily more expensive, but it does require all involved to be well informed about the physical properties of materials. Once built, mistakes become an unfortunate legacy, and retrofitting is technically difficult and expensive. Cities with a large stock of poorly built structures, whether in Italy or Turkey, will remain vulnerable— even if new buildings are better constructed.

Box 3.3 A century's struggle for sound buildings in Italy

The Italian peninsula is seismically active—but even 2,000 years ago, the Romans designed and built large buildings so well that many still survive. Building skills waxed and waned over the centuries, and periodic earthquakes prompted people to act, sometimes through government edicts.

Seismic areas began to be systematically identified after a particularly destructive 1908 earthquake in the southern part of Italy killed 90 percent of Messina's (Sicily) 130,000 inhabitants and a third of the 45,000 inhabitants of Reggio Calabria (mainland). In 1928, building regulations were introduced in seismic areas but applied only to new buildings and to where quakes occurred after 1908 (that had been mapped). Not confined to these areas, earthquakes continued to take a heavy toll.

World War II destroyed many buildings and a construction boom followed. Cities grew, and earthquakes periodically took their toll: the 1968 Belice earthquake in Sicily killed 370 people, injured more than 1,000, and made 70,000 homeless. The patchwork of regulations was replaced by a comprehensive law in 1974 making the Ministry of Public Works responsible for national anti-seismic regulations. The Ministry, with the help of the National Research Center (CNR in Italian) that had been studying the effects of the 1976 Friuli (northeast) and the 1980 Sicily earthquakes, updated the seismic map recording fault zones even where an earthquake had not (yet) occurred. When the Italian bureaucracy was decentralized in the 1990s, responsibility for seismic regulation was shared: the central government set the general criteria to identify seismic areas and the regional authorities demarcated them.

This arrangement changed again after 27 children and a teacher died in a school collapse in southern Italy after a relatively mild earthquake in October 2002 (5.4 Richter scale). Revisions to the Italian building code underway since early 2000 to reflect the rapid advances in seismic research and building technology accelerated, and the seismic map of 2004 distinguished areas with four categories of risk. The national government reduced the regional and city governments' discretion over building regulations for three more ris ky areas, partly reflecting the preferences of the political parties that formed the shifting coalition government and perhaps to protect people against local authorities' diluting the standards.

These changes did make quakes less deadly. But on April 7, 2009, another mild (5.5 Richter scale) earthquake became the deadliest in 30 years, killing almost 300 people in L'Aquila, Abruzzo region's largest city just off the main seismic fault line that runs down the spine of the peninsula. Some old buildings collapsed, but many apartment buildings constructed during the 1950s and 1960s also collapsed, and these were built of reinforced cement concrete.

Concrete, widely used since Roman times, is strong in compression but weak in tension. So reinforcing parts of beams and columns subject to tension using steel bars (which withstand tension well) allows larger structures to be built economically. Such reinforced concrete takes static loads well; but it is brittle and withstands lateral forces (released in earthquakes) poorly—unless specifically designed to do so. The head of Italy's Society of Engineers observed that many structures built in the 1950s and 1960s are vulnerable because the concrete did not use effective reinforcement techniques (though they may have conformed to the building codes of the time). Retrofitting such buildings is expensive and often not worthwhile.

Public anger erupted when even the "state of the art" San Salvatore regional hospital, which opened in 2000, had to be closed just when it was most needed. The damage may have been more superficial than structural, and an inquiry is underway, but blame is being passed around. News reports quote a Milanese architect describing provincial counterparts as "surveyors with no more than a diploma."

Such understandable anger is often misdirected, and even a century ago in San Francisco, accusations of corruption flew when large sections of the grand and costly City Hall collapsed in the 1906

(continued)

Box 3.3 A century's struggle for sound buildings in Italy *(continued)*

earthquake. While corruption was rampant in the city, the state, and even the national government at the time, a careful subsequent analysis tells a more complex tale (Tobriner 2006). The building was designed with newly developed steel reinforcement frames, but funds ran short (some may well have been stolen) during its extended construction, and no additional sums were authorized. The committee overseeing its construction, aware that the public expected a completed building, changed its design after construction had begun to reduce costs. It retained the heavy and ornate features in the façade and sacrificed the less visible structural features. Poor decisions and oversight (including the public's overseeing committee decisions) were responsible. Making better public decisions is the role of institutions—one of the central themes of this report.

Source: World Bank staff.

What role for a building code?

Many developed countries have good building codes, and many developing countries have none (or ignore them), making it natural to propose building codes in countries without one. Engineers and architects find a building code as useful and convenient as the tables that list the strength of various cross-sections of steel beams. Codes as convenient starting designs or rules of thumb may be helpful. But should they be mandated, carrying the force of law with penalties for violations, as minimum standards in every situation?

It is quite appropriate for one government agency to tell another less knowledgeable about construction: so there is no debate when the Ministry of Construction or the Public Works Department insists that the Ministry of Education build schools a certain way. These strictures could extend to buildings constructed or financed by donors and NGOs that help the government deliver public services. It may also be appropriate to make a builder liable for hefty damages if the building does not adhere to a code if the government, as owner, gives the builder leeway in design or construction: this is being proposed in Madagascar, where government schools serve as shelters against annual cyclones that cause many deaths. Countries with a different legal structure may not need a code to establish builders' negligence (or owners' liability if a building collapses).

While the government as owner has the right to specify what it wants done, should it, as regulator, insist on how private owners should build? This is often advocated even in countries where government owned buildings collapse more often than those privately owned.

Economists are often swayed by theoretical arguments, and we examine them before turning to some practical concerns. Economists may accept that a private owner has an incentive to build a good structure, but invoke externalities—the owner may not incur the expense of building well if others bear the cost of a building collapse. One classic example often invoked of a public good that a government should supply is lighthouses. However, Ronald Coase (1974), in a seminal article, notes that although economists often use lighthouses as examples of public goods, governments did not build lighthouses until very recently. Instead, lighthouses were built at considerable expense in remote and difficult locations to help ships ply dangerous waters and were financed by various associations of shipping companies (whose competitors would also benefit) and associations of seamen's widows and orphans (who would not get their loved ones back).

Cohen and Noll (1981) construct an elaborate model to determine the optimal building code in seismic areas, motivating the discussion by correctly stating that fires caused 90 percent of the damage following the 1906 San Francisco earthquake, leaving the reader with the impression that fire *spread* (the externality). A careful history of the San Francisco earthquake shows that numerous fires started *simultaneously*: 95 percent of residential chimneys were damaged, gas mains burst in numerous locations, street lanterns fell, and boilers exploded starting fires in multiple locations. People were overwhelmed, and there was not enough water to put out the fires.

Economists also invoke asymmetric information—that one party to a contract (such as renter or home buyer) knows less than the other (the landlord or developer)—to explain "market failures" that government interventions could correct. Despite Akerlof's (1970) elegant analysis of a market for lemons, used car markets thrive with dealers offering warranties, and workplaces have bulletin boards that allow employees to rely implicitly on their colleagues' honesty. Similarly, every society deals differently with the enormous informational asymmetry in choosing a spouse: dating or living together first is accepted in some settings while extended family networks gather information and arrange a match in others.

It is important to recognize the diverse arrangements that people devise without fixating on one that a few countries have found useful. Elinor Ostrom, whose work is better known after her 2009 Nobel Prize in economics, has long studied such mechanisms that have the advantage of self-enforcement. In some countries, builders establish a reputation for quality. In others, banks or insurers set standards for buildings they finance or insure. And in some, people rely on government, either through state ownership or regulations.

History matters and arrangements are path-dependent, but important underlying differences influence what is effective and appropriate. Germany industrialized earlier and became more urban than France or Italy. This both influenced and reflected the mobility of labor and the type of dwellings (single family homes, abutting townhouses, and building with multiple units) and their ownership. Only 40 percent of German homes are owner-occupied, while the proportion is 68 percent in the United States, 80 percent in Spain, and 78 percent in Mexico.[10] Rentals both require and reflect the ability to enforce contracts (such as evicting defaulting tenants without undue delay or expense).

A building code is but one cog in this complex mechanism that differs from one country to another, and copying one cog does not ensure its working in a different mechanism. Some may recognize this but nevertheless seek a strong building code to "set a goal." But this can do more harm than good, especially when laws are easier to write than to enforce. The code may provide a false sense of security if hazards are infrequent and violations go undetected, making the code obsolete. Codes are rarely revised, not just because of bureaucratic lethargy, but because arriving at a consensus is time consuming and difficult. On the other hand, no one cares about codes that will be ignored, which may be why some governments are quick to adopt them at donors' bidding; but donors are subsequently frustrated when the codes are not enforced. And worse, if laws meant to protect become an excuse to harass (and cudgels in the hands of the corrupt), laws and regulations come to be seen as hurdles to be overcome. It is not surprising that building codes are poorly enforced: the World Bank's *Doing Business* reports use them to measure delays indicating the extent to which businesses are hindered. Box 3.4 provides a thumbnail sketch of codes' differing roles in history.

Better building practices and the differing roles of codes

Questioning an ubiquitous or central role for a building code is not to deny the importance of good building practices—or a role for governments. To do this usefully, a code could be specific in two ways. One ("normative") is to specify the standards to be met, such as withstanding wind speeds of x kilometers per hour. But enforcement requires a facility to test the design before authorizing construction and a system of inspection to verify that what is built conforms to the approved design. Few governments have such testing capabilities. And if tests are delegated to a university or engineering association, there must be a trustworthy system to prevent counterfeit certificates or buying permits and passing inspections with bribes. The second way ("prescriptive") is to specify how to build, such as foundation at least y meters deep, or walls z centimeters thick with reinforcement bars. But this also requires inspection capabilities. Governments can help institute those capabilities, and in conjunction with other complementary measures, improve building practices, as in Pakistan and in Sri Lanka.[11]

Pakistan: Improving and not ignoring vernacular architecture

Most housing in developing countries is constructed without architects or engineers ("vernacular" buildings or architecture). People build their own homes or contract and oversee workmen who do. Available materials, their prices, worker skills, and construction techniques all change—sometimes rapidly. Reinforced concrete has become ubiquitous with the introduction of manufactured cement and steel rods, leading to the decline of wood framed structures. As residents from Italy to Istanbul are discovering, deaths and destruction from earthquakes rise as buildings without sufficient lateral strength and flexibility collapse. Concrete could be made resilient

Box 3.4 Building codes BC and their later kin

Building codes are not new. They have appeared—and disappeared—periodically. Hammurabi's code in 1750 BC sought, among other things, to make Sumerian buildings safe by adding punitive penalties to the builders' liabilities for any resulting damage:

- If a builder does not construct a house well and it falls and kills the owner, then the builder shall be put to death
- If the owner's son is killed, the builder's son shall be put to death.
- If the owner's slave is killed, the builder shall pay the owner, slave for slave.
- If it ruins goods, the builder shall compensate the owner for all that has been ruined, and shall re-erect the house at his own expense.
- If the walls of an incomplete house collapse, the builder shall rebuild the walls at his own expense.

Unlike Hammurabi's code specifying penalties, recent building codes specify what a safe building must have (thickness of walls, depth of foundation). But not all countries with a code got them for the same reasons, and such codes are not always mandatory for private owners.

Wooden houses were common in the United States, and while they resist earthquakes if constructed well (walls fastened to stiffen the structure against lateral movement), they are susceptible to fires that were common because wood, and later coal, were used to heat and cook. Fires spread rapidly when houses, especially those in poor neighborhoods, were built with a common wall (townhouses). Privately owned fire companies extinguished fires, but doused only homes that subscribed to their services (indicated by a medallion outside each house, and neighbors often chose different companies). There were endless disputes, some violent, when the fire company that a passerby summoned simply watched because the medallion was not its own: clearly not the best arrangement.

Many city governments responded to residents' concerns and took over the task of extinguishing fires. Some also instituted fire codes that specified such relevant items as chimney size and material, and the type of roof. Fires became less frequent as wood and coal gave way to kerosene and oil, and then to gas and electricity. Cheaper transport allowed people to move to the suburbs in the 20th century, and fires rarely spread when houses are built far apart.

But as with many regulations, vested interests sought to use them to their advantage: brick-layers in California—threatened by newer emerging technologies (steel and reinforced concrete)—prevailed in drafting the 1933 code, even though unreinforced brick buildings are dangerous in seismically active areas. Fire codes evolved into building codes, and the interests they protect are often apparent: many codes specified who does the construction and repair (such as licensed plumbers), not what is done. Nevertheless, such regulations are not onerous in the United States because courts are reluctant to infringe on the rights of owners to do what they please. Codes remain as a convenience because other laws (such as laws on renting) refer to the standards they set without creditors and insurers having to specify them.

Places where stone or brick was the main construction material had no need for codes—unless in a seismic area. All stone balconies were banned after a 1763 earthquake in Palermo, Italy. Such regulations, not always effective, can be captured by vested interests. But they are also path-dependent, allowing both improvements (as peoples' oversight becomes more effective) and the accretion of other unrelated features. It is well recognized that the content of a code should be appropriate, but its role depends on many other elements in a country. Regulations are supplemented and often substituted by other arrangements as well: licensing professions (strict in Germany) and trade associations (widely prevalent in Britain until a few decades ago) augment standards sought in a building code.

(continued)

Box 3.4 Building codes BC and their later kin *(continued)*

So the code's role in implementing better building practices will differ from country to country. "Building to code" in developed countries now often signifies minimal standards that most buildings easily surpass, but having a code to bring the few laggards into line is different—and easier than improving building quality of the majority.

Source: World Bank staff.

---

with sufficient care in design and construction, but all too often, traditional building practices are discarded and modern ones embraced without knowing their different characteristics. Newer concrete structures can fail—in Italy, Istanbul, Kashmir, and Gujarat—when earthquakes strike while traditional buildings remain standing (Jigyasu 2008).

The devastating 7.6 magnitude earthquake that struck the northern mountainous parts of Pakistan in October 2005 killed 73,300 people, seriously injured 62,400, and displaced 3.5 million from their homes. Of the estimated $3.5 billion reconstruction cost, almost half was for housing. Some 462,000 private homes were completely destroyed, another 99,300 severely damaged, many perched precariously on hillsides. Entire villages were cut off when 6,440 kilometers of roads were damaged. The few houses of concrete, whose brittle properties have already been described, collapsed as did others of "kutcha" construction—stone masonry with heavy roofs.

The government, quickly deciding that people should be entrusted to rebuild their own houses, assisted them financially and with technical advice on seismically resilient structures. This was a wise decision but controversial because NGOs were eager to rebuild. The government decided on a uniform grant equivalent to $2,900 for every family whose house was destroyed (450,000 households received this), and $1,250 for damaged homes (110,000 households). In addition, grants of $300 per household for livelihood support went to about 260,000 families, and $1,660 for deaths to $250 for minor injuries went to about 200,000 families. The total of $1.7 billion was sizable, and to reduce theft and corruption as it wended its way to the affected families, the funds were deposited directly in a bank account that the beneficiary opened.

The government created the Earthquake Reconstruction and Rehabilitation Authority (ERRA) to provide grants directly to the affected families conditional on houses being built to acceptable standards. Donors who helped fund the ERRA wanted the rebuilt houses to conform to a building code, and several multilateral donors consulted engineering experts in developed countries with experience in seismic design. Their advice on the minimum size and appropriate placement of reinforcement bars was undoubtedly good. But it was clear to those on the ground that such codes were unlikely to be adhered to. Although Pakistan has many engineers, few were trained in seismically resistant structures: university curricula simply did not cover the topic. Nor did engineers ply their trade in the remote communities affected. Only traditional techniques would enable houses to be rebuilt quickly.

Some international financial institutions, including the World Bank, were reluctant to finance houses because they were not convinced that indigenous buildings could be safe. They were familiar with industrial materials of known properties and designs. Few Pakistani engineers understood the strength of the local materials or the techniques of local construction. Persuading skeptics that sound structures could be built with traditional materials and techniques took long discussions under ERRA's aegis, consultations with centers of excellence from around the world, demonstrations of the techniques by local craftsmen, and smaller scale models on shaking tables.

The houses that collapsed were of *kutcha* construction, not the traditional techniques in areas known to be earthquake prone. As the population grew and wood became scarce and costly, builders largely abandoned the intricacies of traditional building techniques (Langenbach 2009).[12] Two traditional construction techniques considered seismically safe are *dhajji*, with timber frames common in Kashmir and *Bhatar*, with timber-reinforced dry stone masonry in the Northwestern Frontier Province. Each of these traditional quake-resistant building techniques had been developed over centuries making good use of local lumber and other materials, and some local builders were still familiar with their construction.

The National Engineering Services of Pakistan, the country's largest engineering consulting firm and the government's general consultant on reconstruction, played a central role in developing safe housing guidelines for local construction techniques. They initially used the Californian codes that specified metal devices to connect timbers, but later adopted the excellent joints that local carpenters used without any metal. This was not the only contribution of local carpenters: they insisted, for example, that it was better for the base plate (the timber tying the bottom of the box) to lie on a dry stone, not concrete plinth (capillary action allows water to seep up), to allow drainage, preventing the timber from decay.

Once the international financial institutions agreed to fund such construction, ERRA began training construction workers. The army corps of engineers and Pakistani architects and technicians taught quake-resistant design and construction to 300,000 workers in three years.[13] Working with the UN's International Strategy for Disaster Reduction and other partners, the National Society of Earthquake Technology, a Nepalese NGO of earthquake engineers, and the Citizen's Foundation, a Pakistani NGO, brought their unique mix of community-based artisans' training and seismically resistant construction techniques that included (but was not exclusively) vernacular architecture. Many trainees were local artisans; others were migrant workers who had moved to the area seeking employment, who, after training and working would spread the skills as they moved elsewhere.

As people began rebuilding their homes, many families chose reinforced masonry using cement blocks. Almost overnight, hundreds of small cement block factories mushroomed by the roadside throughout the area. Men and mules carried manufactured building materials like cement and steel over steep mountain paths to get to the affected villages, greatly adding to the cost of materials. Cement blocks had never been used at this scale, and it quickly became evident that the blocks were often of inferior quality. ERRA then instituted quality control mechanisms with mobile testing units; but it also recognized that home owners had a tremendous incentive to avoid these substandard blocks if they could tell the difference. So it began a public information campaign about the importance of quality, both to manufacturers (given information on how to make sufficiently strong blocks) and customers (asked not to buy them if they shattered when dropped from shoulder height). Quality quickly improved.

Advice was occasionally ignored, sometimes for good reasons. In a few areas, technical specialists were disappointed to see that their advice for lighter roofs and walls was ignored. And homes were rebuilt with thick mud and stone walls that proved deadly in the earthquake—but gun battles are more common than earthquakes in the area, and thick walls offer better protection against bullets. This underscored the larger point that homeowners are good judges of their circumstances.

Four years after the earthquake, ERRA reports that more than 90 percent of the 400,000 rebuilt houses complied with safe construction guidelines (not a code mandated by law), and more than 30 percent used vernacular architecture. So, tens of thousands of families who preferred traditional techniques rebuilt with greater safety and are more aware of disasters and the importance of prevention—much more than if others had rebuilt their houses for them. People learned not only the importance of earthquake-resistant construction but also what it takes (construction details) to ensure it. Such construction has also boosted both the standing and understanding of skilled craftsmen, who will likely pass these skills on to the next generation of builders. Pakistan shows that building practices ensure safer structures, that this takes many skills, and that it is possible even with artisan materials and local construction techniques.

Sri Lanka: Building seismically resistant structures

Italy was among many countries helping the Sri Lankan government rebuild after the December 2004 tsunami. A team from Italy's civil protection unit was entrusted with reconstructing 12 schools and two hospitals, all government buildings. The Ministries of Education and Health in Colombo approved the concept and working drawings; and the proposed structural design incorporated recent developments in building seismically resilient structures.

Such structures must dissipate, not resist, energy released by an earthquake and have braced supporting pillars to withstand lateral forces. A recent development is to make the columns strong but elastic and to intentionally weaken the beams at a well-defined plastic hinge to yield to excessive forces and gently deform without causing excessive injuries. Such techniques allow buildings to resist forces up to a particular level and to reduce injuries when they fail under stronger forces. Appropriately placed transverse reinforcing bars are securely tied before the concrete is cast. And the structure's strength also depends on the composition of cement, sand, and aggregate mixture and the care during curing. Such buildings require careful design and construction but are not much costlier.

The Italian team had many technical discussions with Sri Lankan engineers who were keen to learn these recent advances that had not yet entered the curriculum of local engineering universities. The Sri Lankan building code—based on relatively recent British standards, where seismic risks are not a major concern—does not incorporate modern engineering designs that the Eurocode endorses.[14] Sri Lankan universities do not research such topics; so the country's building code is adapted from other countries. But better engineering specifications alone would not improve local building practices, especially those using local building materials and construction techniques.

Once the plans were finalized and such technical requirements as the number and size of reinforcement bars were set, guidelines were defined for private construction firms to submit bids. The biggest effort was in monitoring every aspect of the construction because builders have an incentive to skimp on the specified materials, especially when this cannot be easily detected in the finished building. The local builders and construction workers were familiar with normal reinforced concrete construction. But they needed close supervision in the placement and fastening of reinforcement bars for the design that allowed the planned deformation. The hospital building was finished on time and budget.

Corruption and safety

Detailed systematic data are difficult to find, but some descriptions of disasters note that publicly owned buildings collapse while private buildings of similar size and vintage remain standing. The engineering and architectural history of San Francisco notes that many large hotel and bank buildings survived in 1906 while the City Hall did not. Similarly, news accounts in 2008 note that government schools in Sichuan collapsed, while commercial buildings of the same size and vintage nearby did not.

Corruption, the usual suspect, is unfortunately common, especially in public construction (figure 3.3). In photographs from some projects supervised by the World Bank where corruption was suspected, it is easy to see the inclusion of debris in the concrete (material not removed before the concrete is poured) and air bubbles (showing insufficient tamping before it sets) (figures 3.4 and 3.5) (Kenny and Musatova 2008). Is this corruption or lack

Figure 3.3 Corruption perception by industry

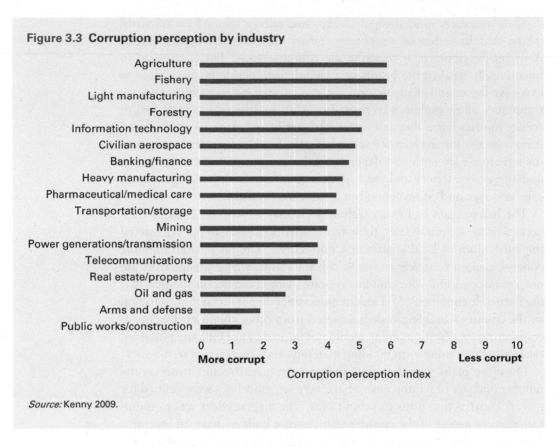

Source: Kenny 2009.

of supervision? The photographs are evidence of inadequate supervision during construction (hasty concrete pour, an absent foreman, inexperienced workers, or absent equipment), not necessarily corruption (Olken 2005).[15]

Corruption is reprehensible but does not excuse or explain poor supervision and management. Stolen funds (corruption) make a building costlier, not necessarily weaker: buildings may fail less in a country with high corruption but with good building practices. As the San Francisco City Hall collapse in 1906 showed, defects in design and shortcomings in supervision are commonly—but not uniquely—associated with public ownership (even of enterprises) (World Bank 1995).[16] This is especially the case in countries where public involvement and oversight of government are deficient.

Three lessons

Three lessons can be drawn from the experiences of Italy, Sri Lanka, and Pakistan as well as from the San Francisco earthquake of a century ago. First, safe buildings require better construction *practices*. A building involves many people (owner, financer, designer, workers, overseers), any one of whom could cut corners and subvert a good structure. Each person responds to complex incentives, not all financial, but the owner oversees and manages the process and ultimately benefits; happily for the hospital in Sri Lanka, engineers supervised the construction closely. Perhaps the

Figure 3.4 Debris embedded in a concrete support beam

Source: Kenny 2009.

Figure 3.5 "Honeycombing" showing shoddy construction

Source: Kenny 2009.

hospital cannot be "scaled up," but if a few Sri Lankan engineers became aware of the new techniques, and if teaching and research in local universities were encouraged, better design and construction would follow. But this requires patience, persistence, and local champions.

Second, owners have the incentive to build well. The government as owner has to ensure that its agents are properly overseen, so the appropriate agency should specify how other government entities should build. The government as owner could build well, and this is more likely when its officials do their jobs well—but it ultimately rests on oversight by the public and a responsive political system. Private owners, however, need information (about the hazards, the materials' characteristics, and so on), not necessarily compulsion, which may be harmful when the rules are difficult to enforce. A government entity already has and collects information about hazards that could be made easily accessible. Insufficient funds to print, or security concerns, are excuses that rarely withstand scrutiny.

Third, "limited human and institutional capabilities" and corruption in poor countries can be weak excuses: better construction is possible both for government structures and for vernacular dwellings that many build without the benefit of engineers or architects. But more funds may be needed to improve the quality of education and research in local universities. Such research could be usefully extended to testing the strength of nonengineered materials widely used in vernacular buildings. Better structures follow, even in areas with low literacy and daunting logistics, when both information and incentives work in tandem.

What people do individually is entwined with what is done collectively—the subject of the next chapter. How well individuals do for themselves, given their environment, is not the same as how satisfactory the environment is—often a result of many individual actions put together.

Jakarta illustrates this interconnectedness and the greater importance and challenge in collective decisions (Financial Times 2009). After doubling its population between 1980 and 2005, the already flood-prone Greater

Jakarta still attracts a quarter of a million new residents every year. Residents of the Kamal Muara district have to raise their houses because the ground is sinking. The ground level is falling with the water table because industrial estates and other commercial enterprises without reliable piped water supply extract fresh groundwater from borewells hundreds of meters deep. Northern parts of Jakarta are predicted to be four to five meters below sea level within 20 years, and simulations show that floods would affect up to 5 million people. Essential for prevention is collective government action, the subject of the next chapter.

Spotlight 3 on Haiti

Preventing Haiti's horrors

The earthquake that struck Haiti in January 2010 was devastating: a third of its 9 million people were directly affected, a million lost their homes, and more than 200,000 lost their lives. Government officials struggle to respond in the aftermath of destroyed buildings, hospitals, schools— even the President's palace. The world has shown commendable concern: donations flooded into charities, the United States military, along with Canada and France, organized logistics for relief and recovery, and other governments are acting bilaterally and through multilateral agencies.

Haiti and its development partners are determined to look ahead, not back. But the lessons of the past are useful for the future, and this spotlight mainly examines the 2008 hurricanes because distance provides a better perspective. The death and destruction in the recent earthquake was far greater than in 2008, yet many of the underlying issues are the same.

Haiti's 2008 hurricanes

Not since 1944 did so many hurricanes affect Haiti in such quick succession: while each of the four 2008 storms and hurricanes (Fay, Gustav, Hanna, and Ike from August 16 to September 8) may have caused some damage, their cumulative effect was devastating. Although Hanna did not make landfall, its unexpected turn to the south brought more rain to already saturated ground (spotlight map 1). Mud slid down hills, rivers swelled with water and sediment, and the Category 4 Ike that followed delivered the *coup de grâce*.

Spotlight map 1 Storm paths through Haiti in 2008

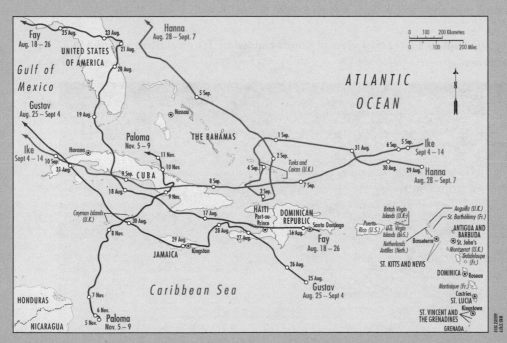

Source: NOAA.

Disparate destruction

The human toll was high: 793 dead, 548 injured, 310 missing.[1] More people were affected, though fewer died than after Hurricane Jeanne in 2004, when mud flows at night caught many sleeping. People were better prepared and more alert in 2008. But as with the comparison with California's earthquakes, fatalities are far greater in Haiti than in neighboring Dominican Republic or Cuba, exposed to many of the same hurricanes (spotlight table 1).

Spotlight table 1 More killed by hurricanes in Haiti than in neighboring Cuba and Dominican Republic

	Haiti	Dominican Republic	Cuba
2002	65	3	6
2003	88	18	
2004	5,422	773	4
2005	88	12	20
2006	16		2
2007	163	175	1
2008	698	13	7

Source: EM-DAT.

Artibonite, with 13.4 percent of Haiti's population, is one of the more vulnerable regions, a low lying fertile delta where four watercourses empty into the sea.[2] Artibonite grows 80 percent of Haiti's rice, and three-quarters of the cultivated areas are on hillsides with terraced fields. (80 percent of the area has steep slopes.) Haiti's hills have been denuded of trees, and heavy rains wash mud from the deforested hills and terraced slopes, carrying rock and debris into Artibonite's port and capital, Gonaïves (spotlight figure 1).

Spotlight figure 1 An aerial view of floods caused by Tropical Storm Hanna in Gonaïves

Source: Reuters http://www.alertnet.org/thenews/photoalbum/1220614932.htm.

Deluge, drainage, or deforestation?

Soil fertility in the uplands is rapidly declining, reportedly at 0.5 to 1.2 percent a year. About 3 centimeters of fertile top soil have been washed away over the last four decades, and settling silt enriches the low lying delta attracting people to cultivate rice—and exposing them to mud flows during heavy rains. So a heavy deluge, poor drainage, and deforested hills all contribute to the disaster.

Soil erosion and deforestation have continued unchecked for decades. The island Hispaniola was almost entirely forested when Columbus arrived, but timber began to be stripped from Haiti's third of the island starting in the mid-19th century. Forests covered 60 percent of Haiti as recently as 1920, but only 1 percent is left (Diamond 2005). The remaining two-thirds of the island—the Dominican Republic—is visibly greener with 28 percent still covered in forests: more rainfall and lower population density help (spotlight figure 2). Wangari Maathai, before winning the Nobel Peace Prize in 2004, wrote after flying over the island (Maathai 2007, pp. 228–29):

> "As I looked down, I realized that I had never seen a country so devastated. People were cultivating crops on the tops of hills, and nearly every tree had been cut down. It looked like someone had taken a razor blade to the land and shaved it bare. When the rains came, the soil just washed away."

Spotlight figure 2 The visible border between Haiti and the Dominican Republic

Source: National Geographic.

Deforestation: Symptom or cause?

International assistance has sought to improve peoples' plight through government spending, but Haiti's government struggles to balance its budget and to deliver many public services such as schooling. Tax revenues were under 11 percent of GDP, while government spending exceeded

18 percent.[3] Building more schools versus planting more trees is a false tradeoff that begs the question of why hills are denuded. Is deforestation the cause or a symptom of a deeper problem? Maathai (2007, pp. 228–29) describes her unsuccessful attempt to help Haiti's nascent environmental movement:

> "In 2000, two Haitian women supported by GROOTS International came to Kenya to learn about the Green Belt Movement. When they returned to Haiti, however, they were unsuccessful in establishing an initiative. When, in September 2004, I heard the news that Hurricane Ivan and Jeanne had together caused the deaths of more than three thousand people in Haiti through landslides and floods, I thought immediately of what I had seen a decade earlier."

Charcoal, a popular fuel, is made from wood, and the damage to trees is exacerbated by livestock grazing and trampling on vegetation and saplings. Economists are quick to diagnose "the problem of the commons," where each has the incentive to over-exploit commonly owned resources. Haiti's land titles may have shortcomings (not being able to borrow with land as collateral), but the law allows the landowner to seize livestock found grazing on his property. If the law is not flawed, enforcement is often thought to be so, though neither may be at fault.

Only thriving communities can ensure that trees are not thoughtlessly felled and that saplings planted will grow. Even if the interest of uplanders who cut the trees may diverge from lowlanders who get the mud flows, communities bridge these differences and manage the fair use of the commons. Elinor Ostrom, whom the 2009 Nobel Prize Committee honored for her insights into how communities share common pool resources, describes how such arrangements develop, be they to share the use of pastures, fisheries, forests or irrigation systems (Ostrom 1990). Such studies in Haiti find that communities suffered from decades of misrule; and replacing local leaders killed or silenced is not easy even with the help of international environmental activists.[4]

Having freed itself of colonial rule and abolished slavery in the early 19th century, Haiti withered under the Duvalier family from 1957 to 1986. Both François "Papa Doc" Duvalier and his son and successor Jean-Claude or "Baby Doc" were presidents for life who ruled with the help of the *Tonton Macoute,* a brutal band unpaid except for what they got through extortion and looting.[5] By 1961 the *Tonton*s were more powerful than the army and feared by the people: they arrested, tortured, and murdered those they considered troublesome and specifically targeted social and community activists—precisely those who also constitute the backbone of civic institutions. Rebuilding these institutions is difficult, especially when armed predatory gangs still roam the countryside forming uneasy alliances with different political factions and criminal gangs, many with a *Macoute* past. More recently, Aristide's election was a beacon of democratic hope after the Duvalier regime—until he was forced out of power.

The way ahead: Rebuild, reforest, or resettle?

Before the January 2010 earthquake, international donors were helping Haiti's government integrate vulnerability reduction measures into national strategy documents and to ensure the implementing of these measures. A multisectoral committee for land use planning was established in the Prime Minister's Office to provide strategic guidance for future preventive investments. A vulnerability reduction cell was established in the Ministry of Planning and External Cooperation to ensure the integration of these preventive investments. And plans were under way to strengthen line ministries and the local authorities as well. Among international actors, there was growing consensus to rethink and integrate vulnerability reduction measures in their programs. This consensus is now driving Haiti's subsequent recovery and reconstruction strategy.

The earthquake has shattered any illusions of quick progress, and the immense challenges are now being used to marshal international support. The prospects of massive aid create expectations that may be difficult to meet. Donors, coming forward with considerable goodwill, are looking past relief for a development strategy. Such a strategy should come from the government and reflect the wishes of the people; but newspapers report frustrated Haitians asking the United States or the United Nations to explicitly take over the government's responsibilities. None is keen to grasp this nettle, though many are generous with aid, advice, and offers to rebuild. Rebuilding bridges and buildings to ameliorate effects of future disasters—promise high rates of return, enabling foreign donors to fund reconstruction. But Paul Collier (2009, p. 9) warns about "unrealistic donor behavior":

> "At the heart of the maintenance problem is the past behaviour of donors. Donors have structured their activities so as to deliver 'projects,' a procedure for which the construction of infrastructure is well suited: a road can be built by a donor and handed to the government. If over the decade the road falls apart due to lack of maintenance, then eventually the same donor, or another one, rebuilds it. Not only does this approach delink the capital budget from the recurrent budget, but inadvertently it destroys the incentive for the government to provide maintenance. It is a donor responsibility to ensure that any construction of infrastructure is supported by a credible process for its maintenance. Currently such a system is in its infancy as a result of a rudimentary Road Fund (Fonds d'Entretien Routier). However, at present this is a further example of unrealistic donor behaviour. First, there is no effective system to ensure that the Fund actually receives revenue, (e.g. the supposedly automatic earmarking of revenue is not operative). Second, there is no link from construction to revenue so that as more roads get constructed whatever is provided for maintenance will simply be spread more thinly."

Collier proposes promoting reforestation by establishing clear land rights for new mango-planting, regulating the commercial use of charcoal, and introducing a subsidy for gas bombs, though they may be less effective than they appear: regulations on charcoal use may be no easier to enforce than other widely flouted laws. Worse, the black market that will likely emerge could be detrimental to both honest government and the environment. Also, environmental experts warn that trees may not take root where the topsoil has already been washed away. So despite good intentions, such centralized attempts at development may be no more likely to succeed than previous ones. As Ostrom observes:

> "International donors and nongovernmental organizations, as well as national governments and charities have often acted, under the banner of environmental conservation, in a way that has unwittingly destroyed the very social capital—shared relationships, norms, knowledge and understanding—that has been used by resource users to sustain the productivity of natural capital over the ages. The effort to preserve biodiversity should not lead to the destruction of institutional diversity. We have yet to recognize how wide the diversity of rules groups has devised through the

ages to work to protect the resources on which they rely. These institutions are most in jeopardy when central government officials assume they do not exist (or are not effective) simply because the government has not put them in place."[6]

Ostrom's work underscores the importance of good institutions and ways in which communities could improve their functioning. People in particularly vulnerable areas of a large country often move elsewhere: many residents of New Orleans resettled in other areas of the United States after Hurricane Katrina. But those in Haiti have nowhere to go except abroad, and crossing international boundaries is extremely difficult.[7] Even so, Haitians abroad have alleviated their suffering by sending remittances that averaged 20 percent of GDP (roughly 4 times grants from donors) between 2006 and 2008.

Donors are responding to victims' obvious plight, and while they are doing much, it is equally important to recognize where their attempts may fall short. Haiti's prosperity ultimately depends on rebuilding the trust and social capital that was lost even before the earthquakes and hurricanes struck. It would be unfortunate if shortcuts to hasten reconstruction were allowed to trump the slower restoration of trust in government and society. This report's chapters emphasize that measures to preventing death and destruction are possible, but effective government spending requires Haiti's people to participate and oversee all aspects of such measures.

CHAPTER 4

Prevention through Governments

National, state, and local governments with the power to tax are responsible for many major prevention measures; but regardless of the political system, they respond to the wishes of the people—at least some of them. People also act collectively through other entities, formal or ad hoc, many rooted in traditions: villages gathering to clean out the irrigation ditches for example. These organizations play an important though unheralded role in many economies: without them, governments are less effective.

The chapter begins by discussing how much governments spend on prevention. This requires a detailed grasp of budget accounting because prevention is not a specific budget item, and prevention is embedded in infrastructure investments, maintenance, and other spending. In four chosen countries, identified prevention spending was lower than post-disaster spending. But this does not necessarily imply it is "too little," only that disasters increase spending on relief and that such expenditures remain high for several subsequent years, perhaps for good reasons. The effectiveness of prevention spending is more important than its magnitude, and some indicators can suggest the benefits of reversing the past neglect of maintenance and other types of preparedness spending.

The chapter next examines who determines government spending. It is easy to assert that politicians are shortsighted. But competition in the markets for votes, like other competitions, provides the public with the services they want—with a twist that arises when voters can observe inputs (building a levee), not outputs (protection from floods, also requiring other unobservable actions). So, even if voters want prevention, they could vote against such spending if they doubt that it would result in effective protection.

The chapter then discusses how to improve collective decisions. Institutions and political competition improve collective decision making, and against this backdrop, cost-benefit analysis is a useful guide to spend effectively. For disaster prevention in particular, ignoring the value of life tilts the balance against prevention; but using such values requires ethical considerations and a deeper appreciation of the tool. Cost-benefit analysis is a filter, not a scoop: it can rank alternatives, but the alternatives must be conceived by others.

Last, it examines three items that have public-good characteristics related directly to prevention. An early warning system is one such choice of great benefit to some countries and in some places because warnings save lives and property. They are based on hazard warnings. All countries can benefit from modest but well-allocated spending on such systems and from sharing data among themselves.

Critical infrastructure reduces the loss of life and property during and after a disaster, and what is critical depends on the situation and the hazard. In Bangladesh, safe schools are important shelters during disasters. In Turkey, hospitals may be critical because earthquakes result in injuries. But critical is not a synonym for its importance in normal times, and the choice requires informed judgment.

For environmental buffers, it is cheaper to protect than to restore them. Development, including sustainable development, involves change, and choosing what to protect requires a broader understanding of the forces of nature and their effects. Much of the cost-benefit analysis in this area is flawed, and careful analysis is difficult, but important.

How much do governments spend?

Governments do not routinely collect or monitor spending on disaster prevention. Budgets are often allocated by ministries, but even if a "Ministry of Disaster Prevention" existed, it would have little to do. Most preventive measures are embedded in the design and construction of infrastructure (such as the location and height of a dam) or in other spending (such as school buildings that serve as shelters). So, measuring prevention spending requires much effort and considerable judgment to identify spending categories across sectors and levels of government and to collect budgeted amounts. This was attempted for this report in Colombia, Indonesia, Mexico, and Nepal.

Local consultants drew on their own knowledge and that of the governments' disaster management organizations using a common template to separate spending on prevention and relief. Pre-disaster spending includes expenditures on identifying risks (risk mapping and hazard assessments), risk reduction (physical/structural works to withstand damage), risk transfer (insurance), and disaster preparedness (early warning systems and public training and awareness about risks and prevention). Post-disaster spending includes expenditures on emergency response (search and rescue operations, relief), rehabilitation, and reconstruction (repairing and reconstructing houses, commercial establishments, and public buildings). Except in Colombia, pre-disaster spending was generally lower than post-, spending on relief fluctuates far more than on prevention, and relief expenditures rise after a disaster and remain higher than prevention spending for several

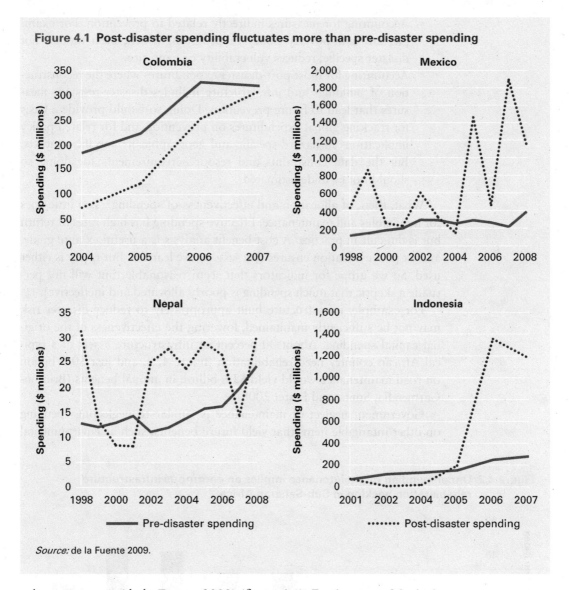

Figure 4.1 Post-disaster spending fluctuates more than pre-disaster spending

Source: de la Fuente 2009.

subsequent years (de la Fuente 2009) (figure 4.1). For instance, Mexico's relief spending rose after the 2005 hurricanes and the 2007 floods (in the southeastern state of Tabasco) and remained three times higher than prevention spending from 1998 to 2008.

Though one cannot conclude from this alone that prevention is "too little" (or that relief is "too much"), this exercise is the first step in systematically estimating how much is spent on pre- and post-disaster management. If and when data are available, these estimates can be further refined by:

- Tracking expenditures at subnational levels. With decentralization in many countries, many prevention measures are now undertaken at subnational levels, as in Turkey, where the disaster risk management cycle was highly centralized but is now being decentralized (see Spotlight 2).

- Accounting for measures indirectly related to prevention. For example, any anti-poverty policy or program, which, even though not disaster specific, reduces vulnerability or exposure.
- Accounting for those post-disaster expenditures where the reconstruction of buildings and infrastructure includes disaster-resistant measures that lead to future prevention. Doing so would provide a basis for tracking global expenditures on prevention and for related policy implications in hazard-specific and geographically specific contexts. But the data constraints and resource requirements for doing so should not be underestimated.

What, then, of allocation and effectiveness of spending? Too little goes for intangibles and maintenance. Effective spending has high rates of return but is difficult in practice. A cost-benefit analysis is a useful ex ante guide, and ex post evaluation ensures that lessons are learned. But rarely is either used. So we grope for indicators that seem reasonable (but will not persuade a skeptic that much spending is poorly allocated and ineffective).

For example, infrastructure built appropriately to reduce disaster risk may not be sufficiently maintained, lowering the effectiveness of the original capital spending. About 30 percent of infrastructure assets of a typical African country need rehabilitation (figure 4.2), and just $0.6 billion on road maintenance would yield $2.6 billion in annual benefits (Briceño-Garmendia, Smits, and Foster 2008).

Government neglect of maintenance is similar to neglecting spending on other intangible items that yield future benefits, such as environmental

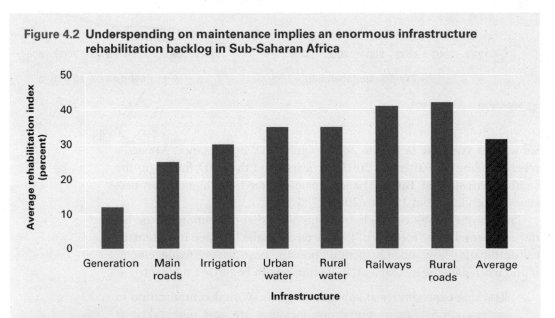

Figure 4.2 Underspending on maintenance implies an enormous infrastructure rehabilitation backlog in Sub-Saharan Africa

Note: The rehabilitation index shows the average percentage across countries of each type of infrastructure that is in poor condition and thus in need of rehabilitation.
Source: Briceño-Garmendia, Smits, and Foster 2008.

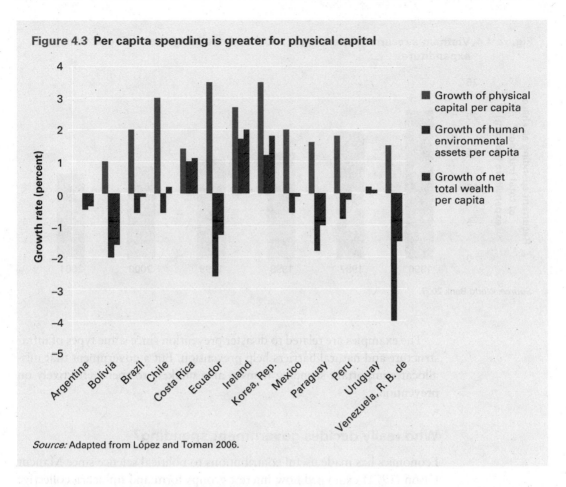

Figure 4.3 **Per capita spending is greater for physical capital**

Source: Adapted from López and Toman 2006.

protection and education (World Bank 2000; López and Toman 2006). Per capita spending, except for rapidly growing Ireland and the Republic of Korea, is greater for physical capital than for intangibles, which also have high rates of return (figure 4.3).[1]

In Vietnam, because of a rule that the growth rate of capital expenditure should be higher than the growth rate of recurrent expenditure, capital budgets grew faster than recurrent budgets. A decline in recurrent expenditure has been particularly acute in transport (figure 4.4) while capital expenditure boomed. Were expenditure to remain at its current level, the percentage of national roads in good condition would fall to just 10 percent of the total network. In its funding request for 2003 to 2005, the Vietnam Roads Agency secured less than half of the finance required to cover all maintenance needs on national highways (World Bank 2007).

Poor coordination between capital and maintenance expenditure is common in countries that operate dual budgeting systems. The introduction of medium-term expenditure frameworks may help address the issue, since a medium-term perspective helps highlight the capital savings offered by adequate maintenance. Implementing such frameworks effectively, however, is fraught with difficulties if the institutional environment remains poor.

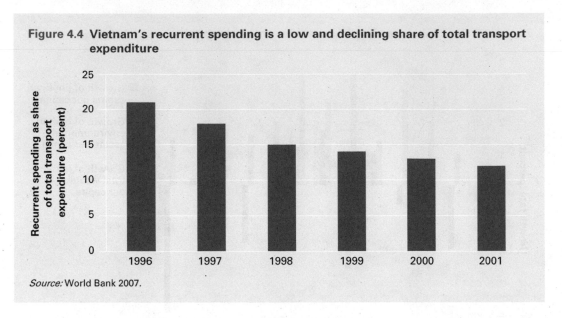

Figure 4.4 Vietnam's recurrent spending is a low and declining share of total transport expenditure

Source: World Bank 2007.

The examples are related to disaster prevention since some types of infrastructure and natural barriers help prevention. But a government that misallocates important spending items is also unlikely to spend effectively on prevention.

Who really decides government spending?

Economics has made useful contributions to political science since Mancur Olson (1971) examined how interest groups form and influence collective decision making. The benefits and costs of government spending are spread unevenly, providing an incentive for groups to form and influence spending and policies in their favor. This holds for all governments: democracies differ only in that some aspects are voted on periodically. A government is a complex organism, and its inner workings are rarely visible and poorly understood. Yet it provides important services that require funding. So who really decides how much to spend and on what? The public, neither fully informed nor entirely selfless, may prefer the government to spend on what benefits them yet accept spending that benefits others. Similarly, politicians are neither completely corrupt nor wholly idealistic. And civil servants are not always civil or serving the public.

Empirical studies complement this analytical strand, but they are limited by what one can observe and measure: voting patterns, who funds politicians, what legislation officials approve, and so on. Such work requires data that are available in democracies (mainly available for the United States and India), though the same forces operate elsewhere, including under closed dictatorships.

Two different groups that influence the adoption of prevention and relief measures are politicians, voters, and the media on one hand; and foreign donors on the other, especially in poor countries where they may have some influence. The following section examines the first group, and foreign donors are discussed in the next chapter.

Relief spending responds to media attention

Spending on relief increases with media coverage. Besley and Burgess (2002) find that politicians respond with greater alacrity to disasters that the media cover. And though their regressions reflect correlation (and a common underlying cause), a causal direction is plausible. They find that newspaper circulation increases the government's disaster responsiveness: a 10 percent drop in harvests increases public food distribution by 1 percent in states with median per capita newspaper circulation, but in states at the 75th percentile in circulation, food distribution rises by 2.3 percent for the same drop in harvests.

Francken, Minten, and Swinnen (2008) investigate what drove relief to 249 communities affected by cyclone Gafilo in March 2004 in Madagascar. Access to radio increased the probability of government relief by 24 percentage points, consistent with the results of focus group discussions where half the communes believe that the media influence politicians' decisions and improve responsiveness. And the probability of government relief was 65 percentage points higher in communities where the majority supported the president during the 2001 elections.

Such effects are the same in developed countries. For about 5,000 disasters occurring outside the United States between 1968 and 2002, the U.S. government's relief response was often crowded out by other noteworthy media events clearly unrelated to disasters (such as the Olympics or the World Series) that coincided with the disaster (Eisensee and Strömberg 2007). For example, disasters are on average 5 percent less likely to receive relief during the Olympics than at other times. A disaster occurring during the Olympics must also have three times as many fatalities than a disaster on an ordinary day to have an equal chance of receiving relief.

Nearly half of all Federal Emergency Management Administration (FEMA) disaster relief payments in the United States were motivated by politics rather than need (Garrett and Sobel 2003). And presidential disaster declarations, often a prerequisite for federal aid, are more frequent in election years, though disasters and electoral cycles themselves are clearly unrelated (Sobel and Leeson 2008).

Under the current U.S. system of disaster assistance, a state governor may ask the president to declare a "major disaster." The president does not unilaterally determine the amount of aid that follows (the House and Senate must approve, though they usually concur), but is responsible for a necessary step and may benefit politically as a consequence. What drives the declaration, when some states benefit and others share the cost?

Many (though not all) of the peaks correspond to presidential election years, consistent with disaster assistance often being an electoral issue that rewards incumbents (figure 4.5).[2]

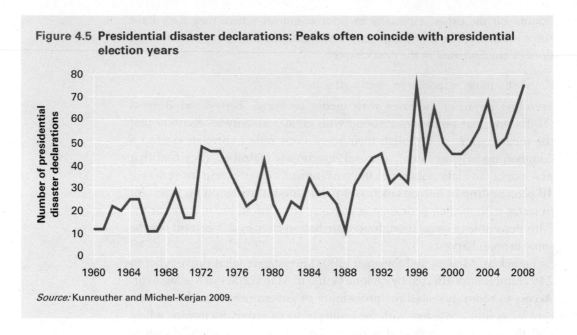

Figure 4.5 Presidential disaster declarations: Peaks often coincide with presidential election years

Source: Kunreuther and Michel-Kerjan 2009.

So while disasters may strike at any time, presidents are more likely to declare disasters during re-election campaigns. When analyzing flood-related presidential disaster declarations between 1965 and 1997, the higher number of declarations in re-election years (28.4 versus 19.4) is statistically significant (Downton and Pielke 2001).[3]

When relief spending rises but prevention measures are ignored, does it suggest politicians' collective myopia, or is it a result of voter preferences? Analyses of electoral data in the United States and India shed some light on this.

Do voters or politicians prefer relief over prevention?

Voters appear to favor relief over prevention spending. Healy and Malhotra (2009) examine voting patterns, disaster damage, and federal government spending for five U.S. presidential electoral cycles (1988, 1992, 1996, 2000, and 2004) in all 3,141 counties. They disentangle voters' responses to events outside the incumbents' control (such as hurricanes) from those that they do control (such as relief and prevention spending). They find evidence of underinvestment in disaster prevention and conclude that a dollar spent on prevention is more than ten times more valuable than a dollar spent on relief in net present value. They are careful in their interpretation: they contrast this finding on disasters with the excessive spending to protect against a repeat of the 2001 attacks using passenger aircraft; so it is just preparedness against natural hazards that is insufficient. Voters appear to behave this way when policies have future benefits and when issues have low salience for political platforms, as with disasters.

In India, there are more votes against incumbents from the ruling party after rain-related disasters—even when the government provides large assistance to farmers (Cole, Healy, and Werker 2008). Voters reward incumbents for relief if they think the losses were from bad luck, not government neglect (presumably the maintenance and operation of dams and irrigation canals)—more evidence of voter sophistication. Voters appreciate relief, but relief spending has only a small effect on re-election prospects: average relief spending reduces the probability of losing the election by one-seventh relative to no relief spending.

There is also a robust link between public food distribution and disaster relief (droughts, floods) as well as political measures such as election turnout, political competition, and the timing of elections (Besley and Burgess 2002). For a given fall in food production or increase in crop damage, greater political competition (turnout in state elections in the previous period) is associated with higher public food distribution and calamity relief. The Indian government's disaster relief measures seem to reflect voter preferences.

So, if politicians are responsive in elected periods, are the voters myopic (cannot see the future benefits) or do they misperceive the risk of disasters (think expected future benefits of prevention are low)? Chapter 2 discussed and put aside the third possibility of a high discount rate for the poor and summarized recent research on risk misperception. That people misperceive risk in experimental settings lends credence to the view that voters may misperceive risks; but insufficient prevention is equally consistent with far-sighted—but skeptical—voters acting in their self-interest.

Effective prevention requires myriad measures that work harmoniously together: for example, flood prevention requires appropriately sited dams and, when there is heavy rainfall or snowmelt upstream, their sluices must be opened and closed at the right time and sequence to hold the rushing waters in the available reservoirs. With enough storage capacity, floods could be prevented. But if reservoirs were already mostly filled, the authorities must quickly decide where to redirect the floods: ideally, where the least value would be lost. Warnings and evacuations must also be coordinated. While voters may not know all the intricate details, they do know (given the history of floods) when they are not protected. If, under these circumstances, the voter must choose between getting cash relief and spending on a levee—just one note in the intricate prevention symphony—they may vote for relief even if everyone wants effective prevention.

Voters may be less prone to vote for public goods provision when there is a substantial ethnic diversity or social fragmentation. Productive public goods—roads, sewers, and trash pickup—in American cities are inversely related to the city's ethnic fragmentation, which in turn is negatively related to the share of local spending on welfare (Alesina, Baqir, and Easterly 1999). Voters chose lower public goods when a significant fraction of tax revenues collected on any given ethnic group was used to provide public goods shared with other ethnic groups. These results suggest that public good provision requires some sense of community and could increase with a more cohesive society.

The empirical findings are striking, but the intelligence of voters, when fully informed, to look past the labels and promises should not be underestimated. Indeed, voter preferences tend to result in more prevention in countries that have more effective governments and better institutions.

Incidence and voice: Why they matter

Ignoring incidence—who ultimately bears the burden of an intervention—can also undermine collective prevention measures, particularly for those most affected. It is easy—and all too common—to use country and governments synonymously with victims. But victims are overwhelmingly poor households, most official aid goes to governments, and relief and prevention spending does not always benefit victims. Government actions reflect the preferences of those who influence its decisionmaking; if marginalized sections of society—often the very poor—have little economic clout or political voice, their well-being gets ignored. So incidence is of great concern, particularly if choices on collective prevention do not reflect their preferences. If the poor have little voice, decisions to spend and locate large scale protective infrastructure may either bypass the poor completely or result in their dislocation—with often little or no compensation—if it turns undesirable land where they reside into coveted real estate. Developing this land may well displace poor residents to other risk-prone parts of a city or places far from economic opportunity. Moreover, because they would be dislocated, the poor would not even reap the benefits of protective infrastructure put in place. If the poor therefore do not have the opportunity to influence public goods decision making, spending and allocation of collective prevention measures could be biased against those most at risk. In this illustration, early warning systems rather than protective infrastructure may have served the poor better. What happened in Indian states when the poor were not consulted in the use of anti-drought funds (box 4.1)?

Box 4.1 India and anti-drought funds

In his book *Everybody Loves a Good Drought: Stories from India's Poorest Districts*, journalist Palagummi Sainath details how measures to manage drought in the mid-1990s in the states of Bihar, Maharashtra, and Orissa were appropriated by the influential at the expense of the poor. The central government Drought Prone Areas Programme (DPAP) was put in place to manage and reduce the effects of drought. But the selection of the DPAP block became politicized because monetary benefits followed. For example, the town of Lonavla—with abundant rainfall (seldom below 1,650 millimeters annually and sometimes as much as 2,000 millimeters)—was designated as a DPAP block. DPAP blocks in Maharashtra grew 73 percent of sugar cane, a highly water-intensive crop, and the irrigated area in DPAP blocks was almost 50 percent higher than the state average. Meanwhile the poor in drought-stricken areas were not consulted and did not participate in the use of anti-drought funds.

Source: World Bank staff.

How to improve collective prevention measures

Having examined how much is spent on prevention and who decides on such spending, the chapter turns to how collective prevention could be improved. Prevention need not be only through governments, and Ostrom's work is a good reminder that alternatives abound, especially in cohesive communities (see Spotlight 3). But governments do provide collective goods and services. Much of the discussion is on how governments could improve prevention, particularly through institutions and political competition. Because specific actions are often at a country level, we outline a useful tool—the familiar but oft-neglected cost-benefit analysis, which must be used with care and sensitivity, especially when choices require ethical judgments such as putting an explicit value on lives. We then turn to early warning systems, critical infrastructure, and environmental buffers, where all countries can expect to reap large benefits by reducing the deaths and damage from disasters.

Institutions and political competition improve decisions

Well informed citizens are more likely to vote, especially for candidates who further their interests (World Bank 2002). A better informed electorate makes a government more responsive, especially if the information is translated into easily understandable "scores," as has been done in Bangalore, India.[4] So the development of trustworthy entities that "digest" information would improve accountability and thus the effectiveness of government relief spending.

But what makes for the emergence of trustworthy entities? Countries that prevent death and destruction better than others appear to have something—institutions—that work better. What these institutions are and the mechanisms they operate through are unclear, but they manage to inform voters and politicians who approve the needed spending and ensure prevention. Two studies drive home the point: Kahn (2005) finds that rich countries do better, and Keefer, Neumayer, and Plümper (2009) underscore the salubrious effect of competing political interests.

Kahn (2005) finds that geography matters: Asia is 28 percent more likely to have a disaster than Africa.[5] But income—which proxies for the quality of institutions—also matters. Richer countries, even though they do not experience fewer disasters, incur fewer fatalities. Deaths are less likely (statistically significant) in countries with higher per capita income: 28 percent less likely in a country with a per capita income of more than $2,000. Less democratic countries and those with greater inequality suffer more deaths. Sen's (1982) observation that famines became less frequent in India after independence suggests that self-rule and democracy ensure greater government responsiveness to people's needs. But some states within India do better than others, and similarly some democratic countries do better than others.

In background work for the report, Keefer, Neumayer, and Plümper (2009) find that differences across countries in disaster mortality can be explained by more than just whether political decision makers are chosen in competitive elections (the conventional notion of democracy). Also critical is the degree to which citizens are informed and the ability of politicians to make credible commitments to (most) citizens.

Key components of political credibility are political parties that allow citizens to hold them accountable for success or failure and that allow individual politicians to make credible promises to pursue public policies in the broad public interest. Across both non-democracies and democracies, the existence of "institutionalized" political parties is significantly associated with reductions in disaster mortality. For example, mortality from earthquakes falls by 6 percent for an additional year of competitive elections and by 2 percent when the average party age rises by a year. Institutionalized party systems are therefore more likely to respond to citizens' needs, with or without competitive elections. Some non-democracies embrace institutionalized ruling parties, bureaucracies, or militaries that facilitate effective responses to disaster; others do not.

The broad finding is consistent with Sen's (1982) observation that democracy helps in responding to emergencies and disasters because voters hold governments accountable. But voting alone is neither necessary nor sufficient. A wide variety of political systems can serve the purpose, and "institutions" are needed to inform all concerned about the alternative prevention measures available, their cost, and their effectiveness. Incentives matter, and political competition could drive the spread of information; but some institutions work better than others for reasons not fully understood.

Cost-benefit analysis: A subtle and sensitive scalpel

Information and new technology increases choices, but how to choose among them? Collective choice requires alternatives to be narrowed and, if not ranked, their distributional implications examined. Cost-benefit analysis is especially useful when the issues are complex and there are several competing proposals.

An investment whose benefits exceed the costs should be undertaken; and if there are competing proposals, the one with the highest benefit-cost ratio should be preferred.[6] Cost-benefit analysis is a well-known tool, particularly useful for governments seeking to compare alternatives (such as the private sector's profit measure). Its use has declined over the years, even at the World Bank (Garcia, forthcoming 2010).

To arrive at the right choice when prevention saves lives requires valuing them. Valuing lives may be abhorrent to many and is always controversial. But ignoring it implicitly considers people useless—and it would be unethical and unfortunate if property is protected but lives are not. For example, background work done for the report shows how, if the value of lives saved were ignored, retrofitting buildings in the Turkish district of Atakoy would not be cost-effective, with a benefit-cost ratio lower than 1. Background work done for the report finds that including a value of life of $750,000 in the benefits, however, tips the scales toward retrofitting (IIASA/RMS/Wharton 2009). And only by including the value of lives saved (at $400,000 each) did earthquake strengthening measures for apartment

Box 4.2 Valuing life: Worthless, priceless, or useless statistic?

Some consider life priceless—and it is. But people make choices regarding the value of life both for themselves and for others, if implicitly (mandating polio vaccine for children benefits many but a few succumb).

"Human capital" is a dehumanizing term but a useful concept. One could measure the "cost" of education (that parents or "the country" spend); but this is an "input" that together with nutrition, parents' time, and so on "produces" human capital. Such human capital is combined with its physical (machines) and natural (land) counterparts to produce output. While the cost of education is the usual measure of human capital, one could infer its value from what it produces, and the two measures differ: Bill Gates or Warren Buffet earn far more than their education cost, while scientists like Albert Einstein may not. The point is that such measures, while useful for some purposes, cannot value the sum total of a person's life or their contributions to society.

Individuals often make choices from which one could infer the value they attach to their own lives. For example, the willingness to take up riskier jobs for higher pay allows one to use the increased risk and reward to calculate the value of statistical life, or VSL. Such estimates are based on revealed preference and not surveys, an alternative but highly flawed technique. Even so, the result is a wide range of values, in part because data and econometric techniques have limitations. Moreover, because the estimation technique assumes a particular functional form, these estimates are valid only within the range of risk observed.

VSLs are often used in cost-benefit analysis; but they are not a measure of what is "lost" when a person dies. The family also values a breadwinner's companionship and contributions to raising children. How to value these? If injured, valuing pain and suffering is also difficult.

In a background paper for the report, Cropper and Sahin (2009) review the literature on valuing death and injury and suggest how they could be roughly estimated. There are few empirical estimates of VSL for developing countries, but estimates from high-income countries could be transferred for use in middle- and low-income countries. When reductions in deaths and injuries are an important part of project benefits, calculating the reduction in injuries and deaths in terms of quality-adjusted life years (or "QALY," a year of life adjusted for its quality) is reasonable. The costs of the project, minus the non-health benefits of the project, can then be divided by the QALYs saved to calculate a cost per QALY avoided. One advantage of this approach is that it would be easy to compare the cost per QALY across policies—to reduce disaster risks and across health and safety policies in various sectors—to encourage consistency in decisionmaking.

Source: World Bank staff.

buildings and schools in Turkey pass the cost-benefit test (Smyth and others 2004a, 2004b).

Deep ethical and philosophical factors must be considered in attaching a value to life, especially if the decisions affect others (as collective actions do). Economists must be aware of their tools' limits (box 4.2).

Regardless of whether lives are valued and what value is attached to them, prevention measures do not reduce risk for all. Building an embankment, for example, diverts water from one area to another, and in doing so may reduce death and damage. But some groups are adversely affected, even if these are fewer in number and their possessions have lower values. And prevention measures often twist the damage-probability distribution, not reduce it everywhere: even for those protected by the embankment, there is a lower risk of damage from small floods but far greater in the event the embankment fails—which is why cost-benefit analysis is a useful guide but should not become the sole judge.

Early warning systems: Spending on improving weather forecasting and sharing data have high returns

Even a few minutes of warning gives people time to flee from a flash flood, tornado, or tsunami.[7] Local authorities use early warnings of tropical cyclones to evacuate large numbers to safer ground. Warnings issued well before an event (lead time) also enable people to protect some property and infrastructure. Reservoir operators could reduce levels gradually to accommodate incoming floodwaters. Local authorities could position equipment for emergency response. People could shutter their windows and reinforce rooftops when warned of severe winds or a cyclone. Chapter 1 showed how deaths and damage from extreme weather events have risen, though more slowly than population and economic activity, largely because of successful prevention measures including better hydro-meteorological forecasts combined with effective emergency preparedness.

Several lower income countries with recurrent disasters like Bangladesh and Cuba, by developing effective early warning systems, experience far less mortality (Golnaraghi 2010). Cuba's Tropical Cyclone Early Warning System is credited with reducing deaths dramatically for weather-related hazards such as tropical cyclones, storm surges, and related flooding: five successive hurricanes in 2008 left only seven dead. Bangladesh's similar efforts are described in Spotlight 1. France continually updates all aspects of its Vigilance System developed after the December 1999 winter storm Lothar. After the 2003 heat wave that killed 15,000, the system was upgraded to include heat/health warnings. Flood warnings were added after 2007 when two large cities, Nimes and Montpellier, had major floods.[8] Mortality in the United States declined significantly over the years because its early warning systems for recurring hazards such as lightning, floods, storms, and heat waves are continually improved: mortality fell by 45 percent and injuries by 40 percent in 15,000 tornadoes from 1986 to 1999 (Teisberg and Weiher 2009). Yet many countries have not benefited as much as they could have, and this section discusses what is needed for them to do so.

Four parts of effective early warning systems require coordination across many agencies from national to community levels: detecting, monitoring, and forecasting hazards; analyzing risks; issuing timely warnings, which should carry the authority of government; and activating community-based emergency plans to respond to the warnings.[9] The focus here is mostly on the first component—also the most technically complex—since the economics of detecting, monitoring, and forecasting hazards plays out at a global scale, unlike the economics of analyzing risks, issuing timely warnings, and requiring emergency evacuations, which are dictated largely by local, social, economic, and cultural circumstances. It is important to emphasize, however, that the strength of a chain is in its weakest link, and all four parts are necessary for an effective early warning system.[10]

Detecting, monitoring, and forecasting hazards

There is an obvious and important difference in the lead times available for responding to hazards that can be forecasted (or predicted) in advance and those that can be detected and monitored only after they have occurred. Many geological hazards can be detected and monitored but not yet forecast, so earthquakes and landslides remain largely unpredictable, though their risks in various zones can be estimated.[11] But detecting underwater earthquakes, landslides, or volcanic eruptions using sophisticated ocean monitoring networks and modeling techniques allows issuance of tsunami warnings and evacuations along coastal zones because the lead time varies from a few minutes to several hours (the 2009 tsunami in Samoa).

In contrast, meteorological hazards can be forecast with lead times ranging from a few minutes (enough to save lives) to several days (enough to save lives and protect property, at least to some extent). Weather forecasting is fundamental to an early warning system for meteorological, hydrological, and climate-related hazards, and advances in technology are only making it more accurate (figure 4.6).

All countries should be able to benefit from more accurate weather forecasting yet many do not. Generating forecasts is complex and requires the following elements:

- Collecting and sharing data in a systematic and timely manner.
- Telecommunication systems that allow exchange of information.
- Numerical weather prediction models, which simulates the physics of the atmosphere.

Figure 4.6 Increasing the accuracy of weather forecasts

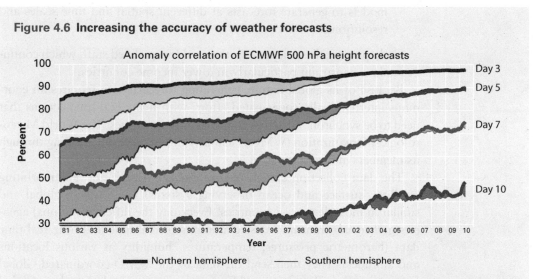

Note: The colored pairs of lines on the top (for the northern hemisphere) and on the bottom (for the southern hemisphere) show that forecasts (3-day, 5-day, 7-day, and 10-day) in the northern hemisphere are generally more accurate than in the southern hemisphere, but that this difference has narrowed over the years. All forecasts are becoming more accurate: the 7-day forecasts today (green) are almost as good as the 3-day forecasts (blue) in the early 1980s. The units of measurement are hectopascal (hPa).
Source: World Bank Working Paper No. 151 2008, Washington, DC.

Figure 4.7 Internationally coordinated network of WMO and 189 national meteorological and hydrological services

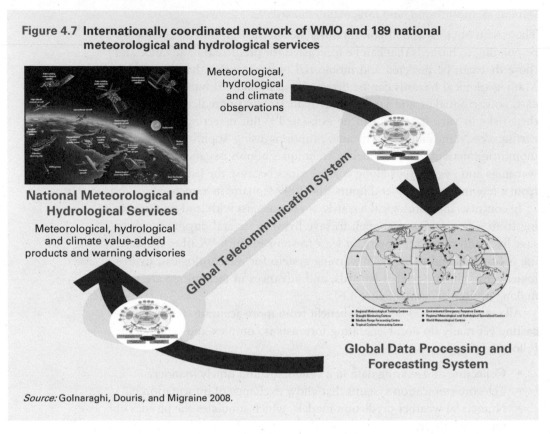

Source: Golnaraghi, Douris, and Migraine 2008.

- Computational facilities and supercomputers for processing data and models to generate forecasts at different spatial and time scales and resolutions.

Underpinning these elements is the need for qualified staff, which continues to be a constraint particularly in lower income countries.

Because of its global nature, generating forecasts also requires an enormous internationally coordinated effort, with many real-time actions that need to be synchronized across countries and time zones. The World Meteorological Organization (WMO) facilitates this massive undertaking through its members' network (figure 4.7).

The data collection system (geostationary weather and polar orbiting satellites, surface and ocean observing systems) is essentially global and similar in most developed countries. Every day the different national agencies gather and transmit massive amounts of real-time and near real-time data (barometric pressures, temperatures, humidity at various locations and altitudes). They then send the data to the WMO-coordinated Global Forecasting Data Processing and Forecasting System, including three Global Meteorological Data Centers (USA, Australia, and Russia), and 40 Regional Specialized Meteorological Centers. The frequency and scope of observed data vary. For instance, as part of the global network, the United States (NOAA) gathers data from upper-atmosphere soundings (weather balloons) every 12 hours, and complete radar scans are available every eight

Map 4.1 Red dots indicate where few, if any, synoptic weather observations are being received

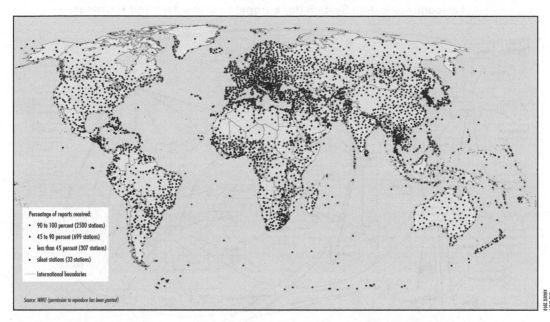

Percentage of reports received:
- 90 to 100 percent (2500 stations)
- 45 to 90 percent (699 stations)
- less than 45 percent (307 stations)
- silent stations (33 stations)

— International boundaries

Source: WMO (permission to reproduce has been granted)

Note: "Synoptic" observations are meteorological observations on the Earth's surface or in the upper-air made at standard time. The above map refers to synoptic weather observations received at Regional Basic Synoptic Network stations.
Source: http://www.wmo.int/pages/prog/www/OSY/Gos-components.html.

minutes; data from ships and aircraft are gathered opportunistically. Radiance data from satellite spectrometers, almost continuous, are being used increasingly in weather forecasting.[12] But not all regions have adequate data collection services (map 4.1).

Global Telecommunications System

Data are disseminated through the WMO Global Telecommunication System (GTS), which connects all countries through their national meteorological services (figure 4.8 shows just a small section). The data and information that flow through the GTS are used for running highly complex weather models. Other analysis supports the meteorological and climate research community. The GTS also distributes tsunami-related information and warnings, where available, so that every country at risk can receive the information in a timely manner.

Global weather forecasts are generated by processing data using various models that differ in complexity and purpose. For example, global models covering the world are operated by different meteorological centers and use different grids ranging from coarse grids (110 kilometers or 1 degree) to fine grids (20 kilometers or 0.18 degree) producing forecasts of large-scale weather systems. One such model produces 10-day forecasts at a coarse spatial resolution used by 31 participating countries ranging from Norway in the north to Morocco in the south and Ireland in the west to Turkey in the east.

Figure 4.8 Coordinating data collection is complex: A section of the Global Telecommunication System (for Europe) to share data and warnings

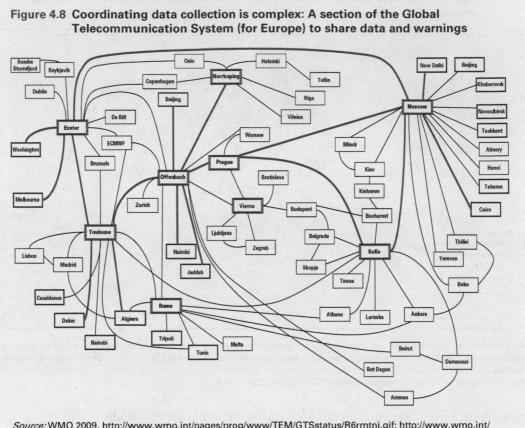

Source: WMO 2009, http://www.wmo.int/pages/prog/www/TEM/GTSstatus/R6rmtni.gif; http://www.wmo.int/pages/prog/www/TEM/GTS/index_en.html.

Every country's meteorological service has free access to the output[13] from global models; but these must be scaled to a finer resolution for local forecasts. Global and regional forecasting models provide boundary conditions for shorter term, geographically focused, and more accurate models that each country's national weather service could generate. But these require more frequent and accurate local observations and the ability to process them. For example, NOAA's and the National Weather Service's national forecasts (for North America) use more frequent data with a 35-square-kilometer grid and an even finer grid for local forecasts to allow greater resolution for densely populated or hazard-prone locations. NOAA also allows direct public access to the output of the models themselves and provides four global forecasts every 24 hours.

Some of the smaller countries (Estonia, Netherlands) have merged to make forecasting more cost-effective. But many countries do not make local forecasts with the accuracy that technology now allows. A 2006-07 WMO survey found that more than 60 percent of their member countries, primarily lower income, have insufficient meteorological capabilities (box 4.3).[14] National meteorological and hydrological services often lack basic

Box 4.3 WMO's 2006–07 country-level assessment

In 2006, WMO surveyed 187 National Meteorological and Hydrological Services (NMHSs) and 139 responded. The survey found:

- Nearly 60 percent of NMHSs were limited by inadequate training of forecasters.
- More than 60 percent either did not have adequate observation stations, telecommunication systems, or 24/7 operational forecasting capacities or could not maintain them or the databases.
- About 90 percent felt the need to improve forecasting and warning capabilities, and half of them wanted better partnerships with other agencies involved in disaster risk reduction.
- Less than half the countries had combined national meteorological with hydrological services. In 44 other countries, the (separate) National Meteorological Service (NMS) and the National Hydrological Service (NHS) collaborated to some extent, particularly for hazard warnings; but most require better coordination to issue warnings.

Source: World Bank staff based on WMO 2006.

equipment and instruments; but even when they have them, they are stymied by the absence of modern computing and telecommunication equipment or the lack of qualified staff.

Collecting data on weather and climate and developing forecasts is costly, but the potential benefits can be huge. Weather-related information and forecasts tell farmers and agribusinesses when to plant, sow, fertilize, and harvest; electricity utilities how to cater to demand; and airlines and shipping companies where to plan routes. Benefits exceed costs sometimes more than tenfold:

- An estimate in China from 1994–96 found a benefit-cost ratio between 35 and 40 (Guocai and Wang 2003).
- Meteorological services in Mozambique were estimated to have a benefit-cost ratio of 70 (World Bank 2008).[15]
- The ratio of the economic benefits of improved hydro-meteorological information (calculated as avoided losses) to the costs of national hydro-meteorological services modernization programs vary between 2.1 to 14.4 for some European and Asian countries (World Bank 2008).
- Benefits of improved weather forecasts estimated for U.S. households exceed the cost of the U.S. National Weather Service modernization program more than threefold (Lazo, Teisberg, and Weiher 2007).

These high benefit-cost ratios suggest that expenditures on improving national hydro-meteorological services are potentially worthwhile. Many governments do not fund their hydro-meteorological services adequately, due to the services' low visibility or the poor funding of public agencies. Some governments—following countries in Europe—want them to partially finance themselves by selling their data and forecasts. So, data and forecasts may not be shared as willingly as before for fear that the recipient is a potential customer—or would pocket the revenue by selling it to one. Generic weather forecasts and warnings are public goods, and such attempts to generate revenues from sale of data or forecasts inhibit the data sharing essential for good regional and global forecasts.

The potential benefits of greater spending on hydro-met services will be realized only if the spending is well directed and organized. The need for a complete meteorological forecasting system must be well identified before spending on expensive technologies, such as Doppler radars, which can run between $1 million to 2 million per unit, and several are needed. A satellite system costs about $380 million. Running it costs about $50 million.[16]

The United States with frequent tornados reduced the annual death toll by an average of 79 and injuries by 1,052 thanks to more accurate forecasting (from 40 to 75 percent) (Simmons and Sutter 2005). And the use of Doppler Radar's ability to identify tornados while still in the clouds has led to the longer lead time for tornado warnings (from 5.3 minutes to 10). But these expenditures may not be warranted in other countries if hazards do not occur or are less frequent.

The point is not that Doppler radars are unwarranted but that spending on expensive equipment has to be carefully assessed against the needs and means of a country. Operational and maintenance costs also need to be considered for long-term sustainability. Also, more mundane needs such as estimating and calibrating models, carrying out hazard analysis, and using past data, which in many countries is stored in warehouses on deteriorating paper, may have high returns. Digitizing these data is low tech with high returns.

In addition to gains from short-term weather forecasts, seasonal forecasts are also improving to support medium and longer term socioeconomic decision making. Recurring climatic patterns (like the El Niño Southern Oscillation) can now be forecast with a few months lead time in some places and for some periods of the year. Predicting droughts (a big killer in Africa) requires not only weather forecasts but also data on air temperature, humidity, soil moisture, vegetation, ground, and reservoir levels. National agencies must begin to gather such data and learn to use it effectively if local droughts are to be forecast accurately.

Analyzing risks, issuing timely warnings, and activating responses

Establishing early warning systems requires much information. The spatial distribution of hazards, their severity, timing, and frequency are largely a matter of science. But their economic effects require assembling data that governments already have in some form. These data must be systematically analyzed to determine whether and where early warning systems should be established. Cost-benefit analysis is a good guide. In some cases, one may only need to identify and analyze one major risk (or a few risks) that is (are) sufficient to justify producing warnings, which would then be available to minimize other risks that may not be as easy to quantify.

Box 4.4 Communications to the community

Almost all households (98 percent) have access to radio and TV in Cuba, so these are the main communication channels that the national meteorological service (with government authority) uses to issue tropical cyclone and related flood warnings.

In Bangladesh, far fewer have televisions and radios, so the Bangladesh Meteorological Department conveys cyclone and storm surge warnings through multiple channels (fax, internet, radio, and TV). But the centralized warning center of the Bangladesh Cyclone Preparedness program ensures the warnings reach coastal communities. The center alerts a network of volunteers through HF/VHF radio broadcasts, and they in turn fan out into the communities to warn the people.

Shanghai also issues warnings though HF/VHF radio, using a network of community volunteers to warn those in rural surroundings and TV broadcasts and mobile phone messages (SMS) for those in urban areas.

Source: World Bank staff.

A warning is based on a forecast, but it should carry the authority of the government. So hazard warnings developed by technical agencies should be communicated to the authorities who must then quickly decide whether to warn the public and to activate evacuation and emergency plans. To decide is to weigh their costs and benefits: false alarms are expensive (much of the cost falls on citizens, not the government) and too many false alarms will result in warnings being ignored (box 4.4).

Such decisions and their responses require much preparation: pre-positioning equipment, emergency responders, sandbagging (a low technology effective only if what is being protected is chosen carefully), and redirecting traffic all require not just planning but also periodic drills in communities. Bangladesh shows that the response can be effective even in poor countries.

Critical infrastructure

All infrastructure should be well designed, constructed, and maintained. But it is especially important that *some* function when most needed. Such "critical" infrastructure must be identified before a disaster to ensure its adequacy.

Every sector has parochial advocates (education specialists favor "safe schools"; doctors, "safe hospitals"), but even jails could be critical because they keep robbers from looting. Governments decide what is critical, but the choice should not be left to officials alone: the government of Myanmar was warned of the intensity and likely path of Cyclone Nargis five days before landfall in 2008, but the military junta did not warn the population, lest it disrupt a referendum under way. The military moved its planes and ships to protect them from damage, but not the people—and 140,000 died.

What is critical depends on local conditions and the likely hazard. In quake-prone Istanbul, hospitals to treat broken bones and crushed bodies may be critical. But in flood-prone Bangladesh, hospitals may be less critical than water treatment plants—or schools, less for the education than to serve as shelters.

Critical assets are specific: a particular bridge, not all bridges. An example illustrates the point. A bridge connecting residential areas with a hospital separated by a river and a bridge that links them to the industrial area must both have sufficiently high economic rates of return. But the bridge to the hospital is "critical" if the area is prone to quakes. The "willingness to pay" for the lost service immediately after a disaster would be a good yardstick to measure which asset qualifies as critical. Once selected, the "margins of safety" (the extra strength that engineers build into designs) should be higher than usual. Designing the bridge to higher standards may raise the cost and so reduce its economic rate of return;[17] but sensible judgments must prevail.

Critical is not a synonym for "socially important." Conversely, noncritical does not mean unimportant: it just implies that interruption of service is tolerable. Even the United States encounters difficulties in keeping "critical infrastructure" manageably small, and other governments will undoubtedly discover this as well (box 4.5). Sectoral ministries may know enough to propose the list, but the decision should not be theirs to make. The choice requires judgment, and while collective judgments have their shortcomings, the country's decision-making structure should be respected.

Box 4.5 The United States tries to identify critical infrastructure

In U.S. public policy, the meaning of "critical infrastructure" has evolved over the years, defined only when a presidential commission on Critical Infrastructure Protection was established in the wake of the 1995 Oklahoma City bombing. The commission identified eight sectors as critical: telecommunications; electrical power systems; gas and oil storage and transportation; banking and finance; transportation; water supply systems; emergency services (including medical, police, fire, and rescue); and continuity of government.

Since then, successive federal laws, reports, and executive orders have sought to clarify the concept, and the number of infrastructure sectors and the types of assets considered "critical" expanded. After the September 2001 attacks, President Bush's new executive orders added nuclear sites, agriculture, and livestock to the list. A year later, the National Strategy for Homeland Security added chemical plants and postal and shipping services as well. The list now has 13 sectors, each including thousands of physical structures in different locations, some privately owned (power stations).

The Information Analysis and Infrastructure Protection Directorate in the Department for Homeland Security is now responsible for identifying critical assets, and there were 1,700 such assets in April 2004. There is much confusion and controversy because of the implications for private owners and because the state governments have their own lists and agenda. Nor are the criteria clear: some electric generating plants, for example, are not in use and others generate little power. And if being on the list attracts resources, potential beneficiaries scramble for the spoils.

The amorphous "threat" results in an unclear and changing list of what is critical, and when it includes too many assets, the costs rise without commensurate benefits. It may well be that the United States now seeks to protect too many facilities, or the wrong ones (or both).

Sources: Motef and Parfomak 2004; Forest 2006.

Figure 4.9 Three modes of operation of the SMART Tunnel

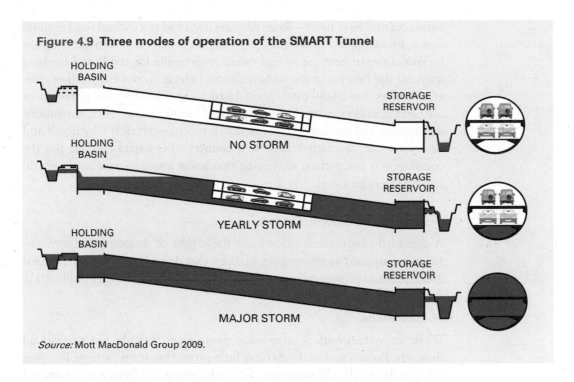

Source: Mott MacDonald Group 2009.

Selection does not conclude the issue: all infrastructure needs maintenance: fixing potholes in the road before the winter or the rain; painting steel bridges before they weaken through corrosion; and inspecting and fixing cracks in concrete bridges. All engineers know this, but they do not obtain budget appropriations—even in the United States, where the 2007 bridge collapse in Minneapolis drew attention to such neglect. Public finance theory suggests that spending should go down a list of projects arranged in descending order of (economic) rates of return. But when subject to arbitrary budget spending limits, lumpiness, and interruption costs, dynamic maximization could put some low-return spending ahead of postponable high-return spending. Since maintenance can be postponed, it gets deferred—repeatedly—until the asset crumbles.

Multipurpose infrastructure, such as Kuala Lumpur's Stormwater Management and Road Tunnel (SMART), is critical infrastructure tailored to the specific hazard. Floods from heavy rains are a hazard, and the 9.7-kilometer-long $514 million tunnel has three levels (figure 4.9), the lowest for drainage and the upper two for road traffic. The drain allows large volumes of flood water to be diverted from the city's financial district to a storage reservoir, holding pond, and bypass tunnel. Combining the drain with the road has two advantages: it ensures maintenance of a drain that otherwise would be used only sporadically, and it costs less than building the road and drain separately.

Critical infrastructure should still pass the cost-benefit criterion, and designs such as the SMART require imagination and innovation. Maintenance remains neglected, and although economists generally disapprove,

earmarks may have merit—some earmarking a fuel tax to fund road maintenance, for example.[18] But it may prove ineffective in other settings: the public works department (or its equivalent responsible for roads and bridges)
may use the funds to paint stone culverts (which do not rust) rather than
steel bridges that do. So many good decisions at many levels of government
are needed, underscoring the importance of "institutions." Such institutions
accompany and promote economic development—which is why death and
destruction are inversely related to a country's per capita income. But the
correlation is not perfect, suggesting that some lower income countries do
better than others.

Protecting environmental buffers

A degraded environment exacerbates the effects of disasters, and environ-
ments are stressed by growing populations that do not protect them. Natural
and manmade prevention measures can complement each other (table 4.1).

Physical limits

While ecosystem buffers offer some protection, they do not prevent all
disasters. Forests and wetlands offer little protection from extreme flooding
when soils are already saturated. Similarly, mangrove belts a few hundred
meters wide can reduce the destruction from a sizeable tsunami but not
significant ones, for example, those taller than 10 meters. A narrow swath
of trees could do more harm than good if they topple and add to the water
borne debris. Many were injured and killed by splintered mangroves in
Papua New Guinea floods. But mangroves also trap floating debris (including tsunami victims who would otherwise be swept out to sea during the
backflow) and over the long term help to protect against coastal erosion
(FAO 2007).

Analytical limits

Several studies report impressive numbers on the value of natural defenses:

- As coastal defenses, Mangrove forests in Malaysia have been estimated to have an economic value of $300,000 per kilometer based on
  comparison with engineered alternatives (ProAct 2008).
- Since 1994, communities have been planting and protecting mangrove
  forests in northern Vietnam to buffer against storms. An initial investment of $1.1 million saved an estimated $7.3 million a year in sea
  dyke maintenance and appeared to significantly reduce losses of life
  and property from typhoon Wukong in 2000, compared with other
  areas (WWF 2008).
- In the Lužnice floodplain—one of the last floodplains in the Czech
  Republic with an unaltered hydrological regime—470 hectares have
  monetary values per hectare of $11,788 for flood mitigation (water
  retention), $15,000 for biodiversity, $144 for carbon sequestration,

Table 4.1 Natural hazards and protection

Natural hazard	Type of ecological protection	Examples
Landslides and avalanches	Dense and deep-rooted vegetation helps to bind soil together, resisting slippage of surface layers. Forests form a physical barrier against upslope avalanches and pin down the snow pack, reducing the chance of a slide beginning.	Reforestation has been used to protect against avalanches in Switzerland, complementing and in some cases substituting for engineered barriers (UNISDR 2009): 17 percent of forests are managed to protect against landslides and avalanches.
Floods	Dense vegetation cover within upper watershed areas increases infiltration of rainfall as opposed to surface run-off, reducing peak flow rates except in the most extreme conditions when soils are already fully saturated. Vegetation also protects against erosion, thereby reducing soil loss and the transport of mud and rock that greatly increase the destructive power of floodwaters. Dense vegetation also protects river banks and adjacent land structures from erosion by floodwaters. Wetlands and floodplain soils absorb water, reducing peak flow rates downstream.	Hurricane Jeanne hit several Caribbean islands, but the number of flood-related deaths was more than 3,000 in Haiti versus only a few dozen in all other affected countries, largely due to Haiti's highly degraded watersheds (Stolton and others 2008). The pattern was similar during the 2008 hurricane season. In 1992, the World Bank committed $85 million to alleviate poverty in three Indian states (Andhra Pradesh, Orissa, and West Bengal) through employment creation at shrimp and fish farms. Mangrove forests were depleted to make space for shrimp farms. When cyclones hit the newly denuded coast, however, they found little resistance. And a significant part of the investment was lost. Two cyclones, one in Andhra Pradesh in 1997 and one in Orissa in 1999, destroyed the newly constructed sites for shrimp farming (Independent Evaluation Group 2007). A study around Mantadia National Park, Madagascar, concluded that conversion from primary forest to swidden (area cleared for temporary cultivation by cutting and burning the vegetation) can increase downstream storm flow by as much as 4.5 times (Stolton and others 2008). Communities have successfully planted bamboo to protect channel embankments from annual floods in Assam (UNISDR 2009). Canalization and drainage in the Mississippi floodplain were estimated to have reduced flood storage capacity by 80 percent, and have subsequently been linked to subsidence of large areas and to the severity of the impact from Hurricane Katrina (WRI 2005).

(continued)

Table 4.1 Natural hazards and protection *(continued)*

Natural hazard	Type of ecological protection	Examples
Tidal waves (tsunami) and storm surges	Coral reefs and sand dunes (which in coastal areas typically depend on associated plant communities for maintenance) provide a physical barrier against waves and currents. Salt marshes and lagoons can divert and contain floodwaters. Mangroves and other coastal forests can absorb wave energy and trap floating debris, greatly reducing the destructive power of waves.	Modeling for the Seychelles suggests that wave energy has doubled partially as a result of changes in coral reef structure due to bleaching and changes in species composition (Stolton and others 2008). In the Caribbean, as a result of reef degradation, more than 15,000 km of shoreline could experience a 10 to 20 percent reduction in protection from waves and storms by 2050 (Stolton and others 2008). Re-establishment of salt marshes forms part of coastal defense measures in areas of the U.K. (UNISDR 2009). Following the 2004 tsunami, studies in Hikkaduwa, Sri Lanka, where reefs are in a marine park, noted that damage reached only 50 meters inland and waves were only 2 to 3 meters high. At nearby Peraliya, where reefs have been extensively affected by coral mining, the waves were 10 meters high, and damage and flooding occurred up to 1.5 kilometers inland. In Japan, where accurate historical records exist, the role of forests in limiting the effects of tsunami damage has been demonstrated (Stolton and others 2008). The Black River Lower Morass is the largest freshwater wetland ecosystem in Jamaica. The marsh acts as a natural buffer against river floodwaters and incursions by the sea (Dudley and others 2010).
Hurricanes and storms	Forests, coral reefs, mangroves, and barrier islands buffer against immediate storm damage.	The protected mangrove system known as the Sundarbans in Bangladesh and India helps to stabilize wetland and coastlines and to buffer inland areas from wind and wave surges resulting from cyclones. Mangroves can break up storm waves that exceed 4 meters during cyclones (Dudley and others 2010).

Sources: Dudley and others 2010; Stolton, Dudley, and Randall 2008; Independent Evaluation Group 2007; and UNISDR 2009.

$78 for hay production, $37 for fish production, and $21 for wood production (ProAct 2008).

- The economic value of forests for preventing avalanches is estimated at around $100 per hectare per year in open expanses of land in the Swiss Alps and up to more than $170,000 per hectare per year in areas with valuable assets (ProAct 2008).

- A recent study on the role of wetlands in reducing flooding associated with hurricanes in the United States calculated an average value of $8,240 per hectare per year, with coastal wetlands estimated to provide $23.2 billion a year in storm protection services (Costanza and others 2008).
- The two reserves that form the Muthurajawella Marsh, in Sri Lanka, cover 3,068 hectares near Colombo. The economic value of flood attenuation (converted to 2003 values) has been estimated at $5 million a year (Costanza and others 2008).
- Benefits from forest protection in the upper watersheds of Mantadia National Park, in Madagascar, in reduced flood damage to crops, have been estimated at $126,700 (Kramer and others 1997).

While the figures are impressive, modeling the effectiveness of alternative vegetation types or land uses needs considerable longitudinal data from the specific area, and subjecting such protection to cost-benefit analysis, while possible in principle, is difficult in practice (box 4.6). Moreover, the benefits of protection are the avoided expected damage; but cost-benefit ratios are sometimes stated on the basis of actual damage without multiplying it by the probability of occurrence.

Benefits are hard to value, and it is easy to make mistakes, especially when environmental protection is sought and quality varies. As Dahdouh-

---

Box 4.6 Costs and benefits of mangroves or shrimp ponds on the Thai coast

Sathirathai and Barbier (2001) calculated the net present value per hectare of Thai mangroves by adding the value of forest products local people collected (around $540), the increase in coastal fishery yields (around $270), and storm protection (around $74,600). Storm protection contributed most of the total net present value (NPV) of more than $75,000 per hectare. It also comprised most of the $1,150 per hectare NPV of converting mangrove to shrimp ponds. The results are reported in several publications.

To evaluate habitat and storm protection services, Barbier (2007) developed a new "dynamic" approach that incorporated the change in wetland area within a multi-period harvesting model of the fishery. The NPV of storm protection was recalculated based on actual storm damage rather than the replacement cost of engineered coastal defenses (the original analysis), yielding a NPV per hectare of around $10,000.

Three points are worth noting about the difficulties of evaluating ecosystem protection services:

1. The NPV per hectare of mangroves declined considerably because replacement cost methods, which essentially use a cost to estimate a benefit, generally overestimate storm protection services.
2. Although mangroves still comprise most of the NPV of shrimp farming, without the value of mangroves for storm protection, it would not be worth converting the shrimp ponds back into mangroves.
3. Because of the lack of data, the estimate of expected storm damage due to protection by mangroves could not control for other possible mitigating factors, such as storm intensity, coastal topography, and other natural barriers, such as coral reefs and seagrass beds.

Source: World Bank staff.

Guebas and others (2005) note about mangroves protective role in storm protection:

> "Our surveys of villages and post-tsunami observations make it clear that mangroves play a critical role in storm protection, but with the subtle point that this all depends on the *quality* [emphasis added] of the mangrove forest."

Timing also complicates the cost-benefit decision of even whether to restore. For example, because mangrove habitats can recover naturally without artificial intervention, restoration projects should be undertaken only if recovery is not happening on its own.[19] Determining why natural recovery is not taking place and removing necessary stresses are essential to any successful artificial restoration effort.

Costs are often difficult to quantify too: costs of restoring mangroves in the United States alone fall into three orders of magnitude, ranging from about $225 per hectare to over $200,000 per hectare.[20] Costs of restoring natural hydrology by "reconnecting" divided mangroves could be lower but may increase exponentially if large-scale earthworks are needed to re-landscape an area. Maintenance costs are often ignored, though they are considerable, particularly if there are ongoing human pressures: effective management of protected areas costs is high even in low-income countries. It is harder to protect wetland habitats (including coral reefs) that are more vulnerable to non-point pollution and the removal or introduction of particular species.

The role of natural ecosystems in reducing the adverse effects of disasters is recognized, but evaluating both their costs and benefits is difficult. Moreover, governments tend to emphasize physical investments at the expense of intangible assets. The Bangladesh spotlight (Spotlight 1) shows how water management authorities initially favored the construction of embankments, and the Haiti spotlight (Spotlight 3) how deforestation, a major cause of the mudslides, remains unaddressed. Other examples from Argentina and the United States show a similar government preference for physical structures (Gentile 1994; Penning-Roswell 1996; Driever and Vaughn 1988). Such policies put people at risk and distort urban development.

Protecting the environment is generally more cost-effective than restoring it, but successful protection requires the participation of users whose livelihoods depend on the resources in question: fences and policing are rarely effective. Well-functioning communities have long found diverse ways to share and protect the commons. Elinor Ostrom (1990)[21] describes a variety of such arrangements among local users, including clearly defined boundaries and effective monitoring by people part of or accountable to the appropriators, complemented by graduated sanctions for resource appropriators who violate community rules. These broad principles underlie successful institutions and have significant ramifications for long-term sustainability for common property regimes (Gibson, Williams, and Ostrom 2005).

To summarize, governments can do more to prevent disasters. This does not always require more spending, but it often requires spending differently. Most important (and this is difficult), preventing disasters requires continual monitoring of the effectiveness of such spending. Transparency and disclosure are important for this reason. And when voters are confident that such spending is not wasted, they will be more willing to reward such spending.

Three spending items generally have high returns. The first is more funding for weather forecasting with accompanying oversight to prevent careless spending. This would allow countries to take advantage of greatly improved technology. Early warning systems and evacuation drills and procedures are warranted in some of the more risky areas. The second is ensuring that certain critical infrastructure remains functional after a disaster. And the third is protecting environmental buffers, sensible but difficult to translate into action: better institutions will help.

Spotlight 4 on Ethiopia

Deaths from droughts or Derg?

Ethiopia is prone to many hazards including earthquakes—the African and Arabian tectonic plates meet in the Rift valley. Although flash floods are more frequent, droughts have been far deadlier. Global data show that almost a million people have died from droughts since 1970, mostly in Africa (chapter 1, figure 1.3). Over the past six decades, Ethiopia has been particularly drought-prone, with one every 3 to 5 years and some lasting over several years. There is rain, averaging 1005 mm annually, but it varies greatly by region and is particularly unpredictable.[1]

Many of these deaths were avoidable, although droughts are not—because a "slow onset" hazard allows ample time for food to reach those who would otherwise starve, but this did not always happen. Chapter 2 reports on the empirical association between disasters and conflicts that continue to simmer in the region; but conflict is not the only reason for food not to reach the starving. Amartya Sen drew attention to the absence of famines in India after independence when the authorities became more responsive to their people.[2] Better institutions, both domestic and external, could prevent deaths from droughts.

Living with unreliable rains

Much of Ethiopia's agriculture—accounting for half its GDP and sustaining 80 percent of its people—is rainfed, and its 80 million people have long adapted to its unpredictability. Farmers and pastoralists cope with droughts differently, and both groups have great difficulty with extended

Spotlight map 1 Rainfall in Ethiopia

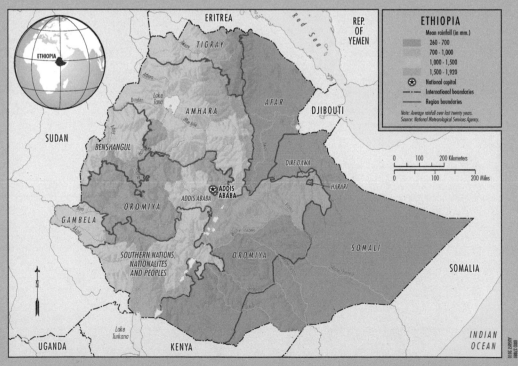

Source: World Bank staff.

droughts. Farmers grow multiple crops (drought-resistant teff, maize, and barley) on small, rain-fed plots.[3] They also keep sheep and goats to sell when needed. Pastoralists' livestock store protein for lean years, and a tenth of the rural population are nomadic pastoralists in Somali and Afar, the Borana zone of Oromiya region, and Benshagul and Gambela (spotlight map 1).[4] Migration helps, but some international borders that now separate related tribes are becoming less porous: Turkana tribesmen's herds are being blamed for spreading foot and mouth disease across the Kenyan and Sudanese borders.[5] Population growth and the settlement of pastoral nomads add to the pressures on the land.

Wars and conflicts inhibit and interfere with these traditional coping mechanisms. These conflicts have local origins and have been fed by regional and super powers with their own concerns. Ethiopia shows how famines happen, but it requires an explanation of its politics and ethnic divisions that overlap with ideology and groups seeking support for their cause.

The Emperor's neglect in the 1972–73 drought

Ethiopia became a nation-state in the 19th century, and its kings managed to keep it from being fully colonized. Italy seized Eritrea in 1889 and occupied parts of present day Ethiopia from 1936 until early World War II, exiling Haile Selassie, the Emperor, after 1930. Selassie was restored to the throne in 1941, though the British administered the territory under a United Nations mandate until 1951 when Eritrea joined the federal state, but its relations with the central government remained difficult. The Amharans and Tigrayans in the north, along with the Agau and Oromo from Wollo, had resisted the shift of power to the south since the late 1800s and, by extension, the Emperor's rule.[6]

The Emperor was widely admired internationally, but became increasingly unpopular domestically. After a 1943 revolt in the north, the Emperor confiscated northern and central Wollo lands (former provinces in northeastern Ethiopia). Making farmers into tenants required rents to be collected even when droughts reduced their harvests (Tigray in 1958 and Wollo in 1966). So resentment simmered, and the incipient independence movement began.

The Emperor became more isolated and autocratic after the 1960 attempted coup, instigated by his bodyguard's commander, was thwarted. During the 1972–73 droughts, grain was taken from the affected areas in the north and sent to Dessie and Addis Ababa, the provincial and national capitals. The resulting famine killed over 100,000 people (although some claim 200,000 died in Wollo alone). The Emperor's rule crumbled when his neglect was exposed.[7] Students and the middle classes revolted in the capital, the military mutinied, and the Derg (Amharic for committee) took over. The Emperor died in custody in 1975, and the Derg's Marxist-Leninist ideology initially attracted student support. Agriculture was collectivized, and kebelles (peasant associations) became instruments of central government control (Wolde 1986).

The ideological shift lost Ethiopia one superpower's support and gained it another's. But domestic ideological divisions overlapped regional and ethnic differences. Disputes within the Derg pulled Colonel Mengistu Haile Mariam out of the shadows to take control in 1977 and unleash the "Red Terror." Thousands who opposed the government were killed and separatist movements strengthened: the Tigray People's Liberation Front (TPLF) sought an independent Tigrayan state, and the Eritrean People's Liberation Front (EPLF) sought the same for themselves further north.

Support and weapons poured in across porous borders. Somalia invaded Ethiopia in 1977 to annex Ogaden where there was much dissatisfaction with Addis Ababa's rule. After fierce fighting in 1977–78, Ethiopia repelled the invasion with the help of Cuban troops. Bitter memories and suspicion lingered long after these troops left, and fighting has since renewed—this time on the Somali side of the border. The deadly drought in 1984 shows what could happen again when food and its denial become weapons of war.

Food as a weapon in the 1984 drought

Rains failed in 1983–84, and the Ethiopia Relief and Rehabilitation Commission, a government agency created after the 1972–73 famine, appealed for help. Fighting in Tigray and Eritrea made donor governments understandably suspicious that the drought was exaggerated to garner aid that could then be diverted (Adejumobi 2007). Only after the international media began reporting on the dying thousands did food aid begin to flow in. But the Derg restricted its movements as well as those of migrants and traders while military offensives and aerial bombardment destroyed opponents' cattle and grain stores (Porter 2008). Some claim that over a million people died in the famine; subsequent studies confirm that mortality, other than direct casualties of the conflict, was greater in areas with more fighting (Kiros and Hogan 2001).

Colonel Mengistu remained president after the 1987 non-competitive election, but fled the country in 1991 after losing both domestic and international support. The TPLF and EPLF movements wrested local control and Eritrea's independence in 1993 left Ethiopia landlocked. Fighting between them erupted in May 1998 over what seemed a minor border dispute, and the peace since the June 2000 Algiers agreement has been intermittent. The Boundary Commission awarded Eritrea the disputed town of Badme, but the transfer remains incomplete, and Eritrea's foreign policy, especially toward Somalia, lost international support.

The tenuous peace makes for intermittent aid. Ethiopia's National Meteorological Service Agency forecast poor *belg* rains (typically from February to May) in January 2000, but donors pledged no aid until April because the war with Eritrea raised the same suspicion of exaggerated need (Broad and Agrawala 2000). The suspicions were mutual, and when food finally became available, the Ethiopian government balked at shipping it through the Eritrean port of Assab that handled three quarters of relief before the conflict. By the time disputes over logistics and control over its distribution were resolved, a localized famine was well underway.

A good beginning: Social safety nets and better preparedness

Widespread starvation was averted during the subsequent and more severe drought of 2002–03 because fighting abated and food aid reached 13.2 million people, although some went hungry and livestock was lost. The government subsequently developed a more permanent safety net and supplemented the emergency food distribution system with the Productive Safety Nets Program (PSNP) in 2005. The PSNP finances public works (such as building terraced fields on hill slopes to reduce soil erosion and increase water retention) paying cash for up to five days a month per household member and six months a year (but for no more than three years to avoid dependency). In addition, about 10 percent of the poorest beneficiaries get unconditional cash or food transfers. The PSNP is also linked to the Other Food Security Program, which provides credit and agricultural extension services and funds irrigation and water harvesting schemes.

The PSNP, sub-Saharan Africa's second largest social safety net (after South Africa), now reaches over 7 million people (spotlight figure 1). It appears to target households well, although the transfer amounts are often small and distribution remains irregular. A survey after the 2008 drought found that beneficiaries living in households that got at least 10 days of work a month in the 3 previous months consumed 30 percent more calories and held more livestock than non-beneficiaries (0.62 TLU).[8] The effectiveness of any single intervention may not be significant, but

Spotlight figure 1 Number of PSNP beneficiaries, (millions) 1992–2009

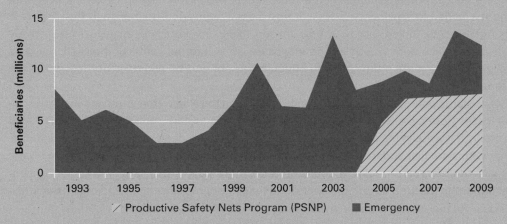

Note: The number of PSNP beneficiaries is a subset of the total number of emergency assistance beneficiaries.
Source: World Bank (2009) Project Appraisal Document for PSNP Phase 3.

public works combined with seeds, credit, and irrigation raised wheat and maize yields by about 200 kilograms per hectare.

Weather forecasting and early warning systems are being improved, and the National Disaster Prevention and Preparedness Fund was established to finance relief and make assistance more timely and predictable. The World Food Programme (WFP) and the World Bank support software (LEAP, for Livelihoods, Early Assessment, and Protection) that projects food shortfalls and calculates funding requirements by linking weather and crop production/rangeland data. This software was used in 2008 to allocate a $25 million World Bank Contingency grant.

Food aid has been sizable, fluctuating between 0.4 and 2.5 percent of GDP between 1996 and 2001.[9] USAID and the WFP now jointly issue monthly early warning bulletins, but the need for food aid sometimes becomes a source of controversy.[10] NGOs sometimes report deaths from starvation that the government disputes. The government is understandably eager to be less dependent on donors, and even if they are correct that there is enough food at the national level, it may not always be aware of local shortages. People can starve even if there is food elsewhere in the country, and this is less likely if information and food flowed more freely internally.

The long view: Increasing investment and irrigation

More food could be grown with better policies and investment. Productivity would increase if farmers' tenures were made secure: there are reports that *kebelles* in some areas threaten to evict farmers who oppose the government.[11] The past neglect of agricultural research could be reversed, and while this has begun, it must be sustained to develop higher yielding drought-resistant crops unique to Ethiopia. Better transport and storage facilities to prevent pockets of shortages would require only modest investments. Irrigation has considerable potential, but requires major investments and potentially difficult international agreements.

Only 2 percent (200,000 hectares) of Ethiopia's cropland is irrigated despite erratic rainfall, using little water (0.3 billion cubic meters) from its plentiful rivers: the Blue Nile begins in Ethiopia's Lake Tana (see spotlight map 1) and joins the White Nile in Khartoum (Sudan) before flowing north through Egypt and into the Mediterranean Sea. Egypt and Sudan's large populations have used much of the Nile waters to irrigate crops since the time of the pharaohs, and many dams were built over the centuries. In the 1950s, Egypt raised the height of the dam at Aswan creating the large but shallow Lake Nasser upstream. Egypt and Sudan signed the 1959 Nile Waters Agreement entitling each to 55.5 billion and 18.5 billion cubic meters a year respectively (though Sudan uses only 13.5 billion now because of its internal conflict). International laws generally recognize these claims, though Ethiopia was not part of, and does not recognize, the 1959 agreement.

There are large potential economic benefits from using the Nile waters more efficiently. Evaporation losses from Lake Nasser of around 10 billion cubic meters annually would be reduced substantially if it were in the cooler Ethiopian highlands, where deep valleys allow dams to create lakes with a smaller surface area. Hydroelectricity generates additional gains: a dam on the Abbay sub-basin (spotlight map 1) could produce more power than Ethiopia currently consumes. Exporting the surplus to its power hungry neighbors requires more and better transmission grids.[12] All these require major investments and the consent of the other riparian countries. But such consent comes with cooperation, not conflict.

Ongoing conflicts in neighboring Somalia and Sudan inevitably engage Ethiopia and Eritrea on opposing sides, and recent reports are worrying: "This cross-border area [i.e. where Kenya, Ethiopia and Somalia meet] is a conveyer belt that moves arms to and from all three countries, and across the African continent."[13] During its 1998–2000 war with Ethiopia, Eritrea assisted Somalia's Ogaden National Liberation Front to relieve pressure on its front by drawing Ethiopian troops southward.

Such alliances continue while tactics and location shift: Ethiopia recently withdrew its troops from Somalia after trying since December 2006 to oust *al-Shabab*, now labeled a terrorist group, from the government. Prospects of large oil and natural gas reserves in Ogaden and similar finds in Sudan complicate matters (Chinese engineers were killed). Fighting in these areas continues, and the flow of weapons and munitions is being financed while food aid appeals are issued during the periodic droughts.

Preventing deaths from droughts: 2009–2010

After meager 2008 rains, particularly in eastern Ethiopia, the main *kiremt* rains in 2009 (June to September) were diminished and delayed by four to six weeks.[14] Better early warning systems and the organization of the safety net notwithstanding, droughts under these circumstances retain their deadly potency. Donors tried to raise $175 million in the last months of 2009, although some government officials dispute the risks of starvation.[15] Even if the appeal for aid is answered, time and transport are necessary for the food to reach the starved.

Starvation is easier to prevent than droughts, but it requires that the authorities be both concerned and informed about the people's predicaments.[16] The WFP reports that in 2009, violence forced 350,000 people from their homes in southern Sudan, where seasonal rains were meager. Centralized controls do not permit the accurate and timely flow of information and food, and conflicts around the borders make relaxing such controls more difficult.

Peace is possible, but has been elusive. The World Bank's forthcoming *2011 World Development Report* will examine conflicts, fragile states, and the roles played by stress—both internal and external (including external interference)—capability, and expectations. Conflicts become more complex when they involve governments of distant superpowers: the long reach of their military and clandestine services supply sophisticated weapons. Better domestic institutions are undermined when the fighting is financed or instigated by foreign powers whose electorates and representatives are not always fully aware of what is happening in distant and unfamiliar lands—so better external institutions would help.

Many scholars have noted that deaths during droughts are associated with conflicts, and the analyses in chapters 4 and 5 found that death and destruction are lower when there are good institutions (typically also associated with democracy and better governance), and that this link operates through political competition, not just periodic elections. Droughts cause death when food does not reach the starving, and spot shortages could occur despite an adequate harvest and ample food stocks. Earlier deaths stemmed from the Emperor's neglect (in 1972–73), conflict (in 1984), and disputes with donors (in 2000). Being ill-informed or ill-prepared are some of the many avoidable reasons for starvation. A more liberated flow of information and goods would reduce these dangers.

CHAPTER 5

Insurance and Coping

T he earlier chapters showed that individuals generally take prevention
measures within their choice set. But full prevention is neither attain-
able nor desirable, and residual disaster risks will remain. Insurance and
complementary measures to have funds when needed (such as borrowing or
setting aside reserve funds), remittances, and relief "soften the blow," and
this chapter examines their roles in turn.

The chapter begins with the basics of the insurance business: the advantages of pooling and transferring risk to those willing to bear it and how
insurers deal with the many complications that arise from adverse selection
and moral hazard. Insurance clearly increases a person's choice and thus
well-being: the contract specifies the resources transferred from one person
to another when the event (such as a disaster) occurs. In doing so, it shifts
the risk from the individual to the pool of the insured. But softening a disaster's blow concomitantly dilutes the incentive to prevent—unless the premium reflects the risk and the prevention measures a person undertakes.

Commercial insurance companies calculate the premia using detailed data
on the frequencies and intensities of hazards and how they affect exposed
assets. The premia must also cover the considerable costs of administration,
marketing, and monitoring. Many people may forgo insurance if the premia are too high. And while parametric insurance—a type of insurance that
specifies the payout based on a parameter related to the hazard but unrelated to actual damages incurred—reduces some of the monitoring costs,
such schemes have low penetration rates in developing countries where they
have been introduced.

When an insurance industry does develop, it invariably draws the government in as regulator, as provider (in many countries), or as reinsurer.
Governments inevitably add a political dimension, and pressures to subsidize the premia may increase. The U.S. experience with flood insurance

shows that this is not just an issue in developing countries. Too low a premium encourages construction in hazard-prone areas, thereby increasing exposure and vulnerability.

The chapter next turns to whether governments should buy insurance to have funds to spend after a disaster, simply borrow, or set aside funds in reserve. Many are already indebted and even those with low debts may find it difficult to borrow when they most need to. Politicians who want to spend on worthy programs tend to deplete funds set aside in a reserve fund. To avoid this "honey pot syndrome," governments may purchase insurance. The World Bank's Catastrophe Risk Deferred Drawdown Option and other such facilities can help countries.

While individuals are risk-averse, there are good reasons for some governments acting on their behalf to be risk-neutral. A risk-neutral entity would buy insurance only if the premium were lower than the probability times the expected loss (which leaves nothing to cover the insurer's costs). But the likelihood of a disaster that is large relative to an economy's size (as in the Caribbean, where the main unknown is which island will be hit) may make some governments risk-averse, especially when rapid access to funds after disasters could be difficult or costly. Such governments, and those seeking to avoid the "honey pot syndrome," would benefit from buying insurance. The Caribbean Catastrophe Risk Insurance Facility pools disaster risks regionally, helping countries purchase insurance less expensively than otherwise. Comparing prices offered by insurance firms against those in capital markets, as Mexico did when issuing catastrophe bonds, is also advantageous.

The chapter then examines remittances sent by private individuals and groups abroad to help people cope with a disaster. Remittances are directed to victims and their survivors, even when the disaster does not attract any media publicity. The funds arrive quickly without the involvement of governments or other organizations. But sometimes unnecessary government policies (controls on capital flows, dual exchange rates) impede arrival of the funds. Remittances that arrive before a disaster also help with prevention. Although remittances augment consumption, particularly consumer durables, they are also used to improve the quality of housing. Mud and straw huts give way to houses built of brick and cement. Private remittances also help develop banking and money transfer facilities, which in turn strengthen the area's commercial ties with other parts of the country and the world.

Last, the chapter examines the role of aid in prevention. Post-disaster aid can also be double-edged: while some aid is warranted, it can also give rise to the Samaritan's dilemma—the inability to credibly deny help following a disaster to those who have not taken sufficient prevention measures. Some new but not very strong evidence shows that post-disaster aid could reduce prevention. Donors should therefore be aware of the disincentives they may create, and concern for the victims should be moderated by the effect on incentives.

Insurance: Useful if the premium is priced right

As with any voluntary transaction, insurance benefits all parties to the contract: the insurer benefits from the business and the insured reduce the adversity of the worst states of nature by giving up some of the benefits in the good states.

The basics of the business

Insurers take pride in covering unique risks like an opera singer catching a cold, or a racehorse breaking a leg. But such insurance is a side show, and the bulk of their business covers more mundane, predictable, and diversifiable risks (such as life and property insurance). Consider insuring houses against fire: one cannot tell when and if a particular house will catch fire, but data on past fires allow the number of house fires in an area to be reliably predicted with probabilities attached. Making the average loss more predictable allows firms to insure individual houses against fire: the insurer collects an annual payment (premium) from risk-averse home owners (the insured) and promises to pay (the insured amount could be actual damages or a specified sum) if their house burns down (the trigger). The aggregate annual premia collected from the insured must cover the insurer's operating costs and the likely payouts. And if unexpectedly fewer houses burn down, the insurer has a surplus beyond its normal profits.

There is always a chance that an unexpectedly large number of houses will catch fire (as in a particularly dry year), so the insurer has a buffer, which is the owners' capital and surpluses accumulated from earlier years. This buffer is invested and the ensuing earnings (dividends or interest) augment the premia the firm collects. If the surpluses accumulate over time, competitive pressures would prompt the insurer to lower the premia; if they are depleted, the premia would be raised. This is the basic principle of insurance; but complexities quickly multiply.

Adverse selection arises when a person buys insurance knowing that his risk exceeds that of the larger pool that is the basis for determining the premium. If only those knowing their risk is greater buy such insurance, the insurer's surplus will fall as the risk of the pool rises. Moral hazard arises when the insured take additional risks because they are insured (not repairing the building sprinklers that extinguish fires if the building is insured against fire). Co-payments (where the insured bears a specified fraction of the loss) and deductibles (where the insured bear losses up to a specified amount) reduce but do not eliminate these difficulties. Contracts become complex and the costs of administering claims, resolving disputes, and increasing monitoring mount. Insurers continually seek observable proxies of the risks they insure, link their premia to these risks, and continually test the insured's price sensitivity to premia that must cover these costs.

The costs result in a premium that greatly exceeds expected losses, but sufficiently risk-averse people buy insurance all the same because it protects them from the devastating financial implications of a disaster. Insurance does not "shift the loss" collectively: the insured pay for the losses through their premia, and those who do not make a claim, essentially pay for others who do.

Insurance can be a competitive industry, but some economists find that there is little competition (insurers are exempt from antitrust laws in the United States) or that costs are not driven down. Administrative and marketing costs are about 35 percent of aggregate premia in the United Kingdom (the insured get roughly 50 percent in payouts, a figure that is broadly similar in the United States) where private insurance firms compete, in contrast to 10 percent in Spain where a state-owned monopoly provides coverage (Von Ungern-Sternberg 2004). Germany privatized its provincial monopoly providers under a European Union directive only to find that operating and administrative costs rose as a consequence and insurance premia were raised between 35 and 75 percent in five years.

Regardless of who owns insurers, governments invariably get involved as regulators if not as providers because buyers "get the product" (the promised payout) only after a disaster; and the insurer may find some reason to refuse payment, reduce coverage, or go out of business.

The government's inevitable involvement

Insurance is limited in the developing world, but a large industry in many developed countries. [1] These countries' governments are involved in each of them, though in different ways. Courts, not governments, enforce contracts, but the payouts to the insured may be delayed or denied. Insurers invariably write and interpret the clauses to their advantage ("the fine print"), and seemingly fair clauses are not always so. British insurers and the insured could cancel a policy with seven days' notice, and insurers cancelled coverage in 1997 when it became apparent that the erupting volcano on Montserrat would destroy every building on the island, akin to cancelling coverage after a fire has started (Von Ungern-Sternberg 2004).

In the 1800s, insurance was for named perils, with covered losses stemming only from the specified risk. In the 1930s, all peril property insurance became more common. Whatever the coverage, governments try to ensure that insurers honor their contracts (consumer protection), and when this requires insurers to have adequate funds (solvency), regulations often extend to approving the premia. The premia are sometimes high, and to ensure coverage, property insurance is sometimes mandatory (as in Germany and many Swiss cantons); but sometimes populist pressures cause premia to be too low (as in the United States with flood insurance), needlessly increasing exposure in hazardous areas.

The fertile lands in the flood plains attract farmers, and many settlements in the United States are periodically inundated. Sympathy for the victims would prompt public assistance, and settlers would rebuild in the same area. After several major floods in the 1950s and 1960s, private insurers were no longer willing to cover floods (which became an "uninsurable" risk), and the U.S. government, recognizing that it was unable or unwilling to deny assistance to those affected, established the National Flood Insurance Program (NFIP) in 1968.

The premia were set low to induce homeowners to buy the NFIP insurance, but very few people voluntarily purchased coverage (Kunreuther and Michel-Kerjan 2009). The federal government then required this coverage as a condition for federally insured mortgages, but the mandate was poorly enforced and many people canceled their policies, especially if there was no flood for several years, and others purchased insurance just after a flood (Michel-Kerjan and Kousky 2010). They examine more than five million insurance policies, the largest flood insurance sample ever studied, and find that of the one million residential NFIP flood insurance policies in place in Florida in 2000, a third were cancelled by 2002 and about two-thirds were cancelled by 2005. There was no effective mechanism to prevent or discourage more people from settling in the areas known to be hazardous: the NFIP is a federal program, while zoning and insurance regulation are state issues, and local politicians reflected the settlers' desires. The number of policies nationwide managed by the NFIP increased from 2.5 million in 1992 to 5.6 million in 2007 and, in nominal terms, the property value covered rose from $237 billion to $1,100 billion during the same period.

The NFIP's other shortcomings were exposed after Hurricane Katrina flooded much of New Orleans in 2005. The NFIP covers floods, but private insurance covers wind damage. Many disputes arose over who should pay when damage from wind could not be easily separated from that by floods (Kunreuther and Michel-Kerjan 2009). Victims were given the runaround and payouts were delayed.

In a background paper for this report, Kunreuther and Michel-Kerjan note how multihazard insurance can address insurer-insured disputes by having homeowners' coverage move from the traditional one-year insurance contract to multiyear contracts (say 10 or 15 years) tied to the property (not the owner as is the case today). The premia would reflect insurers' best estimate of the risk over that period and would assure policy holders of coverage. The possible denial of coverage was a major concern in hazard-prone areas because insurers canceled policies following the 1992 and 2005 hurricane seasons. Following Hurricane Andrew, Florida passed a law in 1992 limiting the cancellation of policies by insurers to 5 percent a year at the state level and to 10 percent at the county level (Jametti and von Ungern-Sternberg 2009). Both insurers and home owners cancel policies for different reasons, and the premia are subject to political pressures. These major changes in government policy require appropriate regulatory authority and decisions (Kunreuther and Michel Kerjan 2008). Comprehensive, multihazard insurance will entail higher premia. Some policyholders may think they are being charged for coverage they do not need (a person in an earthquake area not prone to hurricanes and floods may only have quake insurance), but they would not be overcharged if premia reflect risk accurately. Whether premia accurately reflect risks becomes all the more important.

Government involvement inevitably brings political pressures; and vested interests and populist pressures exist in all countries, though they manifest themselves differently. Insurance subsidies are usually regressive: those with assets to insure are generally better off than the poorer segments that often pay indirect taxes that pay for the subsidies. But underpriced insurance is not always the result of government pressures. Insurers sometimes make mistakes or may take unwarranted risks and then discover that the risks were greater than they assumed. To compensate for these mistakes, insurers often find reasons to deny payments, redefine the risks that are covered (terrorism was made a separate risk that got excluded), and raise deductibles and premia.[2]

Pricing the premium

The premium is an important price: too low, and excessive construction in exposed areas and insufficient prevention result; too high, and few buy insurance. Calculating the appropriate premium is not trivial: probability distributions and loss functions must be estimated, and the relevant pool and observable characteristics that correlate well with the underlying risk (an unobservable) must be identified. These estimates are a firm's "proprietary information." And while competition may drive insurers to continually improve these correlates and hence their contract terms and prices, the European experience (showing the lower operating costs of monopoly providers) suggests that this may not always follow.

Some additional complexities arise with infrequent hazards: diversification among many policy holders (contemporaneous) may not suffice, and diversification over time (intertemporal) is more difficult (box 5.1). Examining data from the largest U.S. catastrophic risk reinsurer for 1970 to 1998, Froot (2001) finds that catastrophe insurance premia are far higher than expected losses (up to seven times greater). The most likely reasons are reinsurance market imperfections (such as government intervention in insurance markets) and the market power exerted by traditional reinsurers.

As noted in several parts of this report, governments can do much to improve data quality and accessibility. Hurricanes are more frequent than earthquakes, but consider what it takes to set the hurricane insurance premium: several sets of detailed data are needed including the frequency, the likely paths and severity of hurricanes, the value and type of construction of all structures in their path (so accurate property records are essential), and how much damage each structure would likely suffer at various wind speeds (so local universities and engineering associations must know and test the strength of materials and designs of existing buildings). Climate science models estimate the forces (such as wind speed and air pressure) and engineering determines how buildings withstand them; allowing estimates of loss exceedance curves (insurers use this combination of cumulative probability distribution function with values at risk).

Even with good data, it is far from clear whether the frequency and severity of hurricanes has changed (chapter 6 discusses how frequency and

Box 5.1 Catastrophe risk in insurance and financial markets

Pooling risks reduces aggregate variance; so losses that are large and unpredictable for a victim become small and predictable in the aggregate pool. Risk pooling could be contemporaneous or intertemporal, but the latter requires the insurer to have enough capital to make the payouts and replenish it over time with annual premia. Catastrophes are infrequent, and insuring against them illustrates the issues with intertemporal diversification.

The risk that an event could generate a large loss for a country (1998 Hurricane Mitch for many Caribbean countries) could be small if that risk were shared worldwide. Reinsurance permits this worldwide sharing of risk through multiple transactions; but some catastrophes may be large enough to exhaust the collective buffer.

When payouts are significant relative to the global capital and surpluses of all insurance companies, it raises two issues. First, it questions the probability distribution that insurers use to set the premia: it is hard to know if a string of large losses are "several heads in a row" or evidence of the probability distribution changing. Second, even if the insurance actuaries were confident that the probability distribution was unchanged, investors in the equity market may be nervous: they drive down the prices of the insurer's equity on the stock exchange, thereby raising its cost of capital. In either case, pressures would build to raise the premium, a tendency exacerbated by any market power that insurers may have. So insurers raise the premium for catastrophe coverage as the likelihood of exhausting their buffer increases. They could augment this buffer by raising more capital (issuing equity), but their cost of capital would reflect the greater perception of risk.

But while insurance and financial markets are linked, they are not entirely integrated, and the price of risk in the two markets could differ substantially. Integration is easier when liabilities of insurers are traded on financial exchanges (some insurers are organized as mutuals, not corporations), and investors can more easily ascertain the insurers' exposure. A premium for nondiversifiable risk in financial markets may differ from that in insurance markets: there are potential gains from placing such risk in capital markets because many natural hazards are uncorrelated with the business cycle. Those who straddle both insurance and capital markets—hedge funds that underwrite insurance, CAT-bond issuers and buyers—could profit from these differences.

Those seeking to place such risks (reinsurers, governments buying insurance) would benefit from comparing prices in the insurance and financial markets. Governments must have the ability to assess their risks comprehensively and independently. Small mistakes can result in huge losses (more precisely, large transfers between the insured, the insurers, the reinsurers and CAT-bond holders).

Source: World Bank staff.

severity might be affected in the future because of climate change). Insurers in the United States had taken note of the dangers to property after 1992's Hurricane Andrew, but were nevertheless caught unprepared for the string of storms and major hurricanes (Katrina, Rita, and Wilma) in 2004 and 2005. Insurers incurred large payouts and raised the premia; but one cannot tell if the string of hurricanes were a low probability drawing from an unchanged distribution (making the premia increase unjustified)—or a shift in the distribution itself.

In a background paper for the report, Seo and Mahul (2009) found that property at risk rose as much in one decade of coastal development in the United States as from five decades of greater hurricane activity. The premia also rose substantially (an average of 76 percent) after 2005. More reliable information on probability distributions of hazards and the values and strength of structures at risk would reduce the premia regardless of whether coverage is from insurers or capital markets. The insurance premia almost double when probability and loss estimates are ambiguous as opposed to specific (Kunreuther, Hogarth, and Meszaros 1993). These complexities notwithstanding, calculating the insurance premium should be commercial, not political. The government is typically involved (even if only as regulator), and political pressures get transmitted regardless of a country's institutional arrangement. Governments also gather relevant data (on weather, property values, location, and the like) and not all governments make them readily accessible.

Parametric insurance

Parametric insurance is a type of insurance that makes the payment of claims conditional on a triggering event (wind speeds exceeding a certain threshold; earthquakes exceeding a particular intensity). Because assessing whether the parameter has been triggered is easy, such insurance obviates the need for detailed loss assessments. Insurers therefore avoid some costs (such as monitoring to reduce fraudulent claims, valuing the structures and their strength) and the insured pay a lower premium as a consequence. Although the premium is not tied to prevention measures (because the payouts are specified and unrelated to damage), the insured retains the incentive to prevent because lower damage is to the insured's benefit alone.

There are now some 20 schemes in low- and middle-income countries including China, Ethiopia, India, Malawi, Nicaragua, Peru, Ukraine, and Thailand (World Bank 2009a). Evaluation was built into the design of two weather-based crop insurance pilots (India in 2003 and Malawi in 2005), and their experiences have been carefully studied. Published evaluations of these schemes find that despite much effort, market penetration has been low. Fewer than 5 percent of eligible households in India and 17 percent of farmers offered insurance/credit in Malawi used these schemes. Subsequent surveys in India found that most farmers did not understand complex contracts or trust those selling insurance (Giné, Townsend, and Vickery 2008; Cole and others 2008).

Parametric insurance has had greater success at the wholesale level. In countries where there is some commercial insurance, domestic insurers reduce their risks by purchasing parametric reinsurance contracts from others. Governments also partake in such schemes directly.

Should governments borrow, set aside funds, or buy insurance?

Government revenues may fall after a disaster, especially if output declines and relief spending rises in the immediate aftermath and later, to rebuild

Figure 5.1 Managing and transferring financial risks to the market

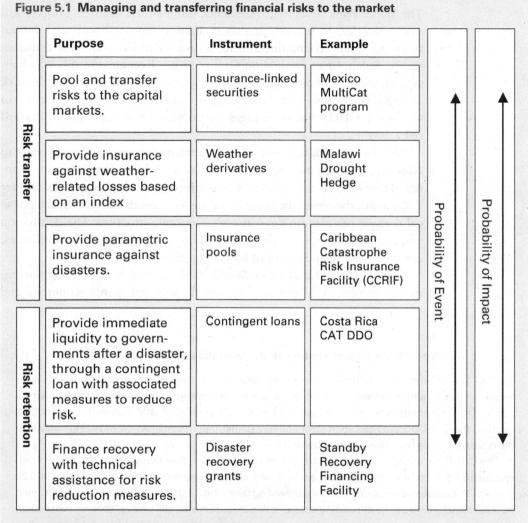

	Purpose	Instrument	Example		
Risk transfer	Pool and transfer risks to the capital markets.	Insurance-linked securities	Mexico MultiCat program	Probability of Event ↑↓	Probability of Impact ↑↓
	Provide insurance against weather-related losses based on an index	Weather derivatives	Malawi Drought Hedge		
	Provide parametric insurance against disasters.	Insurance pools	Caribbean Catastrophe Risk Insurance Facility (CCRIF)		
Risk retention	Provide immediate liquidity to govern-ments after a disaster, through a contingent loan with associated measures to reduce risk.	Contingent loans	Costa Rica CAT DDO		
	Finance recovery with technical assistance for risk reduction measures.	Disaster recovery grants	Standby Recovery Financing Facility		

Note: The figure focuses only on risk transfer/retention schemes and not on risk reduction measures (preventive measures that reduce the risk of death, injury, and damage, such as early warning systems; risk identification and measurement, and safer buildings and structures).
Source: World Bank staff.

damaged and destroyed government property.[3] Governments could borrow domestically and internationally to finance the wider budget deficit, but some may find it difficult. Lenders may be unfamiliar with small countries who do not normally borrow, and countries that do may have large existing debts and may not be able to raise additional sums. In addition to the probability and severity of the hazard, the choice between borrowing, setting funds aside, or buying insurance depends on the country's circumstances (figure 5.1).

Specific examples of contingent loans, insurance pools, and insurance-linked securities are discussed in the remainder of the section.

The World Bank's CAT DDO

The World Bank lends to governments, often after a disaster. Projects and loans take time to process, and those already approved with undisbursed funds are often "restructured" after a disaster to allow quicker disbursements (Independent Evaluation Group 2006). Recognizing this was happening often, the World Bank recently made available the Catastrophe Risk Deferred Drawdown Option (technically called a Development Policy Loan with CAT DDO) that encourages the country to manage natural hazard risks (box 5.2).

The disaster risk management requirement encourages governments to consider preventive measures and view disaster risk in a comprehensive manner. There is merit to considering risk comprehensively because, as chapter 2 discussed, the economic effect of a disaster depends not just on the physical damage but also on the country's economic structure. The destination and composition of its trade, reliance on tourism, sources of tax revenues, reserve holdings, and extent of borrowing all affect risk.

The CAT DDO and other World Bank lending facilities help governments borrow. A MultiCat program allows participants (countries and

---

Box 5.2 The World Bank's catastrophe risk deferred drawdown option (CAT DDO)

The CAT DDO, a World Bank loan to middle-income countries exposed to natural hazards, is approved before a disaster and disburses quickly if and when the borrowing government declares an emergency. The loan amount is limited to $500 million, or 0.25 percent of GDP (whichever is smaller), because the CAT DDO provides short-term liquidity (rather than reconstruction financing) following the disaster. It does not preclude other borrowings.

The CAT DDO, available for three years, can be renewed up to four times. There is a single front-end fee of 0.5 percent of the approved amount, and each subsequent renewal entails a fee of 0.25 percent. The interest is set at the IBRD rate prevailing when the funds are disbursed. The funds could be repaid at any time before the closing date, and this amount would still be available for subsequent borrowing. Borrowers must, however, have an adequate macroeconomic framework in place when the loan is approved and a disaster risk management program monitored by the World Bank.

The World Bank estimates that the CAT DDO is 25 percent less expensive than insurance for the equivalent risk, so it is attractive, though the approved (though undrawn) amount counts when determining the country's borrowing limit from the World Bank.

Costa Rica, the second most exposed country to multiple natural hazards (Natural Disaster Hotspots 2005), was the first to have a CAT DDO approved in September 2008 for $65 million. Domestic politics delayed the payment of the front end fee until after a 6.2 magnitude earthquake on January 8, 2009 struck causing damage estimated at $100 million; but Costa Rica drew down a portion of the loan when the fee was paid. As of December 2009, CAT DDOs had been approved for Costa Rica, Colombia, and Guatemala.

Sources: World Bank 2009a. *Catastrophe Risk Financing in Middle- and Low-Income Countries: Review of the World Bank Group Operations.* April 1, 2009, document prepared for a Technical Briefing to the Board of Executive Directors. http://treasury.worldbank.org: Jose Molina Jr. "Overview of DDO and CAT DDO," World Bank Treasury (power point presentation). Costa Rica: Earthquake OCHA Situation Report No. 2 printed from http://www.relief web.int on 1/15/2009.

regions) to buy insurance for multiple perils using documents and legal help developed for this purpose (World Bank 2009b). In 2009 the government of Mexico used this facility to issue a $290 million series of three-year notes with parametric triggers that replaced those that were maturing.

Should governments purchase insurance? Unlike individuals who are risk-averse, there are good reasons for some governments to be risk-neutral (meaning they should not buy insurance if the premium exceeds the expected loss) (Arrow and Lind 1970).[4] Box 5.1 explained why catastrophe insurance premia exceed expected losses, suggesting that governments should self-insure only by setting aside sufficient reserves—for example, in a contingency fund (holding reserves in such funds has an opportunity cost though)—or have access to ready borrowing.

But some governments may be risk-averse, not risk-neutral, and buy insurance even when the premium exceeds expected losses as with small Caribbean countries. The World Bank and other organizations have been encouraging governments to shop carefully, to consider risks comprehensively, and to think about prevention.

The Caribbean Catastrophe Risk Insurance Facility

Hurricanes form in the Eastern Atlantic Ocean and strengthen as they move west and then north (map 5.1). One or more of the many islands spread

Map 5.1 The Caribbean region—in harm's way

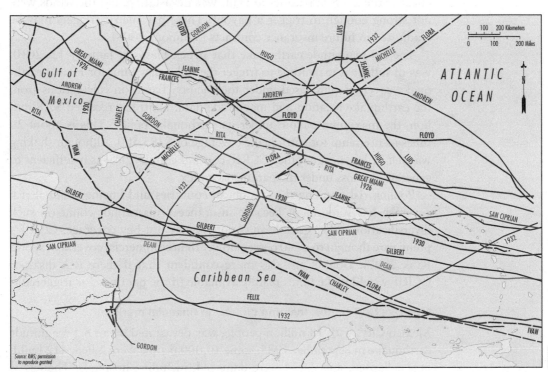

Source: Risk Management Solutions (RMS).

across the Caribbean is hit almost every year: the main unknowns are which island will be hit and how severe the damage will be.

The Caribbean Catastrophe Risk Insurance Facility (CCRIF) was set up in June 2007 for Caribbean island governments to collectively purchase parametric insurance. Commercial insurance is available in the Caribbean region, but the total premia paid by businesses averaged about 1.5 percent of GDP between 1970–99 while losses (insured and uninsured) amounted to only about 0.5 percent of GDP (Auffret 2003).[5]

Donors provided $67 million in start-up capital, and 16 member governments contributed $22 million. Governments purchased parametric insurance paying CCRIF about $20 million in premia for parametric insurance coverage totaling roughly $450 million (Cummins and Mahul 2009). The Facility retains responsibility for the first $20 million of payout (backed by its capital) and transfers the remaining exposure through reinsurance and catastrophe swaps that the World Bank intermediates. Donors expect that its capital and reserves will grow and that it will be self-sustaining.

The Facility paid about $1 million to St. Lucia and Dominica within two weeks of the November 2007 earthquake, the most severe in the eastern Caribbean in 30 years. It paid $6.3 million to the Turks and Caicos Islands after Hurricane Ike hit in September 2008.[6] There have also been disasters that did not trigger the set parameters: Hurricane Dean in 2007 caused considerable damage in Jamaica because of rain, but there was no payout because wind speed was the parametric trigger. Similarly, the cumulative effect of the 2008 hurricanes in Haiti was devastating, but the winds were not strong enough to trigger a payout. These parametric triggers may be readjusted in future insurance contracts (Simmons 2008).

The 7.0 magnitude earthquake that struck Haiti on January 12, 2010, was of sufficient magnitude to trigger the full policy limit for Haiti's earthquake coverage purchased under the Facility. Based on calculations from the earthquake location and magnitude data, Haiti has received $7.8 million, the maximum payout under its earthquake policy. This is about 20 times its premium for earthquake coverage of $385,500. Although shaking was felt in Jamaica, another CCRIF-covered country, it was insufficient to generate any loss under the parametric index.

Pooling risks among the Caribbean countries and buying residual risk coverage has some merit because insurance firms cannot count on such diversification: other Caribbean countries may not buy coverage. CCRIF's premia are thought to be 40 percent lower than commercial coverage (World Bank 2007). Donors are also more confident that if there is a disaster, CCRIF would make funds readily available (if the parameter is triggered).

Mexico's CAT-bonds: Insuring directly in financial markets

Mexico City, with 18 million people, was devastated by an 8.1 magnitude earthquake in September 1985: some 10,000 people were killed, 412 buildings collapsed, and 3,124 were damaged, including hospitals. The city is not on, or near, a fault line—the epicenter was 400 kilometers away—but Mexico City sits on a drained lake bed in an old volcanic crater with soft clay and ash that amplifies ground movement. So even distant quakes cause damage, and high rises are particularly vulnerable because their natural vibrating frequencies resonate with the seismic shocks. Consequently, many older (low-rise) buildings survived while many modern (high-rise) and well-constructed ones did not. Designing new buildings and retrofitting old ones for earthquake risk requires unusually complex engineering skills.

The earthquake came shortly after a humiliating debt default to foreign creditors. The foreign minister spurned international aid, especially from neighboring United States, and the president refused to suspend payments on recently restructured debts to help with the recovery. Consequently, foreign exchange reserves plummeted and economic management became difficult.

To avoid a recurrence, laws were enacted in 1994 requiring federal, state, and municipal public assets to be "insured" through a government entity, FONDEN, created in 1996 with a catastrophe reserve fund in it. FONDEN allowed funds to be spent after a disaster without having to borrow. Reserves were built from nothing in 1999 to about $863 million in 2001 (in 2008 prices) but were almost depleted following subsequent hurricane damage.

The government realized that the amounts needed after an earthquake would have been too large to set aside untouched ("the honey pot syndrome"). Mexico City accounts for 60 percent of the country's GDP and the 1985 earthquake raised the fiscal deficit $1.9 billion over the next four years (Cardenas and others 2007). In 2006, the Mexican government decided to transfer part of its public sector natural catastrophe risk to the international reinsurance and capital markets. Officials estimated that FONDEN could handle disasters up to $500 million (one standard deviation above average annual spending). FONDEN calculated its expected expenses after an earthquake and compared the amount with the insurance premia. The insurance premia had risen substantially since 2001, so it issued a catastrophe bond through a special purpose vehicle.[7]

The details are complex, but the concept of a catastrophe bond is simple: a special purpose vehicle issues the bond, and the proceeds are held in escrow. Bond holders (typically hedge funds or money managers) receive a higher interest rate (235 basis points above LIBOR [London interbank offered rate] as in the case of Mexico) than what the escrow earns. This difference amounts to $26 million on three bonds outstanding that total $450 million.[8]

When triggered by an event (an earthquake of magnitude equal to or greater than 7.5 or 8.0 on the Richter scale depending on specified points in and around Mexico City), the escrowed funds are released to the government and investors get nothing further. So when the earthquake strikes, investors lose financially, not the Mexican government. Meanwhile, Mexico City experienced many significant tremors (a 6.5 magnitude earthquake in Oaxaca in 2008, a 6.0 in April 2009, a 5.7 in May 2009) with little damage. But should a major one strike, the government would have funds to spend on relief and reconstruction as it sees fit.

Mexico was the first government to issue a CAT bond in 2006. While new issues have declined following the financial crisis of 2008, some $9 billion of face value are outstanding (Cummins and Mahul 2009). Issuing a bond has large fixed costs, many hidden, that small countries may find disproportionately expensive.[9] Such governments may find it advantageous to reinsure through regional pools, but it is also important to design and build structures well so damage can be reduced. Many new buildings in Mexico now have dampeners, but earthquakes differ in their forces and the resonating effect of the lake bed adds to the complexity and expense of retrofitting existing buildings.

Quick and direct help for families

What cannot be prevented or insured against must be borne, and a variety of coping mechanisms ("informal insurance," as distinct from market insurance) have developed over the centuries, many embedded in tradition and custom. People often help their friends and neighbors who suffer a broken leg or the death of an ox, and distant friends and relatives send remittances (some as loans). The main sources of help are:

- Remittances and vibrant communities
- Public safety nets
- Foreign aid.

Remittances and vibrant communities

Relatives or friends who live outside the affected community can send food, credit, or transfers from unaffected to affected areas. For example, marriages in six South Indian rural villages appear to have been arranged expressly to help households cope with droughts (Rosenzweig and Stark 1989). But transfers cover less than 10 percent of the shortfalls in income: so while they may avert starvation, they are unlikely to prevent consumption from declining substantially (Rosenzweig 1988).

Remittances are private financial flows to friends and family. Numerous migrant workers send small amounts that quickly add up. Most important, they flow directly to the victims—quickly and without fuss or fanfare, though not to all victims. Not all poor families have relatives working abroad: migration requires a large initial expense to buy tickets and work permits. But they may indirectly benefit from what their neighbors receive if they work for them.

Many studies of remittances and disasters find credit and transfers from relatives in distant areas (inside countries and overseas) to affected areas. Lucas and Stark (1985) find remittances increased from urban areas into rural areas in Botswana during the droughts of 1978–79. Miller and Paulson

(2007) find that in 1988 Thai households living in a province with below average rainfall the previous year got about 118 baht ($4.72) more remittances. Yang and Choi (2007) find that Philippine households with relatives abroad get remittances of 60 cents for every dollar decline in income between 1997 and 1998.

In a background paper for the report, Mohapatra, Joseph, and Ratha (2009) examine the effect of remittances on both the response and the preparedness. They estimate the effect of disasters (damage, numbers killed and affected) on remittances as a percentage of GDP and control for overall and immigrant population and persistence (this year's remittance depends on last year's). Migrant remittance data for 129 developing countries (part of the World Bank's Development Indicators) are augmented by disaster data from EM-DAT for 1970–2006. For a country with 10 percent of its population abroad, remittances rise by $0.50 for every $1 damage in the same year and by $1 in the year following (or $1.50 in the two years). These effects also register as a proportion of GDP: remittances rise by 0.5 percent of GDP in the same year and an additional 0.5 percent in the year following for an additional 1 percent of population affected by a disaster. Remittances are not sensitive to the number of fatalities.

The striking results are consistent with what is known about migrant motives and behavior: many work abroad to augment the income of family left behind. So when their family's assets are destroyed or their livelihoods threatened, migrants abroad send funds to help. While the migrants' earnings and savings over their entire stay abroad may not change, the timing of their remittances responds to the needs of the family left behind.

The remittances are put to different uses: studies find that a large part goes to buying consumer durables (refrigerators, radios, televisions) and much of what is invested is for building homes or adding masonry structures to them (Adams 1991). Houses made sturdier could be considered a prevention measure, though the situation varies. In Turkey, 13 years after the 1970 Gediz earthquake, the reconstructed area was peppered with improperly reinforced concrete houses—mostly paid for by the earnings of family members in Germany (Aysan and Oliver 1987). Better building practices (described in chapter 3) are needed to ensure building safety.

Mohapatra, Joseph, and Ratha (2009) use household survey data for Burkina Faso (2003), Ghana (2005), and Bangladesh (1998–99) to separate consumption increases attributable to remittances from other factors. The remittances allowed households to consume more than otherwise identical nonrecipient households after the 1998 flood in Bangladesh. Recipients in Ghana, especially those receiving remittances from higher income countries, had better housing and were more likely to have fixed and mobile telephones (figure 5.2). International remittance recipients in Ethiopia were less likely to sell their livestock during droughts (when prices may be disadvantageous) because they have cash to buy food (figure 5.3).

Remittances are not only from family members: expatriate "communities" get organized as NGOs to raise and send funds after disasters (not

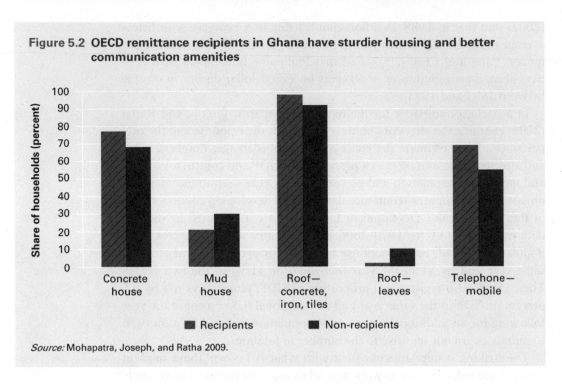

Figure 5.2 OECD remittance recipients in Ghana have sturdier housing and better communication amenities

Source: Mohapatra, Joseph, and Ratha 2009.

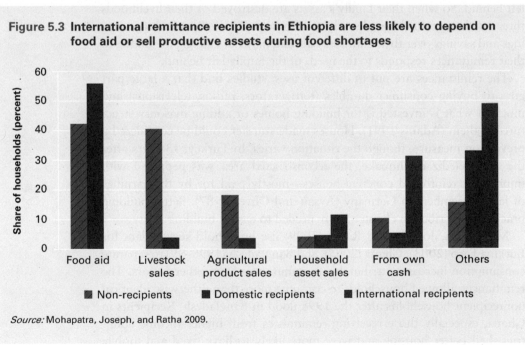

Figure 5.3 International remittance recipients in Ethiopia are less likely to depend on food aid or sell productive assets during food shortages

Source: Mohapatra, Joseph, and Ratha 2009.

classified as remittances in the data). These flows, also well directed, are often spent on relief, not prevention. Private inflows can also take other forms and even factor in longer term reconstruction (box 5.3).

Remittances do not involve governments, but governments affect their flows: dual or parallel exchange rate markets reflect restrictions that the

Box 5.3 Mobilizing Haiti's diaspora

According to official statistics about a million Haitians live overseas, about half of that million in the United States. Unofficial estimates tend to be significantly larger, with newspapers reporting a million Haitians in the neighboring Dominican Republic alone.

This diaspora is important for Haiti's economy. Before the January 2010 earthquake, it sent an estimated $1.5 to $1.8 billion in remittances each year, an amount expected to increase following the earthquake.

Developed countries can take measures to support this process. Following the earthquake, the United States granted temporary protected status (TPS) for 18 months to Haitians already in the United States. The TPS allows more than 200,000 Haitians currently residing in the United States without proper documents to live and work in the United States legally, without fear of deportation. It also allows them to send money home quickly and efficiently through formal remittance channels.

Preliminary calculations indicate that if the TPS resulted in a 20-percent increase in the average remittance per migrant, an additional $360 million in remittance would flow to Haiti in 2010. And if the TPS were to be extended once beyond the currently stipulated 18 months (TPS extensions have been granted before for immigrants from El Salvador, Honduras, Nicaragua, Somalia, and Sudan), additional flows to Haiti would exceed $1 billion over three years. That would be a billion dollars of financial help coupled with goodwill and advice, tailored to the needs of the recipient.

Other mechanisms can mobilize the Haiti diaspora and bring additional resources to the country to assist in recovery and reconstruction. Diaspora bonds could be issued to directly tap the substantial wealth of the Haitian diaspora. Israel and India diaspora bonds have been used to raise more than $35 billion of development financing. Ethiopia, Nepal, the Philippines, Rwanda, and Sri Lanka have issued (or are considering) diaspora bonds to bridge financing gaps.

Diaspora members are usually—though not exclusively—more interested than foreign investors in investing in the home country. Offering a reasonable interest rate—a 5-percent tax-free dollar interest rate, for example—could attract a large number of Haitian investors who are getting close to zero interest on their deposits. If 200,000 Haitians in the United States, Canada, and France were to invest $1,000 each in diaspora bonds, it would add up to $200 million. If these bonds were opened to friends of Haiti, including private charitable organizations, much larger sums could be raised.

If the bond rating were enhanced to investment grade rating through guarantees from the multilateral and bilateral donors, such bonds could even attract institutional investors. Credit enhancement from creditworthy donors would help this process. Support to tax exemption of such bonds, or a public guarantee, could make such a bond more attractive. Recent estimates are that a $100 million grant from official or private donors to guarantee such bonds (say, for 10 years, on an annual rolling basis) could generate $600 million of additional funding for Haiti.

Sources: World Bank staff; Ratha 2010.

government would do well to remove. Remittances—direct private flows from unaffected to affected areas—are an extension of social networks. Some communities have been known to quickly recover largely on their own. What makes some communities "vibrant"—recovering faster than others—is open to interpretation, but two defining characteristics of such communities are social cohesiveness and leadership. Their members help each other and, under able leadership, demand (and get) public services to which they are entitled. A brief account of how the Vietnamese community recovered quickly after Hurricane Katrina, in contrast to other victims, illustrates this point (Chamlee-Wright and Storr 2009).

The Vietnamese community lived mainly in the New Orleans east area, which was severely flooded (from 5 to more than 12 feet), but it recovered faster than both the poorer and wealthier (Lakeview) areas equally devastated. They returned to rebuild within weeks of the storm, and by summer 2007, 90 percent of the 4,000 residents living within a mile of The Mary Queen of Vietnam Catholic Church, the physical and spiritual center of the community, were back. And 70 of the 75 Vietnamese-owned businesses in the vicinity were up and running again. In contrast, only 10 percent of wealthier Lakeview residents had returned 16 months after the storm. Similarly, only 28 percent of the ethnically diverse low- and middle-income residents of Broadmoor (in the uptown area) had returned by 2008.

The Vietnamese community's social cohesiveness accounts for its resilience. Many had come in the mid-1970s after the fall of Saigon, and others arrived later with the help of friends and family. They helped each other evacuate their homes when Katrina struck, remaining in touch with each other when they were displaced. When city officials did not help the elderly repair their homes, other members of the community did. Loans from relatives, labor exchanges, child care services, and rentals of tools and equipment were all organized, spurring the recovery.

The community organized petitions to have public services restored. Father Vien Nguyen was the senior pastor of the church that remained the hub of the community. When municipal officials rebuffed a request to restore electricity in the area, Father Vien Nguyen gave pictures of Mass attendance to *Entergy*, a local power company, and gathered people's names and addresses to show that enough paying customers had returned. Power was restored by the first week of November 2005, enabling the return of non-Vietnamese residents as well.

While the government decided on the many complex issues of relocation, strengthening levees, and redirecting river flows, people rebuilt their lives and livelihoods, underscoring the major role of local communities in recovery.

Public safety nets

The term "safety net" encompasses a wide range of public transfer schemes. Some governments use an existing system to help victims of a disaster, while others begin from scratch. As chapter 2 discussed, disasters can lead to permanent effects on victims, especially on children, where malnutrition in early ages can impair cognition, reducing productivity and lifetime earnings. This suggests a critical role for safety nets: timely assistance—in food aid or cash transfers—can prevent adverse effects from becoming permanent. The need to make food available quickly may require that pre-existing stocks, plans, and systems that quickly disburse food aid are in place, such as food relief outlets in Ethiopia and the World Food Program warehouses in many countries.

Timely food aid can be effective. During Ethiopia's 1995–96 drought, food aid offset the expected increase in child malnutrition (aged between 6 months and 2 years). In contrast, in communities that experienced the drought but did not receive food aid, a 10 percent increase in crop damage reduced child growth (also aged between 6 months and 2 years) by 0.12 centimeters (Yamano, Alderman, and Christiansen 2005). And as Spotlight 4 discusses, Ethiopian households affected by the 2008 drought that received transfers from the Productive Safety Net Program consumed 30 percent more calories than non-beneficiaries. In Bangladesh, free food relief by the government (through the Vulnerable Group Feeding and Gratuitous Relief programs) to those affected by the 1998 floods contributed between 64 and 133 kilocalories a day per person (Pelham, Clay, and Braunholz 2009).

Maintaining adequate food reserves is important, but experiences with cash transfers are becoming increasingly popular (Alderman 2010). Cash transfers, unlike food aid, give users more choice and flexibility and can stimulate domestic supply where local markets exist. Assistance in cash does not, of course, increase the availability of food, cement, or other items that may be needed; but if transport links are functioning, local merchants will ensure availability. Indeed, if they do not, the infusion of cash would raise prices (Spotlight 5). Providing aid in-kind does not require local merchants, but it runs the risk of transporting at great expense some items the victims do not need or like.

The challenges of designing effective safety nets should not be underestimated. The administrative and technical capacities at various levels of government, the size of the affected population, and the depth and liquidity of (food) markets are some factors that determine the appropriate mix of responses in cash and food. Even if well designed, the practical and logistical difficulties of delivering food aid should not be misjudged. In conflict and in fragile situations, food aid can also be a weapon, exacerbating timely provision to those most in need (Spotlight 4). Support sometimes can be inadequate. In Bangladesh, food assistance delivered after the 1998 floods had a positive but limited long-term impact given the small amounts distributed because of delays in delivery (Quisumbing 2005). And bilateral and multilateral aid flows, because they rely on appeals triggered after field assessments, are often slow (figure 5.4).

The central point is that to achieve a quick and organized response, safety nets need to be in place before hazards strike. Trying to put in place safety nets after a hazard strikes is often impractical and ad hoc (table 5.1). There are exceptions—for example, if the affected population is very small, as in Maldives during the tsunami.

The Maldives government devised a cash transfer system from scratch and delivered it to some 53,000 people, about a fifth of the population, within one month of the 2004 tsunami. Teams visited all the affected islands, visually confirmed that the house was damaged, gathered all the people the next day and paid the victims in cash (between $39 and $117 equivalent, depending on the damage). A pre- and post-disaster panel survey found

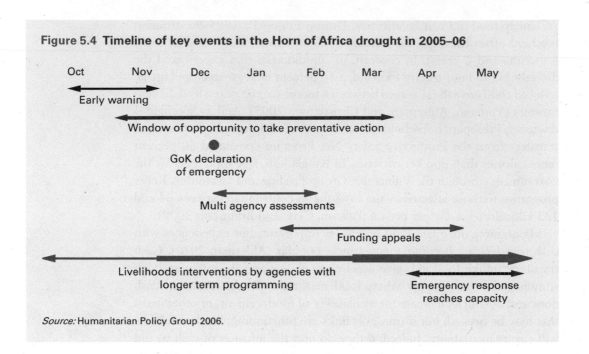

Figure 5.4 Timeline of key events in the Horn of Africa drought in 2005–06

Oct   Nov   Dec   Jan   Feb   Mar   Apr   May

Early warning

Window of opportunity to take preventative action

GoK declaration
of emergency

Multi agency assessments

Funding appeals

Livelihoods interventions by agencies with
longer term programming

Emergency response
reaches capacity

Source: Humanitarian Policy Group 2006.

the targeting to be adequate and that few victims were excluded (Maldives Ministry of Planning and National Development 2006).

For Pakistan's housing reconstruction, a new government agency with no experience in cash transfers rose to the challenge of targeting, disbursing, monitoring, and delivering them to remote locations during the winter. It took four months to identify beneficiaries, and cash grants began disbursing in six monthly tranches in April 2006, six months after the earthquake (Heltberg 2007).

In Sri Lanka, local governments disbursed cash in four rounds, each worth about $50, to the affected households. The first round in March 2005 covered 250,000 households, and while few victims were excluded, many who were unaffected also got the benefits. A survey found that 81 percent of unaffected households received grants (Pelham, Clay, and Braunholz 2009). Subsequent rounds sought to narrow targeting households with damaged houses or with lost income earners.

In Turkey, after the earthquake in 1999, 85 percent of survey respondents were satisfied by the authorities' treatment and grateful for the assistance.[10] Of those who asked for the accommodation and repair allowances, 95 percent got them. The Social Solidarity Fund, with a nationwide network of 900 offices, administered the bulk of the project, quickly mobilizing temporary workers, computers, and other needed resources from around the country.

These varied experiences bring out the challenges in deploying safety nets (Grosh and others 2008). Victims of a disaster may not be exactly those that an existing safety net is designed to catch. Ensuring that only the intended beneficiaries get the benefits requires administrative checks. While normal times allow a wide discussion of who the intended beneficiaries

Table 5.1 Post-disaster safety nets are common

Country	Population covered	Components	Amounts
Maldives (2004 tsunami)	All affected households (one-fifth of population)	Cash grant	$39–$117 per person depending on damage (equivalent to 2 to 6 weeks of average consumption)
		In-kind	
Pakistan (2005 earthquake)	250,000 households (30% of affected)	Cash grant	$300 per household for livelihood support
		Payment for death and injury	$1,660 to next of kin
		Payment for housing	$2,900 per house destroyed. $1,250 per damaged house
Sri Lanka (2004 tsunami)	250,000 households in first round (all affected households covered)	Cash grant	$200 per affected household, plus grants for housing reconstruction
Turkey (1999 earthquake)	206,145 households	Accommodation	$4,000 for accommodation aid and $1,430 per house for damage repairs
		Repair	
		Death and disability	$1,790 to next of kin and $950 (on average) for disability

Source: World Bank staff, based on Heltberg 2007.

should be (rural poor, all poor, not indolent poor), the choice after a disaster requires speed to help the victims. Responsive governments can provide relief quickly, and while small size is an advantage (Maldives), large size need not be a deterrent (Pakistan).

One aspect of safety nets germane to disasters is that traditional safety nets can fail to reach vulnerable groups (children, women, elderly). Why? Because they tend to target beneficiaries by income or indicators not wholly relevant to vulnerable groups, such as land or asset ownership (Baez, de la Fuente, and Santos 2009). More relevant indicators—such as nutritional screening and disabilities—could overcome this, though collecting some of these data for short-term use can be expensive. Keeping in mind the practical difficulties of providing timely in-kind food assistance, better targeting of children may be achieved by adding ready-to-use-foods (RUFs) to general food distribution. RUFs do not require water (compared to powdered milk-based supplements which do), and are increasingly locally produced and do not spoil that easily.

Aid and the Samaritan's dilemma

Buchanan (1975) used the analogy with a Good Samaritan who attempts to assist those in need. But if the Samaritan cannot credibly commit to denying help to the negligent, that could encourage carelessness (Gibson and others 2005). Post-disaster humanitarian aid, whether from bilateral governments, multilateral agencies, or NGOs, is caught in this dilemma.

Several studies have examined the determinants and efficacy of foreign aid in general, but few examine post-disaster aid specifically. Some theoretical models suggest that ex-post aid reduces ex-ante prevention (Raschky and Weck-Hannemann 2007 and Cohen and Werker 2008).

In a background paper for this report, Raschky and Schwindt (2009a) empirically examine this link and find weak evidence that increases in the level of past foreign aid imply higher death tolls resulting from disasters. They construct a model where aid flows could increase collective prevention but predictable ex-post relief could reduce it. They then examine empirically which effect dominates by regressing mortality in 1,763 disasters (divided into three subsamples for storms, floods, and earthquakes) on aid inflow the previous year, controlling for the effects of other factors (hazard exposure, population size, institutional quality, colonial past).

The statistically significant positive coefficient of the main variable of interest, humanitarian aid per capita, implies that more aid in the past is associated with additional deaths from storms. But the results for floods and earthquakes are not significant. There is no apparent reason why the storm results are statistically significant but the flood and earthquake results are not. More research is needed to understand this divergence, and the results need to be interpreted with caution.

In a companion background paper, Raschky and Schwindt (2009b) extend their first study by considering the type and channel of aid. A donor could provide bilateral aid or contribute to multilateral assistance, and could do so in cash or in kind. They examine aid after 228 disasters over eight years (2000–2007). Oil and trade access are two major motives of aid (despite the humanitarian label) that are distinguished. They find that the number of people affected, but not the number of fatalities, are related to the choice between bilateral and multilateral aid. More distant countries get aid multilaterally while those with a higher fraction of fuel exports and better governance indicators get more bilateral aid, perhaps because giving directly bolsters the donor's influence. Multilateral aid may be distributed on a "needs" basis and so the recipient's income, governance indicators—and fatalities—may matter. Bilateral donors also favor more open recipient countries, so a larger fraction of fuel exports makes aid more likely. These findings echo those of Fink and Redaelli (2009), who analyzed 400 recent disasters and found that while needs influence relief aid, so do geographic proximity, cultural and colonial connections, and oil exports. The findings suggest that donor self-interest matters (Olsen, Carstensen, and Hoyen 2003).[11]

Some observers have noted the disincentives of donor programs. For example Nicaragua declined to pursue a weather indexing program after it had been priced in the global reinsurance market: it cited international assistance following Hurricane Mitch in 1998 as an indication of dependable alternatives (Alderman 2010).

It may be unfair, though, to blame countries for neglecting prevention: Mozambique, anticipating major floods in 2002, asked donors for

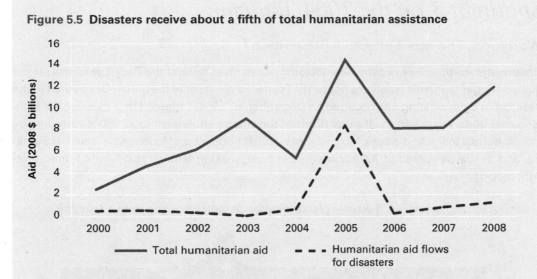

Figure 5.5 Disasters receive about a fifth of total humanitarian assistance

Aid (2008 $ billions)

— Total humanitarian aid   ▬ ▬ ▪ Humanitarian aid flows for disasters

Note: Humanitarian aid is "an intervention to help people who are victims of a natural disaster or conflict meet their basic needs and rights," while official development assistance (ODA) is "money spent on development (education, health, water supply and sanitation, agriculture, and so on) and humanitarian assistance by members of the OECD Development Assistance Committee."
Source: World Bank staff based on data from the Financial Tracking System (FTS) of the UN Office for the Coordination of Humanitarian Affairs.

$2.7 million to prepare and got only half the amount, but $100 million were received in emergency assistance following the floods, with another $450 million pledged for rehabilitation and reconstruction (Revkin 2005).

The report's overarching theme is that not enough is being done to prevent disasters. Donors usually respond to them only after they strike. About a fifth of total humanitarian aid between 2000 and 2008 was devoted to spending on disaster relief/response (figure 5.5).

The share of humanitarian funding going to prevention is small but increasing—from about 0.1 percent in 2001 to 0.7 percent in 2008 (Harmer and others 2009). But prevention endeavors often imply long-term development expenditures whereas the focus of humanitarian aid—already a tiny part of official development assistance—is immediate relief and response. Donors concerned with prevention could specifically earmark development aid (rather than humanitarian aid) for prevention-related activities. And such aid, if used effectively, could reduce issues arising from the Samaritan's dilemma: the inability to deny help following a disaster to those who have not taken sufficient prevention measures.

Spotlight 5 on the 2004 Tsunami

Warnings: The most effective prevention?

Underwater earthquakes occur where tectonic plates meet around the Pacific rim, and severe quakes trigger tsunamis (spotlight figure 1).[1] Tsunamis are rarer in the Indian Ocean than in the Pacific. But a devastating one occurred on December 26, 2004, triggered by a massive 9.3 Richter scale[2] underwater earthquake that released the energy equivalent of 32,000 Hiroshima-size atomic bombs in the first waves. Its epicenter was just northwest of Indonesia's island of Sumatra, and its waves spread at 700 kilometers per hour, making landfall at different times (spotlight map 1).

Spotlight figure 1 Tectonic plates slipping at fault lines generate a tsunami

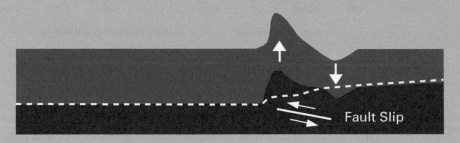

Source: U.S. Geological Survey Web site. http://walrus.wr.usgs.gov/tsunami/basics.html.

Spotlight map 1 Indian Ocean tsunami travel time in hours

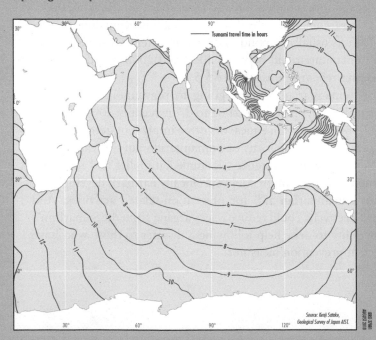

Source: U.S. Geological Survey Web site http://staff.aist.go.jp/kenji.satake/
Sumatra-E.html.

Spotlight figure 2 Banda Aceh's shore, before and after the tsunami

Source: DigitalGlobe.

The force of the waves determines the devastation: distance from the epicenter moderates the force, but the contours of the coast and sea bottom may concentrate it. The slope of the land underwater near the shore slows the waves but raises their height: the first wave that struck Aceh, Indonesia, 15 minutes after the quake was over 20 meters high. In some low lying areas, sea water penetrated three kilometers inland, destroying the crops and ruining the land with salinity. The tsunami reached the Thai coast 40 minutes later, devastating some major tourist resorts but sparing others partially protected by the bays. Waves later reached India's Andaman Islands, villages along India's southeastern coast (Tamil Nadu state), and western parts of Sri Lanka. The severity of damage varied.

Some 230,000 people died, mostly in Indonesia (73 percent) and Sri Lanka (18 percent), many more were bereaved, and 1.7 million were displaced. Damage was particularly severe in Indonesia, especially in Aceh, the poorest of its provinces (spotlight figure 2).

Many survivors lost much of what enabled them to live: coastal fishermen in Aceh, Tamil Nadu, and Sri Lanka lost their boats and nets, and some farmers lost their fields to salinity and permanent inundation.[3] And even though many of Thailand's tourist resorts were physically spared, tourists fled and were reluctant to return. GDP in tourism-dependent Maldives fell 80 percent the following year.

Unprecedented response

News of the devastation spread quickly. Thailand's resorts were filled with camera-toting European tourists enjoying their Christmas break. Although Europeans were fewer than 1.5 percent of the dead, the pictures they took and their heart-rending stories flashed around the world, producing an outpouring of aid.

Government and official aid agencies planned their response in the days following the tsunami, but it became increasingly clear that coordinating private attempts to help would be a challenge considering the amounts. Aid commitments of $13.5 billion greatly exceeded total damage estimated at $9.9 billion, mostly to private property. Most aid went to Indonesia (over $7 billion), and the bulk was through nongovernmental entities. The Indonesian government created a special agency, the BRR, which managed roughly a third of the total contributions. The World Bank managed a multi-donor fund for official bilateral aid.

Unintended effects: Some waste, but avoidable?

A multitude of small nongovernmental organizations (NGOs) eager to help poured in: 435 in Aceh alone. Each brought funds for a specific purpose, but the typical NGO project was small, and "brick and mortar" projects were preferred so that they could "show" contributors how their funds were spent. This preference meant that some spending on intangibles was neglected unless the government did so.

While many projects were well managed, some NGOs bought land and built houses—often before the government decided where they would build roads or provide drinking water, sewerage, and other public infrastructure. So, some newly built houses were in areas unsuitable for townships; some houses that were ceremoniously handed over to victims had no infrastructure and remain unoccupied.

The waste is difficult to estimate: the government, not being involved, keeps no statistics. The report of the Tsunami Evaluation Coalition provides numerous examples of waste in relief spending.[4] Items that were not useful—canned pork to Muslim Indonesia, 75 metric tons of expired drugs, inappropriate western clothes—took up precious cargo space. Masyrafah and McKeon (2008) have other examples: an NGO provided boats to local fishermen that were left to rust because they were poorly constructed and of unfamiliar design.

Waste results from cultural unfamiliarity, especially with well-intentioned help in kind, but the army of aid workers also puts huge demands on the local economy, producing unintended effects. Hiring local workers at "fair" wages so distorted the local labor market that the able-bodied stopped fishing or farming to wait and cook for foreign aid workers on whose continuing presence they had come to depend.

Even "well targeted" aid has unintended effects and can benefit those who may not need help: the incidence of aid (who benefits) is not always obvious. The infusion of cash in the local economy, both as direct grants and spending on services, resulted in inflation (which has distributional effects), as with the spurt of inflation in Banda Aceh (the provincial capital and largest city of Aceh) and in the region's second city, Lhokseumawe (spotlight figure 3). These effects occur in many post-disaster settings, but the scale of the aid after the tsunami enabled the effects to be readily observed.

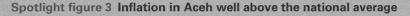

Spotlight figure 3 Inflation in Aceh well above the national average

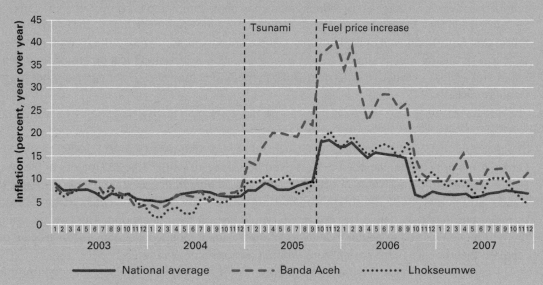

Source: Masyrafah and McKeon 2008.

While some of the waste and unintended effects could have been avoided, many victims and survivors did benefit. Furthermore, the Indonesian government's considerate and efficient response even stilled the conflict with the Aceh provincial government that had been simmering for 30 years. But such humanitarian impulses do not always overcome animosities.

Warnings and preparedness save lives

The tsunami caught most by surprise, but not all. Scientists at the Pacific Tsunami Warning Center in Hawaii frantically called counterparts in the vulnerable countries to alert them of the inevitable tsunami after detecting and locating the massive quake. Those they reached lacked the authority to act; so public warnings were not always issued or acted on.

But some were prepared. A 10-year-old English schoolgirl, having just studied tsunamis in school, deduced from the sudden draining of the sea that a tsunami was imminent. Her family holidaying in the Thai resort of Maikhao Beach fled to safety along with some 100 other tourists. Similarly, the Onge tribe in the Little Andaman Island retreated to higher ground when they felt the quake, as did those on the Indonesian islands of Simeulue, showing that knowledge embedded in culture usefully augments the direct experience of any generation.

Simply asking people to go a short distance inland to higher ground would have saved many lives because the waters quickly abate. Only one person died in Kenya, where radio and television stations discovered news reports on satellite television and broadcast warnings three hours ahead of the tsunami. But 300 died eight hours after the earthquake in neighboring Somalia, because such news was not monitored.

Countries are making efforts now to improve warnings, and many are taking advantage of newer technologies as well. Short message services (SMS) may reach more people quicker, especially with the huge increase in the use of cellular telephones.[5] In the wake of the 2004 tsunami, Sri Lankan authorities sent out a text message for village chiefs and media outlets that could spread the word to people who did not have mobile phones.[6]

Warnings alone are not enough: people must know where to go when they receive one. Before the tsunami in 2004, preparedness plans had been completed for only five of Sri Lanka's 25 districts (de Mel, McKenzie, and Woodruff 2008). But even after the tsunami, an Oxfam survey found that only 14 percent of Sri Lankan survivors knew what to do next time (Oxfam America 2006, p.11). Clearly much remains to be done: evacuation routes and locations must be designated and regular evacuation drills held. Such preparations may also guard against other more frequent hazards.

Zoning for safety: Easier said than done

The tsunami destroyed about 100,000 houses and severely damaged almost 50,000 more in Sri Lanka. A majority of the damaged or destroyed houses were within 100–200 meters of the sea. Residents were told they would not be allowed to reconstruct in the coastal zone. And while UN Habitat and numerous NGOs announced housing projects away from the coast, many refused to move because they fished and the move would disrupt their livelihood. The law requiring them to move was so unpopular that it was later rescinded. Meanwhile, many reconstructed or repaired their houses in the coastal zone without government assistance.[7]

Sri Lanka's experience illustrates the importance of dealing with the social and economic context of communities, not just housing in safe locations. While the speedy rebuilding of shelters is understandable, they may remain unused unless communities move away from unsafe areas—and this requires community involvement and sustained efforts in finding the most appropriate remedy for each situation.

Prediction difficult, detection easy, but cooperation essential

Earthquakes are difficult to predict, though this will undoubtedly improve with technology and our understanding. The ability of some animals to sense impending quakes (notably elephants who move to higher ground) suggests that instruments may be able to measure what these animals can detect in advance. But a tsunami follows a major quake, so its path and likely destructive force could be charted—and warnings issued—if the period between earthquake detection and tsunami prediction could be shortened.

Underwater monitoring instruments and instruments to monitor ocean surface movements help. But while there are several in the Pacific (where the "rim of fire" makes earthquakes and tsunamis common), there were none in the Indian Ocean. Such instruments are now being installed, and this expense may be worthwhile if they also collect data useful for purposes other than the rare tsunami. Not all countries have good seismic facilities, and it would be helpful if those that do shared real-time data. Some countries are reluctant to do so, especially in real time, because they could also be used for other purposes (such as monitoring its nuclear tests).

So, saving lives and reducing damage require an organized response to the warning but this expense is warranted only when exposure and hazard frequency are sufficiently high (chapter 5).

CHAPTER 6

Coming Game-Changers?
Burgeoning Cities, Climate Change,
and Climate-Induced Catastrophes

Future disaster risks (a combination of hazard, exposure, and vulnerability) may change as a result of two powerful trends: burgeoning cities and a changing climate. The latest United Nations (UN) estimates suggest that, globally, the urban population exceeded the rural for the first time in 2008 (UN Populations Division 2008). In less developed regions, this threshold is expected to be reached by around 2020. How will changing distributions of population and income in the context of growing cities change our exposure and vulnerability to natural hazards? How will the incidence of climate and weather extremes affect future economies and well-being? For example, widespread migration to coastal regions may greatly increase risk even if the climate were to remain constant, while increasing prosperity may work to reduce risk, even if the climate hazards themselves are increasing or intensifying.

And what about climate-induced catastrophes, defined here to mean disasters that occur on a global scale and are likely to be irreversible over any realistic time frame for decision-making? For example, the melting of the ice sheet on Greenland, as a consequence of climate change, could raise sea levels by seven meters, and the melting of the West Antarctic ice sheet could raise them by five meters, flooding many major coastal areas.

The chapter starts with a discussion on cities, whose growth, especially in the developing world, substantially changes exposure and vulnerability. It then analyzes how climate change could affect hazards such as tropical cyclones, with a glimpse of the science behind the projections. Note that the focus is on the additional hazards induced by climate change, distinguishing them from changes in hazards without future climate change. Moreover, the focus on hazards means that the analysis does not address all the effects of climate change.[1]

The risks and costs of climate-induced catastrophes, whose global scale and persistence differentiate them from disasters on a more local and regional scale, are examined last.

Institutions are the common thread linking the three possible game-changers. They need to adapt to all risks—not just those from urbanization, climate change, and catastrophe—and function municipally, nationally, and globally. There are no ready recipes to create them, but much can be done to foster them.

Cities: Rising exposure

Cities are economic powerhouses: they occupy only 1.5 percent of the world's land area but produce half the world's GDP. And prosperous cities are economic magnets, attracting people and investments. Their prosperity arises from the division of labor that the density of people and assets allows, and from the lower cost of acquiring productivity-increasing information and technology ("know-how"). There are now 26 megacities (with more than 10 million people), up from eight in 1950. The 2009 *World Development Report* examined these issues in economic geography and concluded that governments should not try to prevent or divert urbanization but should instead better support cities and provide needed services to both urban and rural areas (each has a different set of challenges). Building on the 2009 WDR's framework, this section begins by outlining how and why cities grow and why exposure to hazards may rise but vulnerability may fall in the aggregate as densities and incomes increase.

Cities grow faster than countries

Historically, output has grown by about 1 to 2 percentage points more than population, so per capita income has risen almost everywhere. Much of the growth has been in cities, where per capita income is higher. Among 150 of the world's largest cities, per capita output is about 1.8 times the average national output. And urban per capita income is on average twice the rural.[2] This is not new: cities have long brought prosperity. Cities' population is also growing. The UN estimates the world urban population's share will rise to 70 percent by 2050.[3] About half this growth is "natural" (owing to the fertility of urban dwellers) (Montgomery 2009), and the remainder is due to expansion (when adjoining villages grow to meet) and migration (map 6.1).

Many cities are outgrowing the capacity of roads, water supply, and sewage disposal systems to serve their inhabitants. Services have not kept pace largely because cities have not invested enough in infrastructure—even in the vaunted homes of high-tech industries like Bangalore, India. The reasons differ, but many can be traced to institutions that do not allow city

Map 6.1 Cities projected to have more than 100,000 people by the year 2050

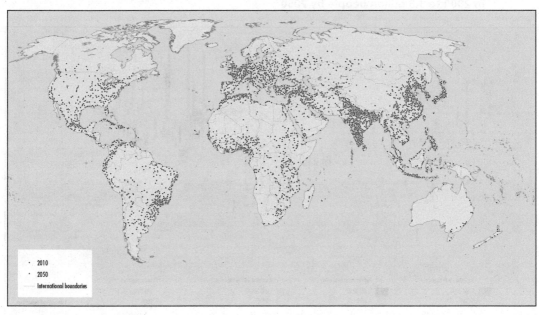

Source: Brecht and others 2010.

administrations to respond to people's needs: for example, the financing arrangements of Indian cities could be faulted (Bahl and Martinez-Vazquez 2008). Congestion, pollution, and frustration may eventually choke the continuing growth of such cities, but their people are exposed to natural hazards today. These are the cities where dangers may be unnecessarily high.

City growth will increase exposure

Cities are largely founded at transport intersections—such as ports, or at the first bridge on a river upstream. Some natural harbors reflect active tectonics. Flat land close to the water was at a premium, reflecting unconsolidated recent sediments, often reclaimed for its value. Such land is vulnerable to both flooding and ground motion amplification. For example, San Francisco was originally a city built of wooden buildings, largely destroyed in the fire that followed the 1906 earthquake. The debris from that earthquake was then pushed into the sea to create more reclaimed land on which the Marina District was constructed, only to suffer high levels of damage and ground settlement in the 1989 earthquake. Such growth increases exposure and vulnerability to hazards unless people take conscious measures to prevent them.

City-specific population projections to 2050[4] for this report are combined with geographic patterns of hazard events representative of the 1975–2007 period. The projected number of people exposed to tropical cyclones and earthquakes in large cities in 2050 more than doubles, rising from

Map 6.2 Exposure to cyclones and earthquakes in large cities rises from 680 million people in 2000 to 1.5 billion people by 2050

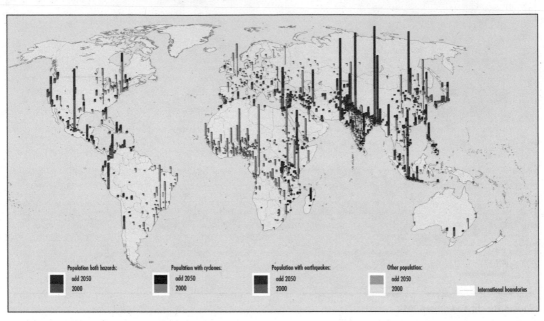

Source: Brecht and others 2010.

310 million in 2000 to 680 million in 2050 for tropical cyclones, and from 370 million to 870 million for earthquakes (map 6.2).

The growing exposure continues to vary by region. By 2050, there will be 246 million city dwellers in cyclone-prone areas in South Asia, but 160 million each in the OECD and in East Asia. Although East Asia has fewer exposed people, the urban population exposed to cyclones is expected to grow at 2.2 percent a year, similar to South Asia's. Sub-Saharan Africa's exposure growth at 3.5 percent is even higher, reaching 21 million urban dwellers by 2050.

Exposure to earthquakes will likely remain the bane of East Asia: 267 million in 2050, up from 83 million in 2000. It is also high in Latin America and the Caribbean (150 million in 2050) and OECD countries (129 million in 2050). But the fastest exposure growth is in South Asia (3.5 percent), followed by Sub-Saharan Africa (2.7 percent).

The density of people and economic activity not only changes the risk equation—it can also change the economics of disaster risk reduction strategies. And what applies to population applies even more to economic assets and output. Cities are engines of growth, and firms prefer to locate in urban centers with good access to labor. Each unit of area therefore generates far more output and hosts a larger stock of economic assets. This reflects the concentration and greater economic value of productive assets—as well as public infrastructure and private assets such as homes—in cities. The exposure of economic assets to natural hazards in cities will thus be considerably higher than in rural areas. But greater exposure need not increase vulnerability: much depends on how cities are managed.

City management will determine vulnerability

A core task for cities is to provide, coordinate, and disseminate information so that land, housing, and insurance markets can operate efficiently. Data on hazard probabilities and the vulnerability of structures and people feed into comprehensive risk assessments. These should be made accessible to all. Such information allows residents to make informed location choices and markets to price hazard risk appropriately. It also provides the basis for the emergence of private insurance markets. And it serves as a sound basis for transparent zoning decisions and other land use restrictions. And while hazard mapping has been performed for many decades, new technologies allow constant updating of information at a fairly low cost. Making these technologies accessible to cities—not only the largest, but also smaller and medium-sized cities with limited local capacity—should be a priority.

For large-scale collective hazard risk reduction investments, the costs and benefits depend in large part on the dynamics of the urban economy, particularly on the value of land. In dynamically growing cities, where land is scarce, large investments to make land habitable or reduce significant risk may well be justified. An example is large-scale land reclamation in Hong Kong SAR, China, and Singapore. Limited expansion options in the vicinity of high economic density raise the value of land significantly. This shifts the cost-benefit ratio in favor of large protective investments. A strict test is whether a developer would, in principle, be willing to pay a price for the reclaimed or protected land that reflects the cost of the intervention.

All cities are not equal, and the viability of large-scale disaster reduction infrastructure will be different in cities with stagnant economies and little or no population growth. Today, this is a phenomenon in mature economies with demographic declines or in countries with strong geographic shifts in economic and population centers (Pallagst 2008). Examples are the former socialist countries in Europe but also parts of Scandinavia and the Mediterranean countries, as well as the old industrial core of the U.S. midwest. Over time, given demographic trends in many middle-income countries, "shrinking cities" may also emerge in some of today's emerging economies, such as those in East Asia.

Public investments in the wake of Hurricane Katrina sparked debate over large-scale protective investments to encourage the rebuilding of New Orleans within the pre-Katrina city limits. More than $200 billion of federal money will be used to rebuild the city. Some have argued for providing residents of areas behind massive flood control infrastructure with checks or vouchers, and letting them make their own decisions about how to spend that money—including the decision about where to locate or relocate. The choice is between spending $200 billion on infrastructure for residents or giving each resident a check for more than $200,000—in a place where annual per capita income is less than $20,000 and which reached its peak of economic importance in 1840.[5] There are, of course, political, cultural, and social factors that have to be considered in the decision whether to reconstruct, but this example nonetheless shows the difficult tradeoffs that shrinking cities face.

Reducing urban hazard risk through large-scale infrastructure must consider the dynamics of city demand. In some developing countries, infrastructure investment—long-lived capital stock—is likely to peak in the coming few decades. These tasks are perhaps more daunting than in the past, given cities' emergence in countries where power is increasingly federal. The challenge is at all levels of government—from federal to urban development ministries to small-town mayors. But the payoffs in saved lives and avoided damages will be high.

Climate change: Changing hazards, changing damages

Climate-related hazards ("extreme events") have resulted in an average of $59 billion a year in global damages (EMDAT 2009) from 1990 through 2008, or 0.1 percent of world product in 2008. Tropical cyclones account for 44 percent, and floods 33 percent.

Even without climate change, economic development and population growth are expected to increase the baseline damages from extreme events over the next century (figure 6.1). If there is no conscious change in adaptation policies to extreme events, baseline damages without climate change are expected to triple to $185 billion a year from economic and population growth alone. Floods and tropical cyclones are expected to continue to be the prominent sources. But heat waves are expected to become more prominent.

There is widespread concern that climate change could increase future damages from extreme events (IPCC 2007a, IPCC 2007b, World Bank 2009). Earlier studies projected increased tropical cyclone activity alone might result in additional annual damages in the United States of $100 to $800 million[6] and global annual damages by $630 million (Pearce and others 1996). More recent studies suggest that a doubling of greenhouse gas concentrations could increase tropical cyclone damage by 54 percent to 100 percent in the United States and double tropical cyclone damage globally.[7] Some studies of historic trends of extreme event insurance claims find that extreme events are rising at a rapid and even exponential rate (Swiss Re 2006; Stern 2007). However, these trend line analyses do not separate changes in the exposed population and changes in the extreme events themselves (Pielke and Downton 2000; Pielke and others 2008).

Analysis commissioned for this report uses an integrated assessment model combining science and economics to estimate the additional damage from hazards as a result of climate change.[8] While the analysis attempted to estimate the additional damage from all hazards, the analysis of potential changes in the location, frequency, and intensity of future tropical cyclones

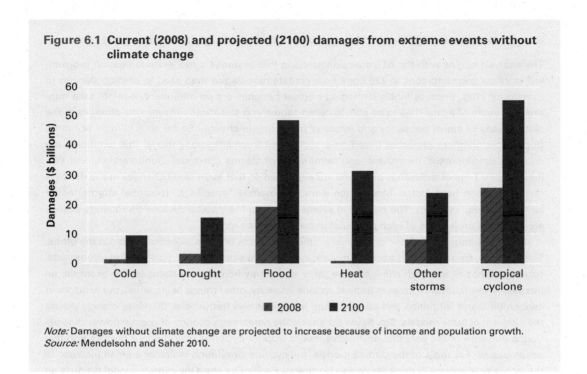

Figure 6.1 Current (2008) and projected (2100) damages from extreme events without climate change

Note: Damages without climate change are projected to increase because of income and population growth.
Source: Mendelsohn and Saher 2010.

is the most complete. Box 6.1 explains the methodology used for tropical cyclones.

A few caveats:

- Aspects of the science remain uncertain. Although all climate models agree the planet will warm, they do not agree on the magnitude of the changes and how they will be distributed across the planet: the results are quite different across the climate models tested (box figure 6.1).

- The analysis does not measure all the impacts of climate change, just those of climate-related hazards.[9]

- The study reports only the direct damages from climate-related hazards. For example, the impacts on ecosystems are not measured. There are other indirect effects of disasters, which are difficult to measure, as discussed in chapter 2.

- The analysis does not address possible interactions with other effects from climate change. For example, although the tropical cyclone analysis does take into account storm surge, it does not consider the interaction between storm surge and sea level rise. Whether the interaction between a rise in sea level and storm surge is "additive" or "super additive" would depend on the assumptions about adaptation to sea level (for example, building sea walls where permissible or locating people out of harm's way). Such interactions are an important area for future work.

Box 6.1 Estimating additional damages from climate change-induced tropical cyclones

The analysis begins with the A1B emission scenario that assumes a moderate mitigation program will stabilize concentrations at 720 ppm. Four climate models are then used to predict changes in climate by 2100. Because highly damaging tropical cyclones are so infrequent, it might take hundreds of years of actual data to be able to detect robust and statistically meaningful changes in the distributions of storm frequency and intensity from climate change. So for each climate scenario, tropical cyclones are predicted based on a specialized tropical cyclone model that simulates the creation, development, movement, and termination of storms (Emanuel, Sundararajan, and Williams 2008). Tens of thousands of storms are simulated so that even small changes in the damage distribution can be detected. Most of the simulated cyclone "seedlings" (potential storms) never become tropical cyclones. The remaining events constitute the tropical cyclone climatology associated with the projections of each particular global circulation model.

Climate change is predicted to have very different impacts on tropical cyclones across the globe. The intensity, frequency, and tracks of tropical cyclones are sensitive to a number of environmental conditions, not all of which change in the same direction when climate changes. For example, an increase in temperature increases tropical cyclone intensity, other things being equal, but wind shear can inhibit storm formation and development. Intensities and frequencies therefore change across the different climate models. Box figure 6.1 shows the percentage change of coastal power dissipation, a measure of the potential destructiveness of tropical cyclones over the four models and five ocean basins. For most of the climate models, the cyclone simulation indicates a small increase in the intensity of storms in the Atlantic and Northwest Pacific Oceans. One climate model predicts an increase in intensity at landfall in the North Indian Ocean and Southern Hemisphere Ocean but most of the models predict a decrease in intensity in these oceans or no effect at all. Note that increases (decreases) in storm intensity imply climate change causes damages (benefits).

Box figure 6.1 Intensity of tropical cyclones will vary over the five ocean basins by 2100

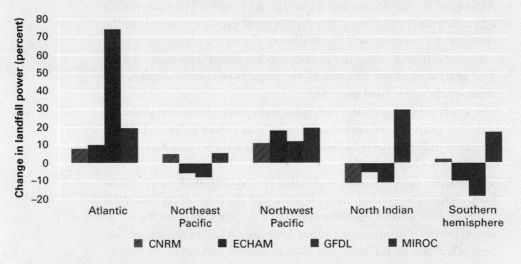

Note: CNRM, ECHAM, GFDL, and MIROC are the climate models used for the projections.
Source: World Bank staff, based on Emanuel, Sundararajan, and Williams 2008.

Box 6.1 Estimating additional damages from climate change-induced tropical cyclones *(continued)*

The damage function is estimated using an international data set of global hazard damages from 1960 to 2008 (EMDAT 2009). Damages per event are regressed on income per capita and population density to determine the sensitivity in different locations. The damage response to the intensity of a tropical cyclone was estimated using US data from the National Oceanic Atmospheric Administration. Future damages (without climate change) are projected using predictions of future income and population. The estimate of climate change damage is the difference between the damage caused by all tropical storms in the future climate minus the damage caused by tropical cyclones in the current climate. Note that the fact that future baselines predict more people and capital will be in harm's way implies that climate change will have larger effects. Empirical results described below reveal that cyclone damages are a highly nonlinear function of storm intensity. A 1.1 percent decline in minimum atmospheric pressure at sea level doubles the damages from tropical cyclones.

- The analysis makes certain assumptions of what the world will look like in 100 years. Economic and population growth may be quite different.
- Relevant policies that would affect adaptation may also change. For example, policies that encourage (discourage) risky development in hazardous areas would increase (decrease) overall damages.
- International reporting of extreme events and damages remains uneven. As data sets improve, it will be possible to improve predictions of international damages.

With these qualifications in mind, the key findings are as follows.

Damages are expected to increase

Without climate change, expected tropical cyclone damages increase from $26 billion today to $55 billion by 2100 because of the growth in income and population.[10] Climate change could add about $54 billion worth of tropical cyclone damages each year, doubling future baseline damage. The estimated increase in damages from climate change varies across climate models between $28 and $68 billion (or 51 to 124 percent of the future baseline). These estimates are sensitive to the elasticity between damages and income. If the income elasticity of damages were unitary (instead of 0.41, as estimated), future baseline damages become $195 billion and climate change adds about $178 billion—almost double the baseline damages.

Averages mask extremes

The estimates of the above damages are in "expected value" terms per year. But the damages are not expected to come in a steady stream. Even with the current climate, 10 percent of tropical cyclones are responsible for 90 percent of the expected damages. Even if climate does not change, damages will vary a great deal from year to year and decade to decade. Climate change is expected to skew the damage distribution of tropical cyclones and is likely to cause rare—but very powerful—tropical cyclones to become more common. With a warmed climate, the 10 percent of tropical cyclones that cause the most damage will be responsible for 93 percent of the expected damages.

Climate change "fattens the tail" of the tropical cyclone damage distribution. For the United States, destructive storms that would come every 38 to 480 years given the current climate, would come every 18 to 89 years with future climate change. Figure 6.2 illustrates this for one specific climate model (MIROC).[11] Most of the cyclones with and without climate change involve damages in the tens of billions of dollars or less. These storms may become even less frequent with climate change. But, very rarely, a very powerful storm will strike a very vulnerable location causing damages up to a trillion dollars. This seemingly small shift in the tail of the distribution is shown as "return years," which show how many years would elapse, on average, between occurrences of a storm causing a specific level of damage (figure 6.2). Even though very rare and damaging storms are part of today's climate, they will become more frequent in a warmer climate. For example, using the future baseline, a $100 billion storm is estimated to happen once in a hundred years in the United States given the current climate. With a future warmed climate, it is expected to happen once in about 56 years.

Figure 6.2 Climate change shortens the return period of large storms

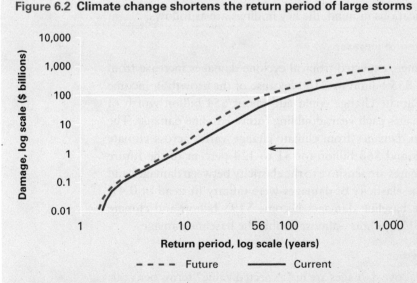

Note: The figure shows the return period for tropical cyclones of different intensity in the United States for one specific climate model (MIROC). A $100 billion storm is estimated to happen once in a 100 years in the United States given the current climate. With a future warmed climate, it is expected to happen once in about 56 years. *Source:* Mendelsohn, Emanuel, and Chonabayashi 2010a.

Damages will vary across locations and within-country variation in damages is likely

The bulk of the tropical cyclone damages from climate change falls on North America ($30 billion) and Asia ($21 billion). Three countries bear 90 percent of global damages: the United States ($30 billion), Japan ($10 billion) and China ($9 billion). However, when damages are scaled by GDP, the Caribbean islands are among the worst hit.

The global tropical cyclone analysis is based on national data sets so that it is not possible to show how effects vary within most countries. However, for the United States, detailed data at state and county levels are available concerning tropical cyclone damages, intensities, and frequencies, allowing spatially detailed analysis to be conducted. Box 6.2 describes these results. At least for the United States, there is a wide range of effects within the country. It is likely that for large countries at least, there will be substantial intracountry variation.

Box 6.2 Within country effects: The case of the United States

The climate change study of tropical cyclones in the United States used information about the counties that each tropical cyclone struck. The spatial scale of the analysis was much finer than the country scale for the global analysis, permitting large intracountry variations in damages to be seen (box figure 6.2). Most of the damages from tropical cyclones in the United States occur in the Gulf states and Florida (87 percent). The damages fall quite rapidly as one moves north along the Atlantic seaboard. At least in large countries, there will be significant intracountry variation in extreme event damages. The estimated damages also vary a great deal across climate models. The GFDL and MIROC models predict much larger damages than does the CNRM model.

Box figure 6.2 Tropical cyclone damages in the United States are concentrated in the Gulf Coast and Florida

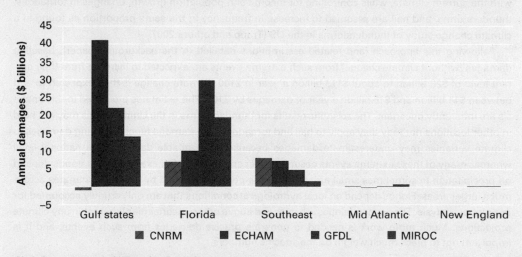

Note: Damages are in billions $/yr for 2100.
Source: Mendelsohn, Emanuel, and Chonabayashi 2010b.

These results provide insight into adaptation to tropical cyclones. The preponderance of damages from tropical cyclones is caused by rare and very powerful storms. To adapt, one may be tempted to build extensive sea walls along the coast as one might against sea level rise. However, very powerful storms are likely to overwhelm such measures making them ineffective. Building higher fortified sea walls in selected places of high value and population density (cities) may be justified but the costs have to be weighed against the damages. Further, in some locations it will be difficult to build sufficiently high sea walls. In this case, retreat may be the only option. In places that cannot be defended, land use rules could be developed to encourage robust land uses, such as open space and agriculture, which can survive occasional storms. Further research into efficient adaptation to such events is a high priority.

The analysis also attempted to estimate additional damages from other (non-tropical cyclone) extreme events (box 6.3). For reasons explained below, estimating such damages is inherently more challenging and uncertain.

Box 6.3 Estimating additional damages from climate change-induced extreme events (other than tropical cyclones)

The analysis for the non-tropical cyclone extreme events (floods, droughts, heat waves, and cold events) follows a similar though not identical approach. It is more uncertain because the link between climate change and these extreme events is more difficult to discern (Mendelsohn and Saher 2010). For the SRES A1 B emission scenario (IPCC 2000), three climate models (CNRM, ECHAM, and GFDL) are used to estimate changes in future temperature and precipitation means and variances. The link between damages from these events and these climate measures is then measured using international data from 1960 through 2008. The climate forecasts are then combined with the coefficients from the damage function to predict future damages in 2100. Damages from climate change were calculated as the difference between damages in 2100 in the warmed climate and damages in 2100 with the current climate, while controlling for income and population growth. Changes in tornadoes, thunderstorms, and hail are assumed to increase in frequency in the same proportion as found in a climate change study of thunderstorms in the US (Trapp and others 2007).

Following this approach (and related assumptions detailed in the background paper), baseline damages (without climate change) from such extreme events are expected to increase from their current level of $28 billion to about $113 billion a year in 2100. Climate change is then expected to add between $11 billion and $16 billion a year of damages by 2100. The estimates presented in this analysis are inherently uncertain. The scientific results for thunderstorms in the United States may not hold in other locations nor may they apply to hail and tornadoes. The damage function linking damages to climate variables may underestimate damages because the available data are at a national level whereas many of these extreme events occur at a finer spatial scale. For example, flash floods depend on precipitation in sometimes small areas, which are poorly measured by variance estimates across much larger areas. Floods depend on local hydrological conditions that are only crudely accounted for in a global analysis. These uncertainties are over and above other uncertainties inherent in any climate projections. Much more work is needed to generate precise damages from such events, and it is important not to place much weight on the specific numbers.

Source: World Bank staff, based on Mendelsohn and Saher 2010.

Consequently, this part of the analysis provides a point of departure for further work on learning about the likely direction and extent of the damages from these events.

Estimating impacts of climate change–induced extreme events is relatively new. Continued research will improve our understanding and ability to estimate the impacts. Better data will also likely help. Disasters are poorly measured even under *current* climatic conditions. Several countries do not even report damages, and the global damage data sets do not report event intensity. Even the very largest extreme events, tropical cyclones, are poorly measured on a global scale. Although the number of storms has been well documented since the advent of satellites, the intensity of these storms is still not measured globally. More accurate and global measurements of both storms and damages will likely lead to better understanding of how climate change leads to damages from hazards. Finally, there is the question of scale. It is likely that sub-national analysis would provide even more accurate estimates.

Climate-related catastrophes: Deep-future disasters with a global footprint

The usual final event of a tragedy is a catastrophe (from the Greek *katastrephein*, to overturn). We define a catastrophe here as an event that is fairly to extremely rare, that severely affects broad swaths of the world, and that is likely to be irreversible over any realistic time frame: examples include a virulent pandemic, a nuclear war, or an asteroid collision. Climate-related catastrophes differ in three ways: they unfold more slowly, providing a potential opportunity to prepare; they result from a cause that the public may not so readily grasp; and numerous actors are responsible. The occurrence of nuclear war, perhaps the greatest threat in the last half of the 20th century, rested on the decision of a few people. So this was analyzed in a game theoretic setting with different degrees of cooperation. The result was deterrence—mutually assured destruction, with the appropriate acronym MAD. In contrast, climate catastrophes result from the conscious self-interested behavior of billions of people in several countries living in different circumstances, so effective international agreements are more difficult.[12]

The scientific community has identified several catastrophes that climate change might trigger. It is also possible that catastrophes could be triggered when several smaller or more localized impacts cascade, though this remains only a theory.

Consider four types of catastrophe:

- *Drastic sea level rise.* Satellite and tide gauge measurements show that sea level rise has accelerated at about 3.4 millimeters per year since satellite measurements began in 1993. The 2007 IPCC report projects a gradual rise of 0.2 to 0.6 meters over the 21st century from thermal expansion of the oceans. But the dislodging and melting of the West

Antarctic or Greenland ice sheets eventually could raise sea levels by 5–7 meters each. The speed of such a massive increase in sea level is a subject of current research. It might take centuries for an impact of this scale to unfold fully, though it is likely that a meter of sea level rise could occur in this century, with a probable upper limit of about two meters (Rahmstorf 2007). In either case, the emissions to trigger large-scale sea level rises could be generated in this century alone. Such rises would flood large inhabited areas and dramatically change human activity. For example, a five-meter rise would require mass migrations of coastal populations and total evacuation of low-lying islands. Although human society could adapt, this change would be extremely difficult and costly.

- *Disruption of ocean currents.* Large-scale melting of polar ice sheets would increase freshwater in the cold North Atlantic Ocean, weakening the flow of warm currents from lower latitudes. This diminution of the Atlantic Thermohaline Circulation (THC) could affect the climate of much of northern Europe.[13]

- *Large-scale disruptions to the global ecosystem.* The impacts of even gradual climate change could suddenly disrupt a variety of ecosystem services. These could include reduced biodiversity, reduced access to water in the current locations of significant populations, acidification of oceans, and rapid changes in land cover on a large scale. The social, economic, and environmental consequences of these losses, not known, could be very large.

- *Accelerated climate change from large releases of trapped methane.* Warming beyond a certain point could release into the atmosphere large quantities of methane in oceans and permafrost. This possibility is an example of a "tipping point," when large and possibly irreversible changes in the climate might result from exceeding a poorly understood threshold. Because methane resides in the atmosphere for only a few decades, the direct effect would be a temporary if powerful acceleration of temperature increase. But such a large and rapid increase in temperature could in itself lead to severe and irreversible consequences. Rapid melting of Arctic sea ice is already happening, and large and rapid warming could set in motion other factors (such as accelerating melting of heat-reflecting snow cover) that cause a further acceleration in climate change.

A second concern is that multiple smaller hardships or disruptions from climate change over a shorter period could combine to create a cumulative effect worse than the sum of the independent hazards. For example, a worsening of droughts and damages to ecosystems in many areas over a short period could lead to economic and social disruption for large numbers of people from the direct effects of the more localized impacts. But it could also lead to forced migration, armed conflict, and widespread failures of institutions.

Gradual or cascading, much is still being discovered and debated. Sea level rise estimates are the most concrete indication of the potential for catastrophic impacts from climate change. But even sea level rise scenarios involve uncertainties about vulnerability and adaptation.[14] The size of losses will depend on the speed of change in sea level rise as well, on the degree of exposure relative to current conditions, and on measures that can be taken to reduce the impacts. The potential magnitudes and likelihoods of other worrisome catastrophe risks, such as abrupt changes in land and ocean ecosystems or the potential for "runaway" acceleration of climate change from methane releases, are difficult to gauge.

A decision framework for catastrophes

The triggers or thresholds that could set off catastrophes are uncertain, as are the probabilities of occurrence and the consequences, though recent scientific assessments indicate that the risks of climate change generally look worse today than some years ago (Smith and others 2009). Expert judgments must be brought to bear in the absence of more concrete information. How then should policymakers weigh the costs and benefits of alternative policy responses?

Standard cost-benefit analyses can be extended to incorporate risks with known or subjectively specified probabilities, but both probabilities and types of potential outcomes are unknown for climate catastrophes. The possibility of catastrophic climate change is characterized by deep structural uncertainties in the science coupled with an economic inability to evaluate meaningfully the welfare losses from high temperatures. (Analyzing the most recent available climate models, Weitzman (2009) concludes that the future holds about a 5 percent chance that temperatures will rise by about 10 degrees Celsius—a world difficult to imagine.) The costs of mitigation also are uncertain, as they depend on the pace of future technological change and the way policies and regulations operate across countries. Nevertheless, some weighing of options by balancing pros and cons is desirable and uncertainty does not justify inaction. But arguing for too rapid and aggressive interventions could lead to measures that are very costly relative to the potential reductions in risk.

While uncertainty cannot justify inaction, it has implications for how decision making is undertaken. Posner (2004) suggests a tolerable-windows approach: a range of plausible estimates are established to ascertain a level of risk-reduction effort where the benefits clearly exceed the costs and a level where costs clearly exceed benefits. Policies then can be adopted that fall within this window.

When costs are incurred well before the benefits, as in taking measures to mitigate the potential for climate change catastrophes, the selection of a discount rate to compare earlier costs with later benefits is a focus of uncertainty and debate. The 2010 WDR notes there is no consensus on the "correct" discount rate for climate change evaluation (and may never be). But decisions about responses to climate change catastrophe risks involve the present generation making altruistic choices on behalf of future generations. The choice of a lower discount rate for valuing reduced long-term climate change hazards involves current generations reducing their well-being for the benefit of future generations. This is also true for other investments that improve the prospective well-being of future generations.

A portfolio of responses

Dealing with catastrophic threats hinges on policies for dealing with "fat tail" risks. Climate change is expected to worsen the distribution of damages from tropical cyclones and this shift will take place in the extreme right hand tail of the damage probability distribution function, fattening the tail. Policies to address tail risks depend in part on society's willingness to devote resources to reduce the probability and likely impact of the risk, relative to benefits from other uses of those resources. Such a comparison is very difficult to quantify, especially when confronted with well-known behavioral biases for catastrophic events and when there are competing catastrophic risks. Without such estimations, prudence in responding to catastrophic threats calls for a portfolio of measures that emphasizes learning and mid-course corrections (noting however the tremendous inertia that exists in the climate system, the built environment, as well as in institutions and behaviors, WDR 2010). A broader portfolio of measures is desirable because of the uncertainties surrounding the costs and potential effectiveness of individual measures. Thus, incorporating several distinct measures makes the resulting set of policy options more robust. The portfolio should include:

- *Rapid emissions reduction* to stabilize greenhouse gas concentrations in the atmosphere at some level low enough to achieve a desired reduction in the perceived risk of catastrophe. Different technological paths could be followed to accomplish this, and it is virtually certain that no single approach would be successful. Rapid scaling up of renewable energy certainly would be part of the response. But given continuing uncertainties about the future cost and physical availability of different types of renewables and our ability to store energy to offset the inherent intermittency of most renewables, this response also would require addressing expanded nuclear power and introducing carbon capture and geological storage on a very large or even global scale.
- *Various large scale adaptation measures* implemented across the world over the medium term, beyond efforts by individuals and single governments, to anticipate and significantly reduce the potential impacts of a climate catastrophe. Priority measures would include extensive changes in land use policies and practices to limit further increases in coastal area vulnerability and to expand and fortify protected areas to safeguard critical ecosystems. The adaptation measures could even include large-scale anticipatory relocations of especially vulnerable populations, such as those vulnerable to anticipated sea level rises and

increases in storm surges. With such relocation would come the need to rebuild infrastructure and other fixed capital.

These two categories of actions may not be enough to satisfactorily lower the chance of catastrophes, particularly if the world cannot come to an agreement about sharing the burden of mitigation efforts. It is therefore also necessary to consider geoengineering as another potential measure to reduce the risk of catastrophe (box 6.4).

Dealing with the threat of catastrophic climate change is an exercise in reducing uncertainty with only a limited ability to assess the results.

Box 6.4 Geoengineering's potential and pitfalls

Some effects of a doubling in CO_2 concentration could in principle be offset by blocking a small percentage of sunlight reaching the Earth's surface. The most commonly discussed option for reducing absorbed solar radiation involves seeding the upper atmosphere with particulate matter to reflect sunlight. Other approaches include increasing the reflectivity of the earth (massive rooftop retro-fits), changing cloud cover, and even building mirrors in space as a planetary "sunshade." Other types of geoengineering include increased absorption of CO_2 by oceans or giant machines to capture CO_2 from the atmosphere. All these measures have known side effects, some of which would induce unknown but possibly large changes in the climate system.

Geoengineering could arrest or potentially avert catastrophes induced by climate change. But adjusting the earth's temperature by reflecting sunlight may adversely affect other climate variables, such as precipitation. One clear pitfall of geoengineering is technological. Launching reflective particles into the upper atmosphere to increase the earth's reflectivity would need to be carefully controlled for two reasons. First, the particles remain in the atmosphere only briefly, so once initiated the method would need to be sustained indefinitely. And if stopped, the effects of manmade global warming would be felt, essentially, all at once. The effect of experiencing accumulated impacts all at once is unknown. Even more fundamental is the current uncertainty about negative side effects, including potential alteration of the hydrologic cycle and ocean acidification. Based on current knowledge, there is no way to know if geoengineering could be carefully controlled to the extent necessary to provide some protection from further warming while effectively limiting any side effects.

A second reason comes from the strong incentives to deploy such technologies unilaterally. The problem of international cooperation in managing geoengineering is the inverse of achieving international coordination for drastic mitigation. With mitigation, the incentives for acting unilaterally are extremely weak because of the strong incentive to free-ride. With geoengineering, given a potential for low direct costs and fairly immediate direct benefits of implementation, incentives to act unilaterally could be very strong—especially in the face of severe threats from climate change.[16] So, it may be impossible for countries to credibly commit to abstaining from geoengineering. Also, how might potentially beneficial uses of geoengineering be distinguished from hostile measures to inflict harm on other countries? Moreover, how would potential conflicts among countries over the implementation of geoengineering be resolved? For example, suppose that country A seeks to locally cool its climate and stimulate rain in an effort to protect its harvest and stave off famine. But what if country A's application of geoengineering had side effects that threatened crops or water supplies in country B? This question is particularly troubling if country B abuts A, and is a historical rival or enemy. For these reasons, it would be preferable to undertake internationally funded and coordinated research on geoengineering precisely so that its potential applicability and risks can be widely understood.

Source: World Bank staff.

Considerations in developing a portfolio of responses include the costs of the various measures, the lead times needed (particularly important when some uncertainties may decline as science and technology improve but inertia remains very large), and the information about their prospective effectiveness. The portfolio can change over time as more is learned about the nature of catastrophe risks and the costs and effectiveness of different responses. Since no climate catastrophe has been experienced in recorded memory, people may underestimate or overestimate this "virgin risk" (Kousky and Zeckhauser 2010).

Examining current and potential costs of alternative measures and considering their effectiveness can help protect against possible biases. The potential for catastrophe certainly makes aggressive action more desirable, but how much more remains uncertain. Postponing sound measures to curtail the growth of greenhouse gas concentrations will reduce the effectiveness of "crash" emissions abatement and massively increase costs.[15] Similarly, postponing stronger land use measures to limit growth of coastal settlements will greatly increase the cost of later adaptation through relocation.

Any portfolio for addressing catastrophe risk will need to be adjusted over time. One robust conclusion from the comparison of response options is that a significant investment in reducing the cost of implementation and increasing the effectiveness of each option should be a high priority. Efforts to improve understanding of the potential of geoengineering and to lower the costs and potential risks of very rapid mitigation options are a high priority. Given the likely high costs of large-scale anticipatory adaptation measures, a more cautious approach would focus first on increasing the prospects for the survival of critical ecosystems and placing some limits on the growth of settlements in more at-risk areas.

Connecting the three Cs: Cities, climate, catastrophes

The future is always uncertain, yet it seems clear that cities will grow and that climate will change, although disparately. Well managed cities can reduce their vulnerability even in a warmer world with stronger storms. Catastrophes are possible, but their likelihood can be reduced with appropriate actions now and preparations for contingency actions later. Climate change poses a troubling risk of increased conflicts: armed struggles have historically been associated with droughts and desertification in Africa, for example. But squabbling over resources leads to conflict when competing claims cannot be peacefully resolved and when institutions to resolve conflicting claims are inadequate. There is thus a large premium on strengthening institutions for resolving tomorrow's resource-related conflicts more peacefully.

These outcomes require much. Urbanization shifts the balance of prevention from individual measures to collective action. Although governments will have a larger role, they must harness the market in better ways, with greater sensitivity to when and how prices get distorted. For collective prevention to be effective, national governments and cities must deliver better services, including prevention. They must design, build, and maintain infrastructure and be more aware of—and responsive to—what individuals can and cannot do: providing detailed seismic maps of fault lines, for example, but allowing developers and people who live in buildings to decide how to construct safe structures. Knowledge and know-how are needed more than funds; without them, the funds would be poorly allocated. Global institutions could also spread word of what can be done and help governments in their tasks.

While there are good reasons for hope, there are also instances of concern. Take Jakarta, where individual prevention measures depend on whether the government, in part, provides adequate water and drainage. If climate change will worsen Jakarta's inundations, should infrastructure and city management be improved today?

Greater Jakarta is a coastal urban area with 24 million people and a catchment area rimmed by volcanoes. Some 13 rivers flow into Jakarta bay, and the city is in the lowest part of the basin. About 40 percent of the city is already below sea level, and floods follow intense rains between November and April (annual rainfall is 15–25 meters a year and up to 4 meters upstream). Major floods hit in 1996, 2002, and then in February 2007, the worst in its history, when heavy rains coincided with a peak in the astronomic tidal cycle that recurs every 18.6 years. Yet, tidal surges and rainfall alone do not explain the floods' severity. A recent study found little difference in total precipitation across five meteorological stations along the Ciliwung River (Jakarta's main river) in 1996, 2002, and 2007 (Texier 2008). How susceptible is an increasingly urbanizing Jakarta to rains and a sea level rise? See figure 6.3.

As in many major cities, public services have not kept pace with population growth. Greater Jakarta's population, doubling from 11.9 million to 23.6 million between 1980 and 2005, is projected to exceed 35 million by 2020. Upstream, numerous secondary residences have been built over the past 50 years. Tea plantations replaced forests on the volcanoes' slopes, reducing the capacity to absorb and store rainwater, increasing peak runoff flows and sedimentation in rivers. Downstream, uncontrolled residential and commercial developments in lakes and reservoirs, which once absorbed the storm water flows into the city, increased flood levels while excessive abstraction of groundwater due to the limited supply of piped water caused rapid land subsidence. In just 15 years, a water absorbing area in Kelapa Gading, a subdistrict in Northeast Jakarta, became a booming commercial and residential area that floods every year (figure 6.4).

Climate change is likely to raise sea levels and increase both the frequency and intensity of storms that will flood Jakarta. People may eventually have to move from Jakarta; so should efforts to improve the city be redirected? A tough question, but framed incorrectly.

Moving should be an individual choice, not an excuse for collective coercion. People now living in Jakarta should not be forced to move, whether by compulsion or by neglecting infrastructure and public services to residents.

Figure 6.3 Greater Jakarta area orographic map with rainfall regime

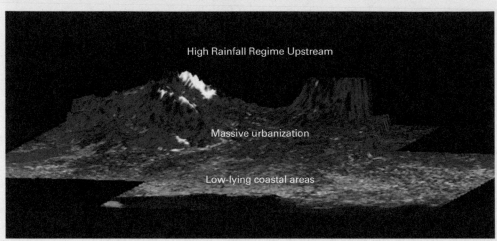

High Rainfall Regime Upstream

Massive urbanization

Low-lying coastal areas

Source: Gunawan 2008.

Investments in Jakarta's infrastructure should continue if they pass the cost-benefit hurdle, and large benefits in the immediate future would weigh heavily in the decision. But it is equally important for investment in and management of other cities to also improve because their growth could accommodate more people and commerce.

Climate change will not adversely affect all cities, and while ports may be important, it is difficult to predict which will thrive. In the 18th century, few thought that New York, which then ranked well behind Boston and Charleston, would become America's largest and richest city, especially since Baltimore and Philadelphia had better ports. Jakarta's prosperity may

Figure 6.4 Fifteen years of urbanization in Jakarta, before and after

1994

2009

Source: Hahm and Fisher 2010.

well continue (it contributes 25 percent of national non-oil GDP). And if it does, it would be in the same situation as Rotterdam today: having to consider expensive measures to protect its people and assets from floods and sea surges. But such choices would be less stark, and ultimately less wasteful, if other Indonesian cities in safer locations grew. Jakarta is not unique; Mexico City, Mumbai, and many others are similar.

Cities, climate, and pending catastrophes are altering the disaster prevention landscape. While hazards will always be with us, disasters show that something has failed. But determining what has failed and deciding on the corrective measures are not always obvious. And debating whether Hurricane Katrina or Cyclone Nargis was a result of climate change detracts attention from policies that continue to misprice risk, subsidize exposure, reduce individuals' incentives to reduce risk, and promote risky behavior in the long run.

People rise out of poverty through better technology, greater market access, and more investment in activities that spill benefits from one set of economic actors to others through greater interdependence, higher productivity, and stronger institutions. Living in cities facing serious risks of inundation is undesirable, but a failure to reduce poverty would be even more undesirable. Fortunately, neither is inherently necessary. People acting individually and through responsive governments can prosper and survive. That, after all, is the basis of sustainable development.

MEMORANDUM TO A CONCERNED CITIZEN

Subject: **Natural Hazards, UnNatural Disasters:**
The Economics of Effective Prevention

We hope you found the report helpful. We cannot presume to tell you anything specific: you know what is best for you and your family. We sought to bring to your attention the experiences of others that are embedded in the statistics and studies.

You may also be interested in hearing directly from two of our colleagues who recently survived harrowing disasters. These are deeply personal narratives, difficult for them to write. We kept them in the first person. A short section following their experience pulls together some common threads.

Reflections as a Gujarat earthquake survivor and humanitarian worker

January 26, 2001. I was a university student and a part-time employee with the state government's remote sensing and communication center in Ahmedabad (Gujarat, India) when the earthquake struck in 2001. It was a little past 8:30 in the morning, and I was still asleep in the flat that I shared with three friends. I remember their shouting through the door to wake me up and the swaying as we took the stairs down four floors. Some things from that day are hazy, but other details are etched permanently in my memory.

It was the Republic Day holiday. The ground was still shaking when we emerged from the flat and I could see the tall telecom tower swaying. I tried to remember what I knew about earthquakes, and it was precious little. Immediately after realizing that I had survived a deadly disaster, and assuming that the earthquake had struck just Ahmedabad, I realized that my parents, who lived in the city of Bhuj some 400 kilometers away, would be worried when they got news of the earthquake, especially because I was not reachable through the mostly disabled phone system.

Meanwhile, the damage in Ahmedabad was becoming apparent: people went about on scooters and motorcycles to make sure that their relatives and friends were safe. As we were unsure of the safety of our multistory building, a close friend visited to check up on me. He took me and my roommates to his uncle's ground floor home, which was rapidly becoming an emergency shelter for others in the neighboring high-rise buildings.

News of the size and scope of the earthquake slowly began trickling in through transistor radios. I learned later in the evening that Delhi and Mumbai had felt the quake too, and only then did I realize that its "epicenter" (we were all learning these terms) was in Bhuj, where my parents were. The tremor we had experienced was of much lower intensity. My concern immediately switched from telling my parents that I was safe to worrying if they had survived, so I decided to leave for Bhuj.

Day 2. I hopped on a private bus for Bhuj early the next day. Drivers slowed to ask others (some in cars, others on foot and carts) about the condition of roads and the towns they came from, and the news was disturbing. People spoke of "all being destroyed," and this was how news spread. I witnessed the destruction first hand, and I had a strange feeling when I saw the many government buildings destroyed, including police quarters. This was strange because I always thought of the *sarkar* (government) as invincible, so it was unnerving to see it as equally vulnerable and incapacitated as the rest of us. In contrast, I was overwhelmed by trucks that stopped to give people bottled water and packets of food, and realized that volunteers were already organizing relief. Someone threw me a bottle of water, and I was about to hand it back when I realized that I should just accept it.

The normal 6 to 8 hour journey took 12 hours. Even though I was used to seeing Bhuj without electricity, it was pitch dark like never before. When I reached my home, to my utmost relief, I found my parents and neighbors assembling a makeshift tarpaulin shelter on the street. They told me what happened: my father was praying indoors and my mother was in the kitchen when they felt the shaking. Instinctively, they ran outdoors from the back door to the garden where they held on to a papaya tree until the violent shaking subsided.

My father had the house built well under his supervision just before I was born, and it withstood the quake but a cantilevered overhang came crashing down. Had they escaped from the front door, the overhang would have hurt them. The quake cracked the walls and had destroyed all electronics and crockery. I also found out then that because power and phone lines were down, my father had the presence of mind to go to the intercity bus terminal and give slips of paper with my name and phone number and that of other relatives to strangers fleeing the city, asking them to call and convey his well-being. Several of these messages got through in coming days to our relatives in various cities.

Day 3. Exhausted physically and emotionally, about 30 of us slept outside that night. Despite the chilly winter night, nobody was willing to enter their homes. Early next morning, we were awakened by an aftershock, only to see an electric pole hanging by the wires just above our tarpaulin. I suppose we were doubly lucky: to have survived the initial quake and then to have survived possible injuries from this aftershock. We realized that such aftershocks would continue for several days, so we decided to lock up our Bhuj home and move to our ancestral home in Rajkot (some 240 kilometers away). It seemed unaffected by the quake, and we monitored the media and got news from friends about the scale of the devastation.

Two weeks later. Grateful for having survived, we were ever more eager to help those affected. We knew that the city of Anjar, around 50 kilometers from Bhuj, was one of the worst affected areas, and our family friend and former neighbor Mr. Kathiwala had relocated there a few months before to help his son set up a business. After several inquiries, we found him, fully bandaged from the waist down at a private hospital in Rajkot. His wife and son survived with minor injuries from their collapsed home, but his 14-year-old daughter never made it out of the bedroom. Mr. Kathiwala was buried under the overhead tank for hours before neighbors rescued him.

Even in the midst of such misfortune and the risk of losing a leg, Mr. Kathiwala recounted how grateful he was to the Daudi Vohra community—a closely knit group of prosperous traders that he belonged to.

When Daudi Vohra members in other towns heard of the dire situation in Anjar, they hired trucks to bring first aid. They transported the injured to hospitals and the more severely hurt to larger cities with better care. In addition to providing for medical treatment, accommodation, meals, and basic household necessities, the Daudi Vohra raised funds to pay for the best available medical care. They also gave families Rs. 5,000 in cash for incidental expenses. This humane support greatly alleviated the trauma of the earthquake.

Three weeks later. Life had to go on, and I eventually returned to Ahmedabad for the scheduled examinations—only to find a notice that they were postponed by three months because of the damaged university building. I stayed with a friend because our fourth floor flat was not considered safe. I came to know one day that the UN disaster management team was seeking volunteers to work in areas ravaged by the disaster, and I joined them exactly three weeks after the earthquake.

Helping with post-disaster assistance enabled me to see things from a different perspective. Statistics cannot fully capture what happened. The poorest suffered most and took longest to recover. In many towns there was little damage in wealthy areas with well-built bungalow-style houses, but the poorly built structures of those less well off mostly collapsed. It was amazing how quickly the government restored life-line services in the worst affected districts. It embarked on a huge reconstruction program, and an efficient model for community-based recovery and reconstruction evolved.

Not all that I saw and heard was this inspiring. The old walled city of Bhuj was largely destroyed, and I heard tales that in *soni bazaar*, where goldsmiths ply their trade, the survived shop owners offered passers-by money to recover the gold ornaments and strong boxes from inside the teetering buildings. I also heard that the foreign food packets were not serving their purpose because the largely vegetarian population was averse to consuming food in wrappers with an undecipherable foreign language. While many volunteers were tirelessly helping with relief and recovery, a few seemed interested only in taking photographs and being "disaster tourists."

Eight years later. Now, after eight years of working in post-disaster and post-conflict situations, not just in India but later in Afghanistan and Sudan, I am struck by several things. Communities respond first in the midst of chaos because people care for others: but with limited resources at their hand, everyone helps their communities and friends first—and only then any others. The Gujarat earthquake was pivotal in the paradigm shift from emergency response to risk reduction and preparedness. Many who believed that natural disasters like earthquakes cannot be prevented are now actively helping reducing the disaster risks in their own lives and around them.

The longest 45 minutes in Aceh

December 26, 2004. It was Sunday morning around 8 a.m. My parents were about to leave for the Hajj that week, expecting friends and relatives to say goodbye. My father was in the shower, and my sister and a cousin were in the kitchen washing dishes. Then, the earthquake struck—big and long. Maybe it was one of God's ways to remind us of our insignificance in the larger scheme of things. We ran outside.

Outside. The shaking finally stopped. But having experienced earthquakes before, we knew there would be aftershocks and waited outside. Then, five minutes later, as expected, another earthquake, this time smaller but longer. More crying. I silently recited my prayers, trusted that God would take care of this, *tawakkal*—that's what we say in Islam. It relaxes us slightly. With the third quake, people started to cry and scream even more.

Then all of a sudden, we saw our neighbors running toward us, screaming "RUN...RUN...TO THE MOSQUE." Without knowing why, we all started to run. Some people tried to lock their houses before running. None knew what was in store. We then heard a horrible, helicopter-like sound, but much louder. While running I looked behind and there it was. Dark brown, high, a monster wave 3–4 meters high! And it was approaching fast.

We made it to the mosque, which was not far from our house. The men quickly asked all the women and children to go upstairs (the mosque had two floors). The mosque was big and had many pillars with no walls so the water could just flow in easily. My dad insisted that he would stay downstairs, and the rest of the family insisted equally that we would not go upstairs. It was a very difficult moment. The water, there already, had risen to my waist.

We had to make a quick decision. Then, we compromised. Since she was physically stronger than both me and my mom, my sister stayed downstairs with my dad while my mom and I went up. We hugged and kissed and cried. The water was now up to my chest and the earth was still shaking. The mosque could have collapsed but we really had no option.

Upstairs. I saw many of my neighbors, crying and praying. Though my heart was full of pain, I did not cry at all. One tearful neighbor told me she didn't know where her son and husband were. They had left early in the morning to go to the beach: it is part of Acehnese tradition to go to the beach on Sunday morning. I felt relieved in my heart, and thanked God quickly because my family was supposed to be on the beach as well. But my little brother, who was studying in Jakarta and supposed to fly back to Aceh that weekend, canceled his plans. So, we decided to cancel our beach picnic that Sunday.

Waiting. I desperately wanted to go downstairs to see how my father and sister were. But my mom stopped me. All we could do was to wait. Then suddenly, a few men appeared upstairs carrying bodies in their hands—my neighbors. More and more bodies were brought up. The upstairs was full of dead bodies. I could not stop thinking that the next one might be my dad or my sister. I just hugged my mom tight. She kept her composure, comforted us, and reminded us to recite God's name.

Downstairs. Someone finally yelled that the water had subsided. We slowly stepped down the stairs. The scene was unimaginable. Water everywhere. Bodies covered with mud. I was expecting the worst. Then I saw my dad and sister, clinging to one of the mosque's pillars, alive.

Finally the tears came. Never before had I cried so much. But the men in my neighborhood were amazing. They worked hand in hand right away to evacuate all the bodies. In less than an hour the mosque up and down was covered with the dead bodies.

I came across a neighbor, a 17-year-old girl, I knew well. We found her with no clothes, entangled in the mud and electricity wires from outside the mosque. She had swallowed dirt water and could not breathe properly. Both her legs were broken. Her head was on my lap, and she kept asking whether we had seen her family. Sadly, her entire family had perished. But we lied to her to motivate her to keep on breathing and it worked. Our plan was to take to her to a nearby hospital. Some men found a volunteer with a car who had come to help. I left for the hospital without having a chance to inform my parents.

Outside. Nearby hospitals—full of mud and water—were not functioning. We finally found a small community health clinic but there was no doctor, only one nurse with no medical supplies left. It was frustrating to think we had come all the way for nothing. We gave my neighbor some water and cookies, while a friend left to find some other help. Knowing this was the best I could do for her, I wanted to go back to the mosque to inform my parents that I was safe. It was 4 p.m. already. But there was no transportation so I decided to walk. It must have been 100 degrees that day, and I had no slippers on. Thank God I found a guy passing by on a motorcycle. He dropped me off at a family friend's place. They got me a pair of slippers, and I resumed walking.

Some other neighbors passing by in a truck picked me up but told me my parents were no longer in the mosque. They had searched for me and eventually went to a relative's place. I somehow reached there around *Maghrib* (sunset) time. My parents were upset but relieved. I told them the story and they understood.

The night. No electricity that night. None of us could sleep; with at least 100 quakes. We kept running outside almost every 5 minutes—so depressing. I kept on hearing sounds. Helicopters or water? Not clear. I felt deeply guilty for leaving my friend in the clinic and prayed that she survived. Later that week I found out that she didn't make it. Better, perhaps, since everybody in her family had also died.

The assistance. We had to ration our food supplies. Fuel was scarce. My mom—so strong throughout—broke down when she found out that her only sister had passed away. She just sat in the corner, praying every day. She had only one dress to wear—the one that she had run in. My sister and I could at least borrow some of the girls' clothes. Underwear was a big issue for all of us. I don't need to explain it further.

We heard rumors that assistance had arrived but was piled up in the airports. Roads remained blocked, so only helicopters could get to people. All we could do was to be patient and tighten our belts.

A few days later, my brother and uncle came with a car full of food. They had flown to Medan—the closest city to Banda Aceh—and driven home. It took them 14 hours. They also brought some clothes, clean underwear, and cash.

Later, we received more cash and other types of humanitarian assistance from many friends from foreign countries. Each day, random people came to the house and brought us assistance. We will never forget that. Indonesian volunteers, national and foreign soldiers, local and international NGOs, religious groups, name it. I would say the Red Cross, volunteers, and soldiers were crucial in removing debris to restore road links.

Things were a lot better after the second week. Among the assistance we received, the only things I disliked were the fortified biscuits from WFP. We stayed in the house for about a month. It had two small bedrooms but somehow we managed, along with many others who came as well for shelter. We wanted to rent another place to lessen the burden but couldn't find anything affordable. It's amazing how rental prices had soared so high. People would rent their homes only to UN and NGO offices. A medium-size house was around 100 dollars a day.

Home? Back home to check the damage, we found out we had lost several walls. Two dead bodies were floating in the kitchen—one of a 5-year-old girl and the other of a man. The house looked scary and dark—full of trees, garbage, and water. I looked at my dad with all his gray hair with water up his waist trying to salvage our belongings. My father is a civil servant about to retire in two years, and my mom is a teacher. We were not poor, but we were not rich either. That was our only home, and my parents had put their life savings into it. Everything they had worked for seemed gone in 45 minutes. It was hard for me to see the future that day. There was no way for him to collect enough money to rebuild. But these are only material things, he told me. I was wrong, he was right.

Some reflections. I was reborn again, even though I do not believe in reincarnation. I see the world differently now. Life is short and unpredictable. My dad says: "You pray hard, you work hard, you rest hard, and you socialize hard—otherwise you will never be happy." I trust him! One could never tell exactly when God wants to take us. In some ways, I consider myself very lucky to have gone through this.

I was deeply touched by all the care that came from all over the world. I just knew that everybody from Banda Aceh or outside was trying their best. I am forever grateful for that, even though I have a different opinion about the reconstruction phase in Banda Aceh.

Indonesia, including Aceh, is highly prone to almost all types of natural hazards: tsunamis, earthquakes, floods, droughts, volcanic eruptions, you name it. The tsunami should be a wake-up call for authorities and communities to reduce these very real risks. I wish I had known more about tsunamis. Perhaps my aunt would be alive now if we had an early warning. The importance of building disaster-resilient infrastructure should also be conveyed to contractors and construction workers. After all, they are the ones who implement policy. Sometimes, the problem is not always the building codes or the institutional framework, but the ignorance of workers who feel that it is acceptable to reduce the amount of cement or concrete or steel to cut down the price. We need to remember that local engagements tend to work better than paper regulations. We need to ensure that policies, regulations, and knowledge arrive where people live.

Common threads

No two disasters unfold the same way, and no two people are exactly alike. But the two narratives reveal common threads. Family, friends, and neighbors are the first to help. Aid, though useful, comes much later. Knowing the hazards and being prepared (knowing what to expect and do) are really up to you.

You can also ask more of your government: not more spending, but more effective prevention measures and more information about hazards, such as maps of fault lines and flood plains. Making it readily accessible would help. And when disasters expose weaknesses, make sure your representatives look into the underlying causes and tell you what is being done to prevent it from happening again.

Notes and References

Chapter 1

Notes

1. See Gall, Borden, and Cutter (2009) for a detailed discussion of the accuracy of hazard databases.

2. The Cuzick test, a variant of the Wilcox or non-parametric test, measures how the change over the years (rank) compares with the variance of the pooled sample. It requires no assumption about the distribution of the data.

3. A drought that affects three countries counts as three events, so an area split into several countries can have more events.

4. Fewer than half of EM-DAT's events (3,577 of 7,788) report damage in U.S. dollars (presumably converted from local currency using the appropriate exchange rate when the event occurred), and these are converted to 2008 dollars using the U.S. GDP deflator and plotted.

5. That property damage is higher in richer countries such as in Europe and North America is well established (UNDP 2004, World Bank 2005, UNISDR 2009).

6. It is important not to scale damage by the country's GDP solely in the year of the event's occurrence. Doing so would be analogous to calculating a rate of return only when one wins at roulette (rather than over the entire visit to the casino). Therefore, whether there is more damage in some countries than in others is better seen by examining damages relative to GDP for each country over a sufficiently long period (the 39 years from 1970 to 2008 may be long enough), and scaling the total by the GDP cumulated over the same span (also adjusted for inflation). At

a global level, inflation-adjusted cumulative damage from 1970 to 2008 is $2.3 trillion or about 0.23 percent of the cumulated world output. Regional averages are weighted by country GDP shares.

References

Altez, R. 2007. "Muertes Bajo Sospecha: Investigacion Sobre el Numero de Fallecidos en el Desastre del Estado de Vargas, Venezuela, en 1999." *Cuadernos de Medicina Forense* 13 (50).

Development Initiatives. 2007. *Global Humanitarian Assistance Report 2007–08*. Wells, U.K.

Eisensee, T., and D. Strömberg. 2007. "New Droughts, New Floods and U.S. Disaster Relief." *Quarterly Journal of Economics* 122 (2): 693–728.

EM-DAT/CRED. Brussels, Belgium: WHO Centre for Research on the Epidemiology of Disasters, University of Louvain School of Medicine. http://www.emdat.be/.

Gall, M., K. Borden, and S. Cutter. 2009. "When Do Losses Count? Six Fallacies of Natural Hazard Loss Data." *Bulletin of the American Meteorological Society* 90 (6): 799–809.

Guha-Sapir, D., and R. Below. 2002. "The Quality and Accuracy of Disaster Data: A Comparative Analysis of Three Global Datasets." Brussels, Belgium: WHO Centre for Research on the Epidemiology of Disasters, University of Louvain School of Medicine.

ReliefWeb Glossary of humanitarian terms. http://www.reliefweb.int/rw/lib.nsf/db900sid/AMMF-7HGBXR/$file/reliefweb_aug2008.pdf?openelement.

UNDP. 2004. *Reducing Disaster Risk: A Challenge for Development*. New York.

UNISDR. 2009. *UNISDR Global Assessment Report 2009*. Geneva.

World Bank. 2005. *Natural Disaster Hotspots: A Global Risk Analysis*. Washington, DC.

World Health Organization. 2009. "The Top 10 Causes of Death." http://www.who.int/media centre/factsheets/fs310/en/.

Spotlight 1

References

Benson, C., and E. J. Clay. 2004. *Understanding the Economic and Financial Impacts of Natural Disasters*. Disaster Risk Management Studies 4. Washington, DC: World Bank.

Government of Bangladesh. 2008. *Cyclone Sidr in Bangladesh: Damage, Loss & Needs Assessment for Disaster Relief and Reconstruction*.

Independent Evaluation Group. 2007. "Development Actions and the Rising Incidence of Disasters." Evaluation Brief 4, World Bank, Washington, DC.

Rogers, P., P. Lydon, and D. Seckler. 1989. "Eastern Waters Study: Strategies to Manage Flood and Drought in the Ganges-Brahmaputra Basin." U.S. Agency for International Development, Office of Technical Resources, Washington, DC.

Rogers, P., P. Lydon, D. Seckler, and G. T. K. Pitman. 1994. "Water and Development in Bangladesh: A Retrospective on the Flood Action Plan." U.S. Agency for International Development, Bureau for Asia and the Near East, Washington, DC.

Salman, M. A. S., and K. Uprety. 2002. *Conflict and Cooperation on South Asia's International Rivers: A Legal Perspective.* Washington, DC: World Bank.

Stolton, S., N. Dudley, and J. Randall. 2008. *Natural Security: Protected Areas and Hazard Mitigation.* Washington, DC: World Wildlife Fund. http://assets.panda.org/downloads/natural_security_final.pdf.

World Bank. 2005. "Project Performance Appraisal Report of the Bangladesh Coastal Embankment Rehabilitation Project." Report 31565, Washington, DC.

Chapter 2

Notes

1. Peter Bauer, the late development economist, provided a vivid example of the distinction between welfare and output: "National income per head . . . takes no account of the satisfaction people derive from having children or from living longer . . . ironically, the birth of a child is registered as a reduction in national income per head, while the birth of a farm animal shows up as an improvement" (Bauer 1990).

2. Consumption is output less savings (or investment). If the purpose is to estimate changes in consumption—a more difficult task—combining changes in output and physical damages (as a proxy of investment) may be useful, so long as what is estimated (consumption, not output) is explicitly stated.

3. Many are summarized in the 2009 *United Nations Global Assessment Report on Disaster Risk Reduction: Risk and Poverty in a Changing Climate.* Blanco Armas, Fengler, and Ihsan (2008); del Ninno and others (2001); Gaiha and Imai (2003); Baez and Santos (2008); Morris and others (2002); Premand and Vakis (2009); Rodríguez-Oreggia, de la Fuente, and de la Torre (2008); de la Fuente and Dercon (2008).

4. The maximum disaster risk-driven effect in the dataset implies a roughly 20 percentage point decrease in secondary school enrollment. The contribution of this work is that it does not rely on a single theory for the explanation of the link between disasters and human capital. Results are not specific to the choice of a particular model, and take into account not only uncertainty of the estimates for a given model but also uncertainty in the choice of a specification. The results give strong evidence of negative long-run effects of geological disaster risk on secondary school enrollment rates.

5. Baez and Santos (2007) examined longitudinal data in Nicaragua before and after 1998 Hurricane Mitch

6. These tests are Raven Matrices and "WISC" for children. Raven measures IQ, but does not measure verbal and numeric intelligence whereas WAIS measures verbal intelligence as well.

7. Height captures several desirable qualities, not just nutrition. Deaton and Arora (2009) find tall people happier and wealthier.

8. Excess mortality was used to measure the degree of famine exposure per region, defined as the deaths exceeding those that would have occurred under normal conditions.

9. One exception to this finding is the influence of PTSR on subsequent depression indexed scores which, presumably, has at least a partially co-determined relationship with PTSR.

10. A conflict is recorded in a particular year for a particular country when there are at least 1,000 deaths and the conflict is national (a civil war) and not international.

11. Meier and others (2007, p. 718) report that the Food and Agriculture Organization (FAO) estimates that pastoral systems use a quarter of the world's land area and provide 10 percent of global meat production.

12. Brancati's data had civil wars in 661 country-years between 1975–99 while peace prevailed in 2,970 country-years. She considered only areas with at least 50 people per square kilometer.

13. The difference is one standard deviation of civil war duration and is statistically significant.

14. Victims also used their own financial resources to rebuild, making reconstruction an imperfect measure of aid intensity. However, Galle District, in the south, is richer than Hambantota District but rebuilt far fewer homes. More generally, the magnitude of the differences in reconstruction far exceeds differences in income per capita across regions of the country. Figures on aid flows reveal similar biases.

15. Disasters reduce a country's endowments, and Collier and Goderis (2007) show that the "natural resource curse" reducing long-run growth is conditional on governance.

16. A potential issue is that rainfall shocks could operate on conflict *through* the rule of law: by precipitating conflicts over resources, rainfall shocks could both undermine the rule of law and trigger civil war. If this were the case, the rule of law effects on civil war should be much larger when estimated without the rainfall variables. In fact, the opposite is true: when omitting the rainfall variables, the rules of law coefficients are practically identical.

17. Large disasters are those whose damage exceeds 1 percent of GDP. The author uses an autoregressive (ARIMA) technique to project what output would have been without a disaster (not a full-fledged model of the economy with massive data needs).

18. The first is a multivariate stepwise regression that finds damage as a percentage of the capital stock to be a good predictor of subsequent GDP declines. (Remittances moderate this decline.) The second is a general linear regression model finding the same effects and that aid and remittances help moderate the decline, though not as much as with the first technique.

19. Variables that the growth literature recognizes to be relevant are adjusted for; but not for every possible factor because this would reduce degrees of freedom. Remittances, relief, and reconstruction aid spending have not been included because these data are not available for all countries over the study period.

20. Loayza and others (2009).

21. The panel is unbalanced, with some countries having more observations than others. A Generalized Method of Moments (GMM) was used to address endogeneity and control for unobserved country specific factors in the estimations.

22. See http://www.nve.no/no/Vann-og-vassdrag/Hydrologi/Bre/Jokulhlaup-GLOF/Messingmalmvatnet-Blamannsisen/ for more information.

23. The Post Disaster Needs Assessment of Haiti estimated damage at 7.75 percent of GDP (or $476.53 million) and losses at or 6.85 percent ($420.86 million). These two numbers were added and widely reported: *The Economist*'s February 12, 2009 issue ("The storms have cost the country $900 million, or 14.6 percent of GDP, according to a donor-funded government study.") and in the World Bank's remarks to the aid consortium on April 14, 2009.

24. In contrast to apartments and buildings, stocks (equity shares in firms) are almost continuously traded in markets, often on organized stock

exchanges that record every transaction. When a hurricane damages a manufacturing facility—as happened after Hurricane Katrina—the price of the affected company's shares would fall, reflecting analysts' estimate of the damage. Markets may not be perfect, and the errors of financial analysts are all too apparent now. But damage estimators are not infallible either. The point is not whether the estimate is accurate but that damage is the present value of the future flow losses for physical assets.

25. If infrastructure is a bottleneck, its economic rate of return would exceed the discount rate. So, the present value of the flow of services would exceed the cost of replacing the infrastructure. Divergence between the present value of the flows and the value of the asset could conceivably occur with privately owned assets; but as note 29 on "Tobin's q" explains, the difference would be small. Even if the two were not exactly equal, however, measuring both is "not exactly double" (may be more, may be less) counting.

26. Conversely, if disasters decrease production capacity, in situations where output is not constrained by capacity, there may be no effect on output.

27. World Bank (2006).

28. Tourism's value added (included in GDP) is lower than revenues because the value of inputs must be subtracted; and because many of these inputs are also imported, the effects on the trade and current account are more modest than the fall in tourism receipts would suggest. More generally, the indirect effects outside the affected area depend on, among other things, the responsiveness of outputs and input supplies to increased demand. Industrial output may not increase if factories are already operating at capacity and cannot be expanded quickly. In many sectors, however, labor supplies can be increased promptly to take advantage of high demand. Other forms of capital can respond as well. In tourism, spare rooms can be rented and fishing vessels used more intensively for recreational purposes. Or construction materials and labor can be shifted to the affected area by postponing some lower value construction projects elsewhere.

29. Tobin's "q" is the ratio of an asset's market value to replacement value. A ratio greater than one gives the firm an incentive to reinvest its earnings. Firms with a ratio below one should distribute any surplus to their shareholders. If the destroyed building has a "$q < 1$," it should not be rebuilt; and if it has a "$q > 1$" market value is the appropriate concept for damage estimates. For q values in the 0.95 to 1.05 range, the differences fall well within measurement errors. It could be outside this range for a disaster that wipes out much of an economy's assets when, as with public infrastructure, each of these valuation concepts may differ more

(and from the present value of flows)—although all prices including the discount rate would change in general equilibrium (Tobin 1969).

30. The farmer's well-being has declined regardless of how quickly he rebuilds. Or more technically, it is the *disaster* that reduces his opportunity cost of time. And reconstruction costs could be higher because of price and wage inflation (as happened temporarily in Aceh after the December 2004 tsunami).

31. Several damage and loss assessments are available on the World Bank website: http://gfdrr.org/index.cfm?Page=home&ItemID=200. Some of those who have undertaken such assessments point out the enormous difficulties in even knowing how many houses were destroyed: property records are inadequate because sales occur infrequently, and even the census often dates back several years and there may have been substantial population increase and migration. These inaccuracies may widen the range of the estimate (or confidence interval), but do not introduce a systematic bias.

32. Disaster impacts are measured as the number of people affected or people affected per capita, and the analysis was carried out for 196 countries in panel data for 1995, 2000, and 2005 using fixed and random effects panel data estimation methods.

33. Mechler uses the same data as Hochrainer, but because not all countries report the needed variables in his analyses, the sample shrinks from 225 to 99.

34. A series of background papers did estimate sectoral declines in output of disasters: Okuyama (2009); Okuyama and Sahin (2009); and Sahin (2009). The interested reader may refer to them but it is worth noting that the estimation techniques are highly elaborate and have vast data requirements.

35. De Mel and others (2008) use three data sets created from surveys of enterprise owners and wage workers.

36. Public infrastructure is not always clearly defined. In some countries, non-government organizations build and operate schools on land that the government provides. Donors may repair the damage to such facilities, not the government.

37. See http://www.eqclearinghouse.org/20100112-haiti/wp-content/uploads/2010/02/ImageCat-Haiti-EQ-Project-Sheet-EERI-20100209.pdf for more details.

References

Albala-Bertrand, J. M. 1993. *The Political Economy of Large Natural Disasters*. Oxford, U.K.: Clarendon Press.

Alderman, H., J. Hodditnott, and B. Kinsey. 2006. "Long-Term Conse-quences of Early Childhood Malnutrition." *Oxford Economic Papers* 58 (3): 450–74.

Alderman H., H. Hoogeveen, and M. Rossi. 2009. "Preschool Nutrition and Subsequent Schooling Attainment: Longitudinal Evidence from Tan-zania." *Economic Development and Cultural Change* 57(2):239–60.

All Africa Global Media. 2009. "Satellite Insurance to Pay Farmers If Land Turns Brown," December 3.

Baez, J., and I. Santos. 2007. "Children's Vulnerability to Weather Shocks: A Natural Disaster as a Natural Experiment." Draft working paper.

———. 2008. "On Shaky Ground: The Effects of Earthquakes on House-hold Income and Poverty." RPP LAC–MDGs and Poverty-02-2009, RBLAC-UNDP, New York.

Bassett, T. 1988. "The Political Ecology of Peasant-Herder Conflicts in Northern Ivory Coast." *Annals of the Association of American Geogra-phers* 78 (3): 453–72.

Bauer, P. 1990. *Population Growth: Curse or Blessing?* Sydney: Center for Independent Studies.

Beegle, K., R. Dehejia, and R. Gatti. 2006. "Child Labor, Crop Shocks, and Credit Constraints." *Journal of Development Economics* 81 (Septem-ber): 80–96.

Benson, C. 1997a. "The Economic Impact of Natural Disasters in Fiji." Working Paper 97, Overseas Development Institute, London.

———. 1997b. "The Economic Impact of Natural Disasters in Viet Nam." Working Paper 98, Overseas Development Institute, London.

———. 1997c. "The Economic Impact of Natural Disasters in the Philip-pines." Working Paper 99, Overseas Development Institute, London.

Benson, C., and E. Clay. 1998. "The Impact of Drought on Sub-Saharan African Economies." Technical Paper 401, World Bank, International Bank for Research and Development, Washington, DC.

———. 2000. "Developing Countries and the Economic Impacts of Catas-trophes." In *Managing Disaster Risk in Emerging Economies,* ed. A. Kreimer and M. Arnold. Washington, DC: World Bank.

———. 2001. "Dominica: Natural Disasters and Economic Development in a Small Island State." Disaster Risk Management Working Paper Series 2. World Bank, Washington, DC.

———. 2004. "Understanding the Economic and Financial Impacts of Nat-ural Disasters." Disaster Risk Management Series 4. World Bank, Wash-ington, DC.

Blanco Armas, E., W. Fengler, and A. Ihsan. 2008. "The Impact of the Tsunami and the Reconstruction Effort on Aceh's Economy." World Bank, East Asia Poverty Reduction and Economic Management, Wash-ington, DC.

Brahmbhatt, M., and A. Dutta. 2008. "On the SARS Type Economic Effects during Infectious Disease Outbreaks." Policy Research Working Paper 4466. World Bank, Washington, DC.

Brancati, D. 2007. "Political Aftershocks: The Impact of Earthquakes on Intrastate Conflict." *Journal of Conflict Resolution* 51 (5): 715–43.

Burr, J. M., and R. O. Collins. 1995. *Requiem for the Sudan: War, Drought, and Disaster Relief on the Nile.* Oxford, U.K.: Westview Press.

Caselli, F., and P. Malhotra. 2004. "Natural Disasters and Growth: From Thought Experiment to Natural Experiment." International Monetary Fund, Washington, DC.

Chen, Y., and L. A. Zhou. 2007. "The Long-Term Health and Economic Consequences of the 1959–1961 Famine in China." *Journal of Health Economics* 26 (4): 659–81.

Ciccone, A. 2008. "Transitory Economic Shocks and Civil Conflict." University of Pompeu Fabra, Department of Economics, Barcelona.

Collier, P., and B. Goderis. 2007. "Commodity Prices, Growth, and the Natural Resource Curse: Reconciling a Conundrum." Working Paper 07-15, Oxford, U.K.: Oxford University, Center for the Study of African Economies.

Cuaresma, J., J. Hlouskova, and M. Obersteiner. 2008. "Natural Disasters as Creative Destruction: Evidence from Developing Countries." *Economic Inquiry* 46 (2): 214–26

Cuaresma, J. 2009. "Natural Disasters and Human Capital Accumulation." Policy Research Working Paper 4862, World Bank, Washington, DC. Background paper for the report.

de Janvry, A., F. Finan, E. Sadoulet, and R. Vakis. 2006. "Can Conditional Cash Transfer Programs Serve as Safety Nets in Keeping Children at School and from Working When Exposed to Shocks?" *Journal of Development Economics* 79 (2): 349–73.

de la Fuente, A., and S. Dercon. 2008. "Disasters, Growth and Poverty in Africa: Revisiting the Microeconomic Evidence." Background paper for the 2009 United Nations Global Assessment Report on Disaster Risk Reduction, *Risk and Poverty in a Changing Climate.*

de Mel, S., D. McKenzie, and C. Woodruff. 2008. "Enterprise Recovery Following Natural Disasters." Policy Research Working Paper 5269, World Bank, Washington, DC. Background paper for the report.

Deaton, A., and R. Arora. 2009. "Life at the Top: The Benefits of Height." Working Paper 15090, National Bureau of Economic Research, Cambridge, MA.

del Ninno, C., P. A. Dorosh, L. C. Smith, and D. K. Roy. 2001. "The 1998 Floods in Bangladesh: Disaster Impacts, Household Coping Strategies and Response." Research Report 122. International Food Policy Research Institute, Washington, DC.

Dercon, S., and I. Outes. 2009. "Income Dynamics in Rural India: Testing for Poverty Traps and Multiple Equilibria." Background paper for the report.

Fiala, N. 2009. "More May Be Too Much: Rethinking the Effect of Rainfall Shocks on Economic Growth and Civil Conflict." Draft, Department of Economics, University of California.

Fomby, T., Y. Ikeda, and N. Loayza. 2009. "The Growth Aftermath of Natural Disasters." Policy Research Working Paper 5002, World Bank, Washington, DC. Background paper for the report.

Foster, A. 1995. "Prices, Credit Markets and Child Growth in Low-Income Rural Areas." *The Economic Journal* 105 (430): 551–70.

Frankenberg, E., J. Friedman, and D. Thomas. 2009. "Medium-Run Consequences of Disaster Induced Psycho-Social Disability: Evidence from Aceh." World Bank, Washington, DC. Background paper for the report.

Gaiha, R., and K. Imai. 2003. *Vulnerability, Shocks and Persistence of Poverty: Estimates for Semi-Arid Rural South India*. Oxford, U.K., and Delhi, India: University of Oxford and University of Delhi.

Grantham-McGregor, S., Y. B. Cheung, S. Cueto, P. Glewwe, L. Richter, B. Strupp, and the International Child Development Steering Group. 2007. "Developmental Potential in the First 5 Years for Children in Developing Countries." *Lancet* 369 (9555): 60–70.

Hallegatte, S., and M. Ghil. 2008. "Natural Disasters Impacting a Macroeconomic Model with Endogenous Dynamics." *Ecological Economics* 68 (1): 582–92.

Hallegatte, S., and P. Dumas. 2009. "Can Natural Disasters Have Positive Consequences? Investigating the Role of Embodied Technical Change." *Ecological Economics* 68 (3): 777–786.

———. 2009. "Think Again: Higher Elasticity of Substitution Increases Economic Resilience." Fondazione Eni Enrico Mattei, Working Paper 66, Milan, Italy. http://www.feem.it/userfiles/attach/Publication/NDL 2009/ NDL2009-066.pdf.

Hamilton, K., and G. Atkinson. 2006. *Wealth, Welfare and Sustainability: Advances in Measuring Sustainable Development*. Cheltenham, U.K.: Edward Elgar.

Hendrix, C. S., and S. M. Glaser. 2007. "Trends and Triggers: Climate, Climate Change and Civil Conflict in Sub-Saharan Africa." *Political Geography* 26 (6): 695–715.

Hinshaw, R. E. 2006. *Hurricane Stan Response in Guatemala* Quick Response Research Report 182, University of Colorado Natural Hazards Center, Boulder, CO. http://www.colorado.edu/hazards/qr/qr182/qr182.html.

Hochrainer, S. 2006. *Macroeconomic Risk Management against Natural Disasters*. Wiesbaden: German University Press.

Hochrainer, S. 2009. "Assessing Macro-economic Impacts of Natural Disasters: Are There Any?" Policy Research Working Paper 4968, World Bank, Washington, DC. Background paper for the report.

Hoddinott, J., J. Maluccion, J. Behrman, R. Flores, and R. Martorell. 2008. "Effect of a Nutrition Intervention During Early Childhood on Economic Productivity in Guatemalan Adults." *Lancet* 371: 411–16.

Homer-Dixon, T. 1999. *Environment, Scarcity, and Violence.* Princeton, NJ: Princeton University Press.

Isard, P. 1977. "How Far Can We Push the 'Law of One Price?' " *American Economic Review* 67 (5): 942–48

Jensen, R. 2000. "Agricultural Volatility and Investments in Children." *American Economic Review* 90 (2): 399–404.

Keefer, P., E. Neumayer, and T. Plümper. 2009. "Putting Off Till Tomorrow: The Politics of Disaster Risk Reduction." Background paper for the report.

Kelman, I. 2007. "Disaster Diplomacy: Can Tragedy Help Build Bridges among Countries?" *UCAR Quarterly* (Fall): 6.

Kuhn, R. Forthcoming. "Conflict, Coastal Vulnerability, and Resiliency in Tsunami-Affected Communities of Sri Lanka." In *Tsunami Recovery in Sri Lanka: Ethnic and Regional Dimensions*, ed. M. Gamburd and D. McGilvray. London: Routledge.

Lis, E. M., and C. Nickel. 2009. "The Impact of Extreme Weather Events on Budget Balances and Implications for Fiscal Policy." Working Paper 1055. European Central Bank, Frankfurt.

Loayza, N., E. Olaberria, J. Rigolini, and L. Christiansen. 2009. "Natural Disasters and Growth: Going Beyond the Averages." Policy Research Working Paper 4980, World Bank, Washington, DC. Background paper for the report.

López, R. 2009. "Natural Disasters and the Dynamics of Intangible Assets." *Ecological Economics* 68 (3): 777–786. Background paper for the report.

Maccini, S. L., and D. Yang. 2008. "Under the Weather: Health, Schooling, and Economic Consequences of Early-Life Rainfall." NBER Working Paper 14031, National Bureau of Economic Research, Cambridge, MA.

Markandya, A., and S. Pedroso-Galinato. 2009. "Economic Modeling of Income, Different Types of Capital and Natural Disasters." Policy Research Working Paper 4875, World Bank, Washington, DC. Background paper for the report.

Mechler, R. 2009. "Can National Savings Measures Help Explain Post Disaster Welfare Changes?" Policy Research Working Paper 4988, World Bank, Washington, DC. Background paper for the report.

Meier, P., D. Bond, and J. Bond. 2007. "Environmental Influences on Pastoral Conflict in the Horn of Africa." *Political Geography* 26: 716–35.

Miguel, E., S. Satyanath, and E. Sergenti. 2004. Economic Shocks and Civil Conflict: An Instrumental Variables Approach. *Journal of Political Economy* 112 (4): 725–53.

Mill, J. S. 1872. *Principles of Political Economy.* London: People's Edition.

Morris, S., O. Neidecker-Gonzales, C. Carletto, M. Munguia, J. M. Medina, and Q. Wodon. 2002. "Hurricane Mitch and the Livelihood of the Rural Poor in Honduras." *World Development* 31 (1): 49–60.

Morris, S., and Q., Wodon. 2003. "The Allocation of Natural Disaster Relief Funds: Hurricane Mitch in Honduras." *World Development* 31 (7): 1279–89.

Murlidharan, T. L. and H. C. Shah. 2001. "Catastrophes and Macro-Economic Risk Factors: An Empirical Study." Paper presented at the International Institute for Applied Systems Analysis conference "Integrated Disaster Risk Management: Reducing Socio-Economic Vulnerability," Laxenburg, Austria, August 1–4.

Norris, F. 2005. Psychosocial Consequences of Natural Disasters in Developing Countries: What Does Past Research Tell Us about the Potential effects of the 2004 Tsunami? National Center for PTSD, Dartmouth College, Hanover, New Hampshire.

Noy, I. 2009. "The Macroeconomic Consequences of Disasters." *Journal of Development Economics* 88 (2): 221–31.

Nyong, A., and C. Fiki. 2005. "Drought-Related Conflicts, Management and Resolution in the West African Sahel." Paper presented at the Global Environmental Change and Human Security Workshop, Oslo, June 21–23.

Okuyama, Y. 2009. "Impact Estimation Methodology: Case Studies." Background paper for the report.

Okuyama, Y., and S. Sahin. 2009. "Impact Estimation of Disasters: A Global Aggregate for 1960 to 2007." Policy Research Working Paper 4963, World Bank, Washington, DC. Background paper for the report.

Otero, R. C., and R. Z. Marti. 1995. "The Impacts of Natural Disasters on Developing Economies: Implications for the International Development and Disaster Community." In *Disaster Prevention for Sustainable Development: Economic and Policy Issues,* ed. M. Munasinghe and C. Clarke. Yokohama, Japan: World Bank.

Porter, C. 2008. "The Long Run Impact of Severe Shocks in Childhood: Evidence from the Ethiopian Famine of 1984." University of Oxford, Department of Economics, Oxford, U.K.

Premand, P., and R. Vakis. 2009. "Do Shocks Affect Poverty Persistence? Evidence Using Welfare Trajectories from Nicaragua." World Bank, Washington, DC.

Renner, M., and Z. Chafe. 2007. "Beyond Disasters: Creating Opportunities for Peace." Worldwatch Institute, Washington, DC.

Rodríguez-Oreggia, E., A. de la Fuente, R. de la Torre, H. Moreno, and C. Rodriguez. 2010. "The Impact of Natural Disasters on Human Development and Poverty at the Municipal Level in Mexico, 2002–05." Center for International Development Working Paper #43, Harvard University, Cambridge, MA.

Sahin, S. 2009. "Valuing Economic Impacts of Disasters within a Global Economy-Wide Model." Background paper for the report.

Santos, I. 2007. *Disentangling the Effects of Natural Disasters on Children: 2001 Earthquakes in El Salvador*. Boston, MA: Harvard University, Kennedy School of Government.

Sen, A. 1987. *Commodities and Capabilities*. New York: Oxford University Press.

Skidmore, M., and H. Toya. 2002. "Do Natural Disasters Promote Long-Run Growth?" *Economic Inquiry* 40 (4): 664–87.

Tobin, J. 1969. "A General Equilibrium Approach to Monetary Theory." *Journal of Money Credit and Banking* 1 (1): 15–29.

Victora, C. G., L. Adair, C. Fall, P. C. Hallal, R. Martorell, L. Richter, and H. S. Sachdev. 2008. "Maternal and Child Undernutrition: Consequences for Adult Health and Human Capital." *Lancet* 371: 340–57.

Wisner, B., P. Blaikie, T. Cannon, and I. Davis. 2004. *At Risk: Natural Hazards, People's Vulnerability and Disasters*. London: Routledge.

World Bank. 2006. "Climate Variability and Water Resources Degradation in Kenya." World Bank Working Paper No. 69, World Bank, Washington, DC.

Yamauchi, F., Y. Yohannes, and A. Quisumbing. 2009a. "Natural Disasters, Self-Insurance and Human Capital Investment Evidence from Bangladesh, Ethiopia and Malawi." Policy Research Working Paper 4909, World Bank, Washington, DC. Background paper for the report.

———. 2009b. "Risks, Ex-Ante Actions, and Public Assistance: Impacts of Natural Disasters on Child Schooling in Bangladesh, Ethiopia, and Malawi." Policy Research Working Paper 4910, World Bank, Washington, DC. Background paper for the report.

Spotlight 2

Notes

1. Japan International Cooperation Agency report (2002) puts the probability at 62 ± 12 percent within the next 30 years and 32 ± 12 percent within the next decade.

2. Gurenko, Lester, Mahul, and Gonulal (2006) describe the intentions and details more fully. Decree Law 587 made TCIP the monopoly insurer up to $25,000, and private insurers may offer coverage only

above TCIP's limit of $62,500. The premium averages $46 monthly now and varies by location (five risk zones) and construction (three types: steel & concrete; masonry; and others). Discounts are also offered for the installation of quake-resistant features.

The TCIP, an entity under the Treasury, is structured to be independent of politics with a seven-member managing board drawn from academia and the public and private sectors. It sells the policies through agents and 24 private insurance companies, may pay any claims directly and quickly (without waiting for the government budget to be approved), and transfers the risks abroad through reinsurance retaining only the risk that the World Bank contingency capital facility could cover.

References

Escaleras, M., N. Anbarci, and C. Register. 2007. "Public Sector Corruption and Major Earthquakes: A Potentially Deadly Interaction." *Public Choice* 132 (1–2): 209–30.

Gurenko, E., R. Lester, O. Mahul, and S. O. Gonulal. 2006. *Earthquake Insurance in Turkey: History of the Turkish Catastrophe Insurance Pool.* Washington, DC: World Bank, International Bank for Reconstruction and Development.

Japan International Cooperation Agency. 2002. "Study on Disaster Prevention/Mitigation Basic Plan in Istanbul." Tokyo.

Chapter 3

Notes

1. The benefits of housing protection against disasters do not always outweigh the costs: protecting windows and doors within a masonry house is not cost-effective in less hurricane-exposed communities of St. Lucia.

2. The most frequently invoked explanations for not adopting preventive measures were: too expensive (57 percent); "we trust in our building" (54 percent); God's will (41 percent); and no use (33 percent). Others included lack of time (29 percent); and lack of knowledge about what to do or being a renter (25 percent).

3. It should be kept in mind, however, that there are many limiting assumptions of the analyses—most of which are conservative in the sense of lowering the benefit-cost ratios.

4. Propensity scores were used to match buildings, and the matching was done non-parametrically to avoid errors associated with a misspecified functional form.

5. See http://pameno.com/news/157-communities-at-odds-with-new-fema-flood-maps.html; http://www.allbusiness.com/government/government-bodies-offices-regional/13171716-1.html.

6. Nguyen Co Thach, former Vietnamese Foreign Minister, famously remarked in 1989 that "The Americans couldn't destroy Hanoi, but we have destroyed our city by very low rents." quoted in Dan Seligman, "Keeping Up," Fortune, February 27, 1989.

7. Under the 1882 Transfer of Property Act and the 1908 Indian Registration Act, only sale deeds drawn up on "stamp paper" worth as much as 20 percent of a real estate transaction's value would be registered. States get the revenue from stamp duties, and the central government gets tax revenues from any capital gain on the sale (through income taxes). So, few transactions (generally to those outside the family) are recorded, and the property registers show the names of long dead owners. Furthermore, even when a transaction is recorded, the value is frequently underreported with the difference paid in cash (black money).

8. Pelling (2003) argues that the peripheries of expanding cities tend to grow more rapidly compared to central business districts. In 2008, in megacities, annual growth rates of peripheral population tend to reach around 10–20 percent compared to central business districts.

9. Such strategies have been implemented successfully in the control of industrial pollution through public disclosure of emission levels of firms using a simple rating system.

10. These data are from the Mexican Statistics office website at: http://www.inegi.org. The *Wall Street Journal* (February 3, 2010) reports different seasonally adjusted numbers for 2008 from the US Commerce Department and Eurostat that show similar ranking of countries: 81.7 percent of Italians own their own homes, 67.3 percent of Americans, and 55.6 percent of Germans.

11. Furthermore, such a code must deal exhaustively with heterogeneous building sites (the foundation in clay soil must differ from that in sandy soil) and alternative designs, making it far less likely to reflect continually improving knowledge and technology.

12. Langenbach's (2009) description of traditional building techniques notes that the *taq* and *dhajji dewari* construction techniques of Kashmir, dating to the 12th century, differ slightly across the line of control. The *taq,* which goes by the Pushtu word *bhatar* in the Northwest Frontier Province, consists of load-bearing masonry with embedded horizontal timbers tied together like horizontal ladders tying the masonry walls together and to the floor.

13. *Guidelines for the Construction of Compliant Rural Homes*, published by ERRA, depicts what to do and what to avoid.

14. The European Union is introducing universal standards, and the Eurocode allows local modification if backed by adequate research and tests. Section n. 6.7.3 of the Eurocode 8 specifies the band in diagonal members in steel frames. A research project by the Polytechnic of Milan, the Instituto Superior Technico de Lisboa, and the University of Athens and Liege proposed the norms for a dissipative connection that limited the seismic damage to a foot-long steel pin connecting the diagonal of the structure to the column. Simulations reproducing different types of shock waves, including those observed during the Kobe earthquake, demonstrated the viability of the design.

15. In Indonesia, a physical audit of a World Bank–financed community-driven development program that constructed roads found that 24 percent of expenditures were "lost" to theft, probably orchestrated by village heads who oversaw projects.

16. Inadequate supervision, lax oversight, and poor choices also characterize the operations of state-owned enterprises for many of the same reasons.

References

Akerlof, G. A. 1970. "The Market for 'Lemons': Quality Uncertainty and the Market Mechanism." *Quarterly Journal of Economics* 84 (3): 488–500.

Baeza, C. C., and T. G. Packard. 2006. *Beyond Survival: Protecting Households from Health Shocks in Latin America*. Palo Alto, CA: Stanford University Press.

Bertaud, A., and J. Brueckner. 2004. "Predicted Impacts, Welfare Costs, and a Case Study of Bangalore, India." Policy Research Working Paper 3290, World Bank, Washington, DC.

Bin, O., C. E. Landry, and G. F. Meyer. 2009. "Riparian Buffers and Hedonic Prices: A Quasi-Experimental Analysis of Residential Property Values in the Neuse River Basin." *American Journal of Agricultural Economics* 91 (4): 1067–79.

Bin, O., and S. Polasky. 2004. "Effects of Flood Hazards on Property Values: Evidence Before and After Hurricane Floyd." *Land Economics* 80 (4): 490–500.

Coase, R. H. 1974. "The Lighthouse in Economics." *Journal of Law and Economics* 17 (2): 357–76

Cohen, L., and R. Noll. 1981. "The Economics of Building Codes to Resist Seismic Shocks." *Public Policy* 29 (1): 1–29.

Collins, D., J. Morduch, S. Rutherford, and O. Ruthven. 2009. *Portfolios of the Poor*. Princeton, NJ: Princeton University Press.

Council of the City of New York. March 2009. Release# 024-2009. http://council.nyc.gov/html/releases/prestated_3_24_09.shtml.

Cruz, P. G. 2009. "The Pros and Cons of Rent Control." *Global Property Guide.* January 19. http://www.globalpropertyguide.com/investment-analysis/The-pros-and-cons-of-rent-control.

de Ferranti, D., G. Perry, I. Gill, and L. Serven. 2000. *Securing Our Future.* Washington, DC: World Bank.

Ehrlich, I., and G. Becker. 1972. "Marker Insurance, Self-Insurance, and Self-Protection." *Journal of Political Economy* 80 (4): 623–48.

Fay, M., T. Yepes, and V. Foster. 2003. *Asset Inequality in Developing Countries: The Case of Housing.* Washington, DC: World Bank

FEMA. 2009. http://www.allbusiness.com/government/government-bodies-offices-regional/13171716-1.html.

———. 2010. http://pameno.com/news/157-communities-at-odds-with-new-fema-flood-maps.html.

Field, E. 2005. "Property Rights and Investment in Urban Slums." *Journal of European Economic Association Papers and Proceedings* 3 (2–3): 279–90.

Financial Times. 2009. "Jakarta's Ecological Crisis Fails to Sink In" July 13.

Fişek, G. O., N. Yeniçeri, S. Müderrisoğlu, and G. Özkarar. 2002. "Risk Perception and Attitudes Towards Mitigation." IIASA-DPRI Meeting: Integrated Disaster Risk Management: Megacity Vulnerability and Resilience. Laxenburg, Austria, July 29–31.

Gill, I. S., and N. Ilahi. 2000. "Economic Insecurity, Individual Behavior and Social Policy," paper prepared for the Regional Study. "Managing Economic Insecurity in Latin America and the Caribbean," The World Bank.

Gill, I. S., T. Packard, and J. Yermo. 2005. *Keeping the Promise of Social Security in Latin America.* Washington, DC: World Bank.

Global Property Guide. 2009. http://www.globalpropertyguide.com

Gómez-Ibáñez, J. A., and F. Ruiz Nunez. 2007. *Inefficient Cities.* Cambridge, MA: Harvard Kennedy School, Taubman Center for State and Local Government.

Grossi, P., and H. Kunreuther. 2005. *Catastrophe Modeling: A New Approach to Managing Risk.* New York: Springer.

Hocrainer, S. 2006. *Macroeconomic Risk Management against Natural Disasters.* Wiesbaden, Germany: German University Press (DUV).

Hung, H. V., R. Shaw, and M. Kobayashi. 2007. "Flood Risk Management for the Riverside Urban Areas of Hanoi." *Disaster Prevention and Management* 16 (2): 245–58.

IIASA/RMS/Wharton. 2009. "The Challenges and Importance of Investing in Cost-Effective Measures for Reducing Losses from Natural Disasters in Emerging Economies." Background paper for the report.

Jackson, E. L. 1981. "Response to Earthquake Hazard: The West Coast of America." *Environment and Behavior* 13 (4): 387–416.

Jigyasu, R. 2008. "Structural Adaptation in South Asia: Learning Lessons from Tradition." In *Hazards and the Built Environment*, ed. L. Bosher. London: Taylor and Francis Group.

Kahneman, D., and A. Tversky. 1979. "Prospect Theory: An Analysis of Decision Under Risk." *Econometrica* 47 (2): 263–91.

Kahneman, D., J. L. Knetsch, and R. H. Thaler. 1990. "Experimental Tests of the Endowment Effect and the Coase Theorem." *Journal of Political Economy* 98 (6): 1325–48.

Keller, C., M. Siegrist, and H. Gutscher. 2006. "The Role of the Affect and Availability Heuristics in Risk Communication." *Risk Analysis* 26 (3): 631–39.

Kenny, C. 2009. "Why Do People Die in Earthquakes? The Costs, Benefits and Institutions of Disaster Risk Reduction in Developing Countries." Policy Research Working Paper 4823, World Bank, Washington, DC. Background paper for the report.

Kenny, C., and M. Musatova. 2008. "'Red Flags' in World Bank Projects: An Analysis of Infrastructure Projects." Policy Research Working Paper 5243, World Bank, Washington, DC. Background paper for the report.

Lall, S., and U. Deichmann. 2009. "Density and Disasters: Economics of Urban Hazard Risk." Policy Research Working Paper 5161, World Bank, Washington, DC. Background paper for the report.

Lall, S. V., H. G. Wang, and D. D. Mata. 2007. "Do Urban Land Regulations Influence Slum Formation? Evidence From Brazilian Cities." In *Proceedings of the 35th Brazilian Economics Meeting*. Washington, DC: World Bank.

Lancaster, K. J. 1966. "A New Approach to Consumer Theory." *Journal of Political Economy* 74: 132–57.

Langenbach, R. 2009. *Don't Tear It Down: Preserving the Earthquake Resistant Vernacular Architecture of Kashmir*. New Delhi: United Nations Education, Scientific and Cultural Organization.

Nakagawa, M., M. Saito, and H. Yamaga. 2007. "Earthquake Risk and Housing Rents: Evidence from the Tokyo Metropolitan Area." *Regional Science and Urban Economics* 37 (1): 87–99.

Olken, B. A. 2005. "Monitoring Corruption: Evidence from a Field Experiment in Indonesia." NBER Working Paper 11753, National Bureau of Economic Research, Cambridge, MA.

Onder, Z., V. Dokmeci, and B. Keskin. 2004. "The Impact of Public Perception of Earthquake Risk on Istanbul's Housing Market." *Journal of Real Estate Literature* 12 (2), 181–94.

Pelling, M. 2003. *The Vulnerability of Cities: Natural Disasters and Urban Resilience*. London: Earthscan.

Peters, J. W. 2009. "Assembly Passes Rent-Regulation Revisions Opposed by Landlords," *New York Times*. February 2. http://www.nytimes.com/2009/02/03/nyregion/03rent.html?_r=1&partner=permalink&exprod=permalink.

Rabin, M. 1998. "Psychology and Economics." *Journal of Economic Literature* 36 (1): 11–46.

———. 2002. "A Perspective on Psychology and Economics." *European Economic Review* 46 (4–5): 657–85.

Ricciardi, V. A. 2007. "Literature Review of Risk Perception Studies in Behavioral Finance: The Emerging Issues." Presented at 25th Annual Meeting of the Society for the Advancement of Behavioral Economics (SABE) Conference, New York, May 15–18. http://ssrn.com/abstract=988342.

Rosen, S. 1974. "Hedonic Prices and Implicit Markets: Product Differentiation in Pure Competition." *Journal of Political Economy* 82 (1): 34–55.

Seligman, D. 1989. "Keeping Up." *Fortune* 119 (February 27): 133–4.

Smith, V. K., J. Carbone, J. C. Pope, D. Hallstrom, and M. Darden. 2006. "Adjusting to Natural Disasters." *Journal of Risk and Uncertainty* 33 (1): 37–54.

Texier, P. 2008. "Floods in Jakarta: When the Extreme Reveals Daily Structural Constraints and Mismanagement." *Disaster Prevention and Management* 17 (3): 358–72.

Tobriner, S. 2006. *Bracing for Disaster: Earthquake-Resistant Architecture and Engineering in San Francisco, 1838–1933*. Berkeley, CA: Heyday Books.

Tversky, A., and D. Kahneman. 1981. "The Framing of Decisions and the Psychology of Choice." *Science* 211 (4481): 453–58.

———. 1991. "Loss Aversion in Riskless Choice: A Reference-Dependent Model." *Quarterly Journal of Economics* 106 (4): 1039–61.

Viscusi, W. K., and R. J. Zeckhauser. 2006 "National Survey Evidence on Disasters and Relief: Risk Beliefs, Self-Interest, and Compassion." NBER Working Paper 12582, National Bureau of Economic Research, Cambridge, MA.

Willis, K., and A. Asgary. 1997. "The Impact of Earthquake Risk on Housing Markets: Evidence from Tehran Real Estate Agents." *Journal of Housing Research* 8 (1): 125–36.

World Bank. 1995. *Bureaucrats in Business: The Economics and Politics of Government Ownership*. Washington, DC.

———. 2000. *Greening Industry: New Roles for Communities, Markets, and Governments*. Policy Research Report. New York: Oxford University Press.

———. 2008. *World Development Report 2009: Reshaping Economic Geography*. Washington, DC.

Yamagishi, K. 1997. "When a 12.86% Mortality Is More Dangerous Than 24.14%: Implications for Risk Communication." *Applied Cognitive Psychology* 11 (6): 495–506.

Spotlight 3

Notes

1. The 2009 Post Disaster Needs Assessment reports more deaths than table 1 (EM-DAT data). Livestock also drowned: 160,000 goats, 60,000 pigs, 25,000 cows.

2. See http://www.alertnet.org/db/crisisprofiles/LA_FLO.htm.

3. IMF (2010). As noted by Diamond there is also "A large but unquantified trade in drugs being transshipped from Colombia to the U.S." (Diamond 2005). GDP or trade statistics may not fully capture this.

4. White and Runge (1994), in a study of how farmers cooperate in a watershed management project in Haiti, find that cooperation is more likely when farmers trained in soil conservation practices perceive the financial benefits. Government grants, whether in cash or in kind, are less effective in eliciting such cooperation.

5. The Creole name of a fabled bogeyman who kidnaps children late at night. Their formal name was *Milice de Volontaires de la Sécurité Nationale* (MVSN).

6. Rethinking Institutional Analysis: Interviews with Vincent and Elinor Ostrom (November 7, 2003) available at: http://mercatus.org/publication/rethinking-institutional-analysis-interviews-vincent-and-elinor-ostrom.

7. The United States, for example, has stopped deporting illegal resident Haitians, but kept seriously injured Haitians from U.S. hospitals until it provoked outrage.

References

Collier, P. 2009. "Haiti: From Natural Catastrophe to Economic Security: A Report for the Secretary-General of the United Nations." Report for the Secretary-General of the United Nations. Oxford University, Department of Economics, Oxford, U.K.

Diamond, J. 2005. *Collapse: How Societies Choose to Fail or Succeed*. New York: Penguin Books.

Hardin, G. 1968. "The Tragedy of the Commons." *Science* 162 (3859): 1243–48.

International Monetary Fund. 2010. "Haiti: Sixth Review Under the Extended Credit Facility, Request for Waiver of Performance Criterion, and Augmentation of Access." Washington, DC.

Maathai, W. 2007. *Unbowed: A Memoir*. New York: Random House.

NOAA (National Oceanic and Atmospheric Administration) http://www.nhc.noaa.gov/2008atlan.shtml.

Ostrom, E. 1990. *Governing the Commons: The Evolution of Institutions for Collective Action*. Cambridge, U.K.: Cambridge University Press.

White, T. A., and C. F. Runge. 1994. "Cooperative Watershed Management in Haiti Common Property and Collective Action." *Economic Development and Cultural Change* 43 (1): 1–41.

Chapter 4

Notes

1. This comes on the heels of Latin America's "lost decade" when infrastructure spending declined drastically as countries kept budget deficits and inflation in check, so these data might reflect some "rebound" as countries then spent more on new infrastructure.

2. Four salient examples are the Alaska earthquake in 1964 (a presidential election year), Tropical Storm Agnes in June 1972, Hurricane Andrew in September 1992, and the four hurricanes in 2004.

3. They analyze covariance techniques and control for differences in the incidence of damaging floods using precipitation and damages as covariates. The adjusted mean is 5.3 in reelection years and 4.4 in other years. Some disasters happened to coincide with presidential election years, such as the 2004 Florida hurricanes.

4. See http://www.pacindia.org.

5. Kahn explores the effect of income, geography, and institutions on deaths from five different disaster types for 73 countries between 1980 and 2002 (CRED data). The disasters considered are earthquakes, extreme temperature, floods, landslides, and windstorms.

6. The highest benefit-cost ratio would be equivalent to the highest economic rate of return—except if cash flows change sign (multiple rates of return) and a more careful analysis is needed.

7. This section has benefited greatly from inputs by Michel Jarraud, Maryam Golnaraghi, and Vladimir Tsirkunov and from background work commissioned for this report by A. R. Subbiah, T. Teisberg, R. Weiher, and L. Hancock.

8. More than 35,000 deaths in Europe were linked to the 2003 heat wave. Much of Europe was affected by heat waves during the summer. Nationwide temperatures were warmest on record in Germany, Switzerland, France, and Spain. At many locations, temperatures rose above 40 degrees Celsius (*Source*: WMO Statement on the Status of the Global Climate in 2003).

9. Second International Conference on Early Warning in 2003, http://www.ewc2.org/pg000001.htm.

10. The 2006 Global Early Warning Survey, launched at the Third International Early Warning Conference (EWC–III) in Bonn, Germany (March 2006) can be downloaded at: www.ewc3.org/upload/downloads/Global_Survey.pdf.

11. Volcanoes are an example of a predictable geological hazard. They typically produce early seismic activity indicating an impending future eruption, and the volcano can then be more carefully monitored with equipment placed near or directly on the volcano. With such monitoring capability in place, eruptions have been predicted with reasonable accuracy in recent years. The Mt. Pinatubo eruption in 1991 is an example where evacuations of increasing scale were ordered starting about 10 days before the actual eruption occurred.

12. GEOSS (Global Earth Observation System of Systems) indicates the many ways (weather forecasting is one) data from satellites are used.

13. Not all products and data are available to national meteorological services through the coordinated WMO network. Specifically, "essential data" are those necessary for the provision of services in support of the protection of the life, property, and well-being of all nations. "Additional data" are those required to sustain WMO Programs at the global, regional, and national levels and, further, as agreed, to assist other Members in the provision of meteorological services in their countries. See WMO Resolutions 40 and 25 (http://www.wmo.int/pages/about/Resolution40_en.html and http://www.wmo.int/pages/prog/hwrp/documents/Resolution_25.pdf). All national meteorological services of WMO Members have access to the essential data. Access to additional data comes with usage restrictions (e.g. intellectual property rights, fees, etc.) negotiated directly with the provider. The main challenge for developing and least developed nations is the bandwidth, which can be expensive, and the technical know-how to use or downscale data.

14. Of the 187 WMO Members, 139 participated in the survey. The survey has been synthesized in the "Assessment Report of National Meteorological and Hydrological Services in Support of Disaster Risk Reduction" and the analysis is available at: http://www.wmo.int/pages/prog/drr/natRegCap_en.html.

15. The explanation as provided in the review for this particularly high ratio is that the agencies (once in possession of a rather strong network) lost most of their capacity during the country's 20-year conflict. Therefore, the investment being valued would in effect make the difference between a forecast and no forecast.

16. Teisberg and Weiher (2009) cite the 1999 testimony of experts before the United States Congressional Subcommittee on Energy and Environ-

ment. "National Weather Service and Fleet Modernization Issues." Testimony of Joel C. Willemsen and L. Nye Stevens before the House Subcommittee on Energy and Environment, February 24, 1999, accessed February 8, 2009 at http://www.gao.gov/archive/1999/a299097t.pdf.

17. Saved lives would be a benefit, and economic rates of return need not be lower, but when the probability of a quake is low, the expected return would be reduced. Too much should not be made of these fine distinctions because the estimates used in cost-benefit analysis are rough and considerable judgment is used. Such judgment is inevitable: the "willingness to pay," for example, is difficult to measure if those using the asset are government agencies whose budgets are allocated.

18. Clever finance ministers could still take these funds away by allocating less to the public works department than the salary bill, forcing the engineers to use the road maintenance funds to pay the salaries.

19. Lewis and Streever (2000) note that "mangrove habitat around the world can self-repair or successfully undergo secondary succession in 15–30 years if: 1) the normal tidal hydrology is not disrupted; and 2) the availability of waterborne seeds or seedlings of mangroves from adjacent stands is not disrupted or blocked."

20. http://www.fao.org/forestry/10560-1-0.pdf.

21. Ostrom (1990) emphasizes how communities develop diverse institutional arrangements for managing natural resources. She identifies eight common property design principles that contribute to successful common property regimes: (1) Clearly defined access rights and boundaries for individuals; (2) A proportional equivalence between benefits and costs; (3) Collective choice arrangements that allow modification of rules; (4) Monitoring to control resource appropriation; (5) Graduated sanctions against violators; (6) Existence of conflict resolution mechanisms; (7) Governmental recognition of minimal rights to organize; and (8) Multiple layers of nested enterprises that take on interrelated responsibilities.

References

Alesina, A., R. Baqir, and W. Easterly. 1999. "Public Goods and Ethnic Divisions." *Quarterly Journal of Economics* 114 (4): 1243–84.

Barbier, E. B. 2007. "Valuing Ecosystem Services as Productive Inputs." *Economic Policy* 22 (1): 177–229.

Besley, T., and R. Burgess. 2002. "The Political Economy of Government Responsiveness: Theory and Evidence from India." *Quarterly Journal of Economics* 117 (4): 1415–51.

Briceño-Garmendia, C., K. Smits, and V. Foster. 2008. "Africa Infrastructure Country Diagnostic." World Bank, Washington, DC.

Cole, S., A. Healy, and E. Werker. 2008. "Do Voters Appreciate Responsive Governments? Evidence from Indian Disaster Relief." Working Paper 09-050, Harvard Business School, Boston.

Costanza, R., O. Perez-Maqueo, M. L. Martinez, P. Sutton, S. J. Anderson, and K Mulder. 2008. "The Value of Coastal Wetlands to Hurricane Prevention." *Ambio* 37 (4): 241–8.

Cropper, M. L., and S. Sahin. 2009. "Valuing Mortality and Morbidity in the Context of Disaster Risks." Policy Research Working Paper 4832, World Bank, Washington, DC. Background paper for the report.

Dahdouh-Guebas, F., L. P. Jayatissa, D. Di Nitto, J. O. Bosire, D. Lo Seen, and N. Koedam. 2005. "How Effective Were Mangroves as a Defence Against the Recent Tsunami?" *Current Biology* 15 (12): 443–7.

de la Fuente, A. 2009. "Government Expenditures in Pre- and Post-Disaster Risk Management." Background note for the report.

Downton, M., and R. Pielke Jr. 2001. "Discretion without Accountability: Politics, Flood Damage, and Climate." *Natural Hazards Review* 2 (4): November 2001, pp. 157–166.

Driever, S. L., and D. M. Vaughn. 1988. "Flood Hazard in Kansas City Since 1880." *Geographical Review* 78 (1): 1–19.

Dudley, N., S. Stolton, A. Belokurov, L. Krueger, N. Lopoukhine, K. MacKinnon, T. Sandwith, and N. Sekhran. 2010. *Natural Solutions: Protected Areas Helping People Cope with Climate Change*. Washington, DC: World Bank and World Wildlife Fund.

Eisensee, T., and D. Strömberg. 2007. "News Droughts, News Floods, and US Disaster Relief." *Quarterly Journal of Economics* 122 (2): 693–728.

FAO (Food and Agriculture Organization). 2007. *The World's Mangroves, 1980–2005: A Thematic Study in the Framework of the Global Forest Resources Assessment 2005*.

Forest, J. J. F. 2006. *Homeland Security. Protecting America's Targets. Volume 3—Critical Infrastructure*. Westport, CT: Praeger Publishers.

Francken, N., B. Minten, and J. F. M. Swinnen. 2008. "Determinants of Aid Allocation: The Impact of Media, Politics, and Economic Factors on Cyclone Relief in Madagascar." LICOS Discussion Paper, Katholieke Universiteit Leuven, Leuven, Belgium.

Garcia, J. 2010. "Economic Analysis in World Bank Financed Projects." Policy Research Working Paper 2564, World Bank, Washington, DC.

Garrett, T. A., and R. S. Sobel. 2003. "The Political Economy of FEMA Disaster Payments." *Economic Inquiry* 41 (3): 496–509.

Gentile, E. 1994. "El Niño no tiene la culpa: Vulnerabilidad en el Noreste Argentino." *Desastres y Sociedad*. 87–104. Red de Estudios Sociales en Prevención de Desastres en América Latina y el Caribe.

Gibson, C. C., J. T. Williams, and E. Ostrom. 2005. "Local Enforcement and Better Forests." *World Development* 33 (2): 273–84.

Golnaraghi, M., ed. 2010. *Institutional Partnerships in Multi-Hazard Early Warning Systems.*

Golnaraghi, M., J. Douris, and J. B. Migraine. 2008. "Saving Lives Through Early Warning Systems and Emergency Preparedness." *Risk Wise.* Geneva: WMO.

Guocai, Z., and H. Wang. 2003. "Evaluating the Benefits of Meteorological Services in China." *WMO Bulletin* 52 (4): 383–7.

Healy, A. J., and N. Malhotra. 2009. "Myopic Voters and Natural Disaster Policy." *American Political Science Review* 103 (3): 387–406.

IIASA/RMS/Wharton. 2009. "The Challenges and Importance of Investing in Cost Effective Measures for Reducing Losses From Natural Disasters in Emerging Economies." Background paper for the report.

Independent Evaluation Group. 2007. *Development Actions and the Rising Incidence of Disasters.* Washington, DC: World Bank.

Kahn, M. E. 2005. "The Death Toll from Natural Disasters: The Role of Income, Geography, and Institution." *Review of Economics and Statistics* 87 (2): 271–84.

Keefer, P., E. Neumayer, and T. Plümper. 2009. "Putting Off Till Tomorrow: The Politics of Disaster Risk Reduction." Background paper for the report.

Kramer, R., D. Richter, S. Pattanayak, and N. Sharma. 1997. "Ecological and Economic Analysis of Watershed Protection in Eastern Madagascar." *Journal of Environmental Management* 49 (3): 277–95.

Kunreuther, H., and E. Michel-Kerjan. 2009. "A Framework for Reducing Vulnerability to Natural Disasters." Philadelphia: Wharton School Publishing. Background paper for the report.

Lazo, J. K., T. J. Teisberg, and R. F. Weiher. 2007. "Methodologies for Assessing the Economic Benefits of National Meteorological and Hydrological Services." *Elements for Life* 174–8. WHO.

Lewis, R.R., and B. Streever. 2000. "Restoration of Mangrove Habitat." WRP Technical Notes Collection (ERDC TN-WRP-VN-RS-3.2). Vicksburg, MS: U.S. Army Engineer Research and Development Center. www.wes.army.mil/el/wrp.

López, R., and M. Toman. 2006. *Economic Development and Environmental Sustainability.* Oxford, U.K.: Oxford University Press.

Motef, J., and P. Parfomak. 2004. "Critical Infrastructure and Key Assets: Definition and Identification." Washington, DC: Congressional Research Service.

Mott MacDonald Group. 2009. "SMART." http://www.geo technics.mott mac.com/projects/smart/.

Olson, M. 1971. *The Logic of Collective Action: Public Goods and the Theory of Groups.* Cambridge, MA: Harvard University Press.

Ostrom, E. 1990. *Governing the Commons: The Evolution of Institutions for Collective Action* Cambridge, U.K.: Cambridge University Press.

Penning-Roswell, E. C. 1996. "Flood-Hazard Response in Argentina." *Geographical Review* 86 (1): 72–90.

ProAct Network. 2008. *The Role of Environmental Management and Eco-Engineering in Disaster Risk Reduction and Climate Change Adaptation.* Nyon, Switzerland.

Sainath, P. 2002. *Everybody Loves a Good Drought: Stories from India's Poorest Districts.* Penguin Book: India.

Sathirathai, S., and E. B. Barbier. 2001. "Valuing Mangrove Conservation in Southern Thailand." *Contemporary Economic Policy* 19 (2): 109–22.

Sen, A. 1982. *Poverty and Famines: An Essay on Entitlements and Deprivation.* Oxford, U.K.: Clarendon Press.

Simmons, K., and D. Sutter. 2005. "WSR-88d Radar, Tornado Warnings, and Tornado Casualties." *Weather and Forecasting* 20 (3): 301–10.

Smyth, A. W., G. Altay, G. Deodatis, M. Erdik, G. Franco, P. Gulkan, H. Kunreuther, H. Lus, E. Mete, N. Seeber, and O. Yuzugullu. 2004a. "Probabilistic Benefit-Cost Analysis for Earthquake Damage Mitigation: Evaluating Measures for Apartment Houses in Turkey." *Earthquake Spectra* 20 (1): 171–203.

Smyth, A.W., G. Deodatis, G. Franco, Y. He, and T. Gurvich. 2004b. "Evaluating Earthquake Retrofitting Measures for Schools: A Demonstration Cost-Benefit Analysis." New York: Columbia University, Department of Civil Engineering and Engineering Mechanics.

Sobel, R., and P. Leeson. 2008. "Government's Response to Hurricane Katrina: A Public Choice Analysis." *Public Choice* 127 (1):55–73.

Stolton, S., N. Dudley, and J. Randall. 2008. *Natural Security: Protected Areas and Hazard Mitigation.* Gland, Switzerland: World Wildlife Fund.

Teisberg, T. J., and R. F. Weiher. 2009. "Benefits and Costs of Early Warning Systems for Major Natural Hazards." Background paper for the report.

UNISDR (United Nations International Strategy for Disaster Redution). 2009. *UNISDR Global Assessment Report 2009.* Geneva.

World Bank. 2000. *The Quality of Growth.* New York: Oxford University Press.

———. 2002. *The Right to Tell: The Role of Mass Media in Economic Development.* Washington, DC.

———. 2007. *Vietnam's Infrastructure Challenge.* Washington, DC.

———. 2008. "Weather and Climate Services in Europe and Central Asia: A Regional Review." Policy Research Working Paper 151, Washington, DC.

WMO (World Meteorological Organization). 2009. http://www.wmo. int/pages/prog/www/TEM/GTSstatus/R6rmtni.gif; http://www.wmo.int/ pages/prog/www/TEM/GTS/index_en.html.

————. 2006. "Analysis of the 2006 WMO Disaster Risk Reduction Country-Level Survey." Geneva: WMO.

WRI (World Resources Institute). 2005. *Millennium Ecosystem Assessment*. Washington, DC.

WWF (World Wildlife Fund). 2008. *Natural Security: Protected Areas and Hazard Mitigation*. Gland, Switzerland.

Spotlight 4

Notes

1. World Bank (2006). Average calculated between 1970–2001.

2. Sen (1981). It is possible for countries to experience deaths from droughts even during times of peace (North Korea in recent years; Ethiopia in 1972–73) as well as to see no significant mortality during a drought or famine even when going through a prolonged period of conflict or civil strife (Sri Lanka during most of the 1980s and 1990s, former Yugoslavia). Chapter 2 reported on empirical analyses of disasters and conflict, and this spotlight is limited to the situation in (and around) Ethiopia.

3. Many barley varieties are unique to Ethiopia and are drought resistant, but there has been little agricultural research to increase their yields. http://www.idrc.ca/en/ev-98727-201-1-DO_TOPIC.html.

4. Dercon (2002).

5. UN-OCHA (2009a).

6. The Oromo, now about 40 percent of Ethiopia's population, is the largest of over 70 ethnic groups and is concentrated in the south. The Amhara and Tigrean groups together are only 32 percent, but they traditionally dominate politics. Somali (6 percent) and Afar (4 percent) inhabit the arid regions of the east and southeast and also suffer from droughts.

7. Jonathan Dimbleby broadcast "The Unknown Famine" on the *BBC*, and $150 million in aid (at current value) poured in.

8. The World Bank (2009) Project Appraisal Document for Productive Safety Net Project. Phase 3. A tropical livestock unit (TLU) measures different animals as cattle equivalents.

9. IMF Country Report No. 02/214. September 2002.

10. *"Ethiopia Jails Seven for Complaining of Aid Abuses,"* Bloomberg, December 29, 2009; The Minister of State for International Development's Statement in U.K. Parliament on December 16, 2009.

11. International Crisis Group Africa (2009).

12. World Bank (2006).

13. UN-OCHA (2009a).

14. FEWS-NET/Ethiopia "ETHIOPIA Food Security Update." November 2009.

15. UN-OCHA (2009b).

16. "Tens of thousands of ethnic Somali civilians living in eastern Ethiopia's Somali regional state are experiencing serious abuses and a looming humanitarian crisis. . . ." according to *Collective Punishment: War Crimes and Crimes against Humanity in the Ogaden Area of Ethiopia's Somali Regional State,* Human Rights Watch (2008).

References

Adejumobi, S. A. 2007. *The History of Ethiopia.* Westport, CT: Greenwood Press.

Broad, K., and S. Agrawala. 2000. "The Ethiopia Food Crisis—Uses and Limits of Climate Forecasts." *Science* 289 (5485): 1693–4.

Dercon, S. 2002. *The Impact of Economic Reforms on Rural Households in Ethiopia: A Study from 1989–1995.* Washington, DC: World Bank.

Human Rights Watch. 2008. *Collective Punishment: War Crimes and Crimes against Humanity in the Ogaden area of Ethiopia's Somali Regional State.* New York.

International Crisis Group Africa. 2009. *Ethiopia: Ethnic Federalism and Its Discontents.* Report No. 153. Brussels, Belgium.

Kiros, G. E., and D. P. Hogan. 2001. "War, Famine and Excess Child Mortality in Africa: the Role of Parental Education." *International Journal of Epidemiology* 30 (3): 447–55.

Porter, C. 2008. *The Long Run Impact of Severe Shocks in Childhood: Evidence from the Ethiopian Famine of 1984.* Oxford, U.K.: University of Oxford, Center for the Study of African Economies.

Sen, A. 1981. *Poverty and Famines: An Essay on Entitlement and Deprivation.* Oxford, U.K.: Clarendon Press.

UN-OCHA (United Nations Office for the Coordination of Humanitarian Affairs). 2009a. "Drought in Kenya: Pastoralism under Threat." *Pastoralist Voices* 1 (16).

UN-OCHA. 2009b. "Ethiopia: Humanitarian Bulletin." November.

Wolde, M. 1986. Cited in Human Rights Watch. 1991. Evil Days: *Thirty Years of War and Famine in Ethiopia.* Washington, DC.

World Bank. 2006. *Ethiopia: Managing Water Resources to Maximize Sustainable Growth*. Washington, DC: Agriculture and Rural Development Department.

World Bank. 2009. Project Appraisal Document for PSNP Phase 3. Washington, DC.

Chapter 5

Notes

1. As reported in the 2010 World Development Report, North America and Europe claimed more than 82 percent of the total nonlife insurance premium volume of $1.5 trillion in 2006. East Asia claimed 13 percent; Latin America and the Caribbean, 3 percent; and South Asia and Africa, 1 percent each.

2. "All cause" or "all perils" contracts can protect against unusual events, but can create problems for insurers and policyholders when a catastrophic "unnamed peril" event, such as September 11, occurs. The United States Congress subsequently passed the "Terrorism Risk Insurance Act" in 2002 to provide limited coverage, essentially permitting private insurers to deny claims stemming from such acts (Kunreuther and Pauly 2005).

3. Revenues depend on the structure of taxation and do not necessarily fall with output. For example, a country that taxes imports rather than domestic production may have higher revenues following a disaster as people import more to consume and rebuild.

4. Arrow and Lind (1970) said the basic intuition is if the net benefits of a public project are distributed independently of national income, and they are spread over a sufficiently large population, the risk of such projects can be shouldered by many individual taxpayers. A social planner could therefore ignore the uncertain returns and act as a risk-neutral entity. One implication is that the discount rate used for public investment should not include a risk premium (which may be embedded in a market rate).

5. It is possible that although hurricanes hit almost every year, one may not be able to accurately price the risk of large hurricanes from 20 years of observations.

6. See CCRIF.org under News & Events section: Tuesday September 9, 2008—"Hurricane Ike Triggers CCRIF's First Hurricane Payout," Tuesday October 14, 2008—"Turks and Caicos Government Receives Payout from Caribbean Catastrophe Risk Insurance Facility."

7. A special purpose vehicle is a subsidiary company with a legal status that makes its obligations secure even if the parent company goes bank-

rupt. The parent company can use it to finance large projects without putting the entire company at risk.

8. As Michel-Kerjan (2010) describes it: "The field of alternative risk transfer (ART; 'alternative' as opposed to traditional insurance and reinsurance mechanisms) grew out of a series of insurance capacity crises in the 1970s through 1990s that led purchasers of traditional reinsurance coverage to seek more robust ways to buy protection. CAT bonds, first developed in 1996–97, transfer part of the risk exposure directly to investors in the financial markets. One of the main advantages for investors (typically catastrophe funds, hedge funds, and money managers) is that these instruments constitute a different class of assets that can enhance their returns since they are not highly correlated with other financial risks (e.g., fluctuations in interest rates)."

9. Measuring and assessing the covariance of probabilities is difficult. Consulting firms provide this service, but they are expensive.

10. A private consulting firm reviewed the operations and Istanbul University assessed the beneficiaries based on interviews of more than 5,000 people.

11. Olsen, Carstensen, and Hoyen (2003) conclude that disasters and complex emergencies have a greater tendency to become forgotten crises when major aid donors, namely western governments, have no particular security interests vested in the afflicted regions.

References

Adams, R. H. 1991. "The Effect of International Remittances on Poverty, Inequality, and Development." Research Report 86, International Food Policy Research Institute, Washington, DC.

Alderman, H. 2010. "Safety Nets Can Help Address the Risks to Nutrition from Increasing Climate Variability." *Journal of Nutrition* 140 (1): 1485–52S.

Arrow, K., and R. Lind. 1970. "Uncertainty and the Evaluation of Public Investment Decision." *American Economic Review* 60 (3): 364–78.

Auffret, P. 2003. "High Consumption Volatility: The Impact of Natural Disasters?" Policy Research Working Paper 2962, World Bank, Washington, DC.

Aysan, Y., and P. Oliver. 1987. *Housing and Culture After Earthquakes*. Oxford, U.K.: Oxford Polytechnic.

Baez, J., A. de la Fuente, and I. Santos. 2009. "Do Natural Disasters Affect Human Capital? An Assessment Based on Existing Empirical Evidence." Background paper for the report.

Buchanan, J. M. 1975. *The Limits of Liberty: Between Anarchy and Leviathan*. Chicago: University of Chicago Press.

Cardenas, V., S. Hochrainer, R. Mechler, G. Pflug, and J. Linnerooth-Bayer. 2007. "Sovereign Financial Disaster Risk Management: The Case of Mexico." *Environmental Hazards* 7 (1): 40–53.

Chamlee-Wright, E., and V. H. Storr. 2009. "Filling the Civil-Society Vacuum: Post-Disaster Policy and Community Response." Policy Comment 22, George Mason University, Mercatus Center, Arlington, VA.

Coate, S. 1995. "Altruism, the Samaritan's Dilemma, and Government Transfer Policy." *American Economic Review* 85 (1): 46–57.

Cohen, C., and E. Werker. 2008. "The Political Economy of 'Natural' Disasters." Working Paper 08-040, Harvard Business School, Boston.

Cole, S., X. Giné, and J. Tobacman. 2008. "Barriers to Household Risk Management: Evidence from India." World Bank, Washington, DC.

Cummins, J. D., and O. Mahul. 2009. *Catastrophe Risk Financing in Developing Countries*. Washington, DC: World Bank.

Fink, G., and S. Redaelli. 2009. "Determinants of International Emergency Aid: Humanitarian Need Only?" Policy Research Working Paper 4839, World Bank, Washington, DC.

Froot, K. A. 2001. "The Market for Catastrophe Risk: A Clinical Examination." *Journal of Financial Economics* 60: 529–71.

Gibson, C., K. Andersson, E. Ostrom, and S. Shivakumar. 2005. *The Samaritan's Dilemma: The Political Economy of Development Aid*. Oxford, U.K.: Oxford University Press.

Giné, X., R. Townsend, and J. Vickery. 2008. "Patterns of Rainfall Insurance Participation in Rural India." *World Bank Economic Review* 22 (3): 539–66.

Grosh, M., C. del Ninno, E. Tesliuc, and A. Ouerghi. 2008. *For Protection and Promotion: The Design and Implementation of Effective Safety Nets*. Washington, DC: World Bank.

Harmer, A., G. Taylor, K. Haver, A. Stoddard, and P. Harvey. 2009. "Thematic CAP for National Disaster Preparedness: Feasibility Study." Humanitarian Outcomes, London.

Heltberg, R. 2007. "Helping South Asia Cope Better with Natural Disasters: The Role of Social Protection." *Development Policy Review* 25 (6): 681–98.

Humanitarian Policy Group. 2006. "Saving Lives through Livelihoods: Critical Gaps in the Response to the Drought in the Greater Horn of Africa." HPG Briefing Note.

Independent Evaluation Group. 2006. *Hazards of Nature, Risks to Development: An IEG Evaluation of World Bank Assistance for Natural Disasters*. Washington, DC: World Bank.

Jametti, M., and T. von Ungern-Sternberg. 2009. "Hurricane Insurance in Florida." Working Paper 2768, CESifo Group, Munich.

Kunreuther, H., R. M. Hogarth, and J. Meszaros. 1993. "Insurer Ambiguity and Market Failure." *Journal of Risk and Uncertainty* 7 (1): 71–87.

Kunreuther, H., R. Ginsberg, L. Miller, P. Sagi, P. Slovic, B. Borkan, and N. Katz. 1979. "Disaster Insurance Protection: Public Policy Lessons." New York: Wiley Interscience.

Kunreuther, H., and E. Michel-Kerjan. 2008. "A Framework for Reducing Vulnerability to Natural Disasters: Ex-Ante and Ex-Post Considerations." Background paper for the report.

———. 2009. *At War with the Weather*. Cambridge, MA: MIT Press.

Kunreuther, H., and M. Pauly. 2005. "Terrorism Losses and All Perils Insurance." *Journal of Insurance Regulation* (Summer).

Lucas, R. E. B., and O. Stark. 1985. "Motivations to Remit: Evidence from Botswana." *Journal of Political Economy* 93 (5): 901–18.

Maldives Ministry of Planning and National Development. 2006. *Tsunami Impact Assessment Survey 2005: A Socio-Economic Countrywide Assessment at Household Level, Six Months after the Tsunami*. Maldives: UNDP/UNFPA. Cited in Heltberg, R. (2007).

Michel-Kerjan, E. 2010. "Hedging Against Tomorrow's Catastrophes: Sustainable Financial Solutions to Help Protect Against Extreme Events." In *Learning from Catastrophes,* ed. H. Kunreuther, and M. Useem. Philadelphia: Wharton School Publishing.

Michel-Kerjan, E., and C. Kousky. 2010. "Come Rain or Shine: Evidence from Flood Insurance Purchases in Florida." *Journal of Risk and Insurance* 77 (2): 369–397.

Miller, D. L., and A. L. Paulson. 2007. "Risk Taking and the Quality of Informal Insurance: Gambling and Remittances in Thailand." Working Paper 07-01, Federal Reserve Bank, Chicago.

Mohapatra, S., G. Joseph, and D. Ratha. 2009. "Remittances and Natural Disasters: Ex-post Response and Contribution to Ex-ante Preparedness." Policy Research Working Paper 4972, World Bank, Washington, DC. Background paper for the report.

Olsen, G., N. Carstensen, and K. Hoyen. 2003. "Media Coverage, Donor Interests, and the Aid Business." *Disasters* 27 (2): 109–26.

Pelham, L., E. Clay, and T. Braunholz. 2009. "Natural Disasters: What Is the Role for Social Safety Nets?" World Bank, Human Development Network—Social Protection, Washington, DC.

Quisumbing, A. R. 2005. *A Drop in the Bucket? The Impact of Food Assistance after the 1998 Floods in Bangladesh*. Washington, DC: International Food Policy Research Institute.

Raschky, P. A., and H. Weck-Hannemann. 2007. "Charity Hazard—A Real Hazard to Natural Disaster Insurance." Working Papers 07-04,

University of Innsbruck, Faculty of Economics and Statistics, Innsbruck, Austria.

Raschky, P. A., and M. Schwindt. 2009a. "Aid, Natural Disasters, and the Samaritan's Dilemma." Policy Research Working Paper 4952, World Bank, Washington, DC. Background paper for the report.

———. 2009b. "On the Channel and Type of International Disaster Aid." Policy Research Working Paper 4953, World Bank, Washington, DC. Background paper for the report.

Ratha, D. 2010. "Mobilize the Diaspora for the Reconstruction of Haiti." Social Science Research Council, New York. http://www.ssrc.org/features/pages/haiti-now-and-next/1338/1438.

Revkin, A. C. 2005. "The Future of Calamity." *New York Times*. January 2.

Rosenzweig, M. R. 1988. "Risk, Implicit Contracts and the Family in Rural Areas of Low-Income Countries." *Economic Journal* 98 (393): 1148–70.

Rosenzweig, M. R., and O. Stark. 1989. "Consumption Smoothing, Migration, and Marriage: Evidence from Rural India." *Journal of Political Economy* 97 (4): 905–26.

Seo, J., and O. Mahul. 2009. "The Impact of Climate Change on Catastrophe Risk Models: Implication for Catastrophe Risk Markets in Developing Countries." Policy Research Working Paper 4959, World Bank, Washington, DC. Background paper for the report.

Simmons, D. 2008. "Catastrophe Insurance Triggers—What Is the Best Fit for the Asia-Pacific?" Paper prepared for the Asian Development Bank conference "Natural Catastrophe Risk Insurance Mechanisms for Asia and the Pacific," Tokyo, November 4–5.

von Ungern-Sternberg, T. 2004. *Efficient Monopolies: The Limits of Competition in the European Property Insurance Market.* Oxford, U.K.: Oxford University Press.

World Bank. 2001. *Implementation Completion Report on a Loan to Turkey for the Emergency Earthquake Recovery Loan.* Report 22484, Washington, DC.

———. 2007. "The Caribbean Catastrophe Risk Insurance Initiative." Results of preparation work on the design of a Caribbean Catastrophe Risk Insurance Facility. Washington, DC.

———. 2009a. *Catastrophe Risk Financing in Middle and Low Income Countries: Review of the World Bank Group Products and Services.* Washington, DC.

———. 2009b. "Helping Governments Insure Against Natural Disaster Risk." Treasury briefing. Washington, DC: International Bank for Reconstruction and Development.

Yamano, T., H. Alderman, and L. Christiaensen. 2005. "Child Growth, Shocks, and Food Aid in Rural Ethiopia." *American Journal of Agricultural Economics* 87 (2): 273–88.

Yang, D., and H. Jung Choi. 2007. "Are Remittances Insurance? Evidence from Rainfall Shocks in the Philippines." *World Bank Economic Review* 21 (2): 219–48.

Spotlight 5

Notes

1. Tsunami is Japanese for a "(great) harbor wave" that is generated when a large body of water is rapidly displaced. The wall of water typically sweeps all in its path, but does not last long. Monecke et al. (2008) estimate the likelihood of Aceh-scale tsunamis at one in 500 years.

2. The most severe earthquake recorded was 9.5 on the Richter scale (Chile 1960). Other severe quakes include 9.0 magnitude earthquake in 1952 Kamchatka (Northern Russia), and two off Alaska (9.1 in 1957 and 9.2 in 1964 off Prince William Sound).

3. The Indian Government reports that 83,788 boats were damaged or destroyed, 31,755 livestock lost and 39,035 hectares of ripe agricultural land was damaged.

4. Tsunami Evaluation Coalition (2007, p.17)

5. Ushahidi, a free software that allows text messages to be mapped by time and location, was used to follow where ethnic violence started and where it intensified in the 2007 Kenyan elections. Since then, it has been used to map conflicts and indirectly monitor elections from Colombia to the Democratic Republic of Congo to Afghanistan. Source: Jason Palmer, Science & Technology Reporter, BBC News.

6. Adele Waugaman, spokesperson for UN Foundation/Vodafone Foundation partnership, BBC News.

7. The Red Cross, for example, constructed 6,100 units themselves, but supported owner-construction for another 24,000 units. (http://www.ifrc.org/docs/news/08/08091202/index.asp).

References

de Mel, S., D. McKenzie, and C. Woodruff. 2008. "Enterprise Recovery Following Natural Disasters." Policy Research Working Paper 5269, World Bank, Washington, DC. Background paper for the report.

Masyrafah, H., and J. Mja Mckeon. 2008. "Post-Tsunami Aid Effectiveness in Aceh Proliferation and Coordination in Reconstruction." Wolfensohn Center for Development Working Paper 6, Brookings Institution, Washington, DC.

Monecke, K., W. Finger, D. Klarer, W. Kongko, B. G. McAdoo, A. L. Moore, and S. U. Sudrajat. 2008. "A 1,000-Year Sediment Record of Tsunami Recurrence in Northern Sumatra." *Nature* 455 (7217): 1232–4.

Oxfam America. 2006. *Disaster Management Policy and Practice: Lessons for Government, Civil Society and the Private Sector in Sri Lanka.* Boston.

Tsunami Evaluation Coalition. 2007. *Report: Expanded Summary: Joint Evaluation of the International Response to the Indian Ocean Tsunami.* London. Available at http://www.alnap.org/resource/5536.aspx.

United States Geological Survey. 2008. *Poster of the Sumatra-Andaman Islands Earthquake of 26 December 2004.* http://earthquake.usgs.gov/eqcenter/eqarchives/poster/2004/20041226.php.

Chapter 6

Notes

1. For a discussion of the overall effects of climate change and the costs of adaptation, see IPCC (2007a) and World Bank (2009, 2010).

2. Sources:

    (a) Based on estimates for 1820–1998, excess GPD growth above population growth has varied beween 0.7 percent in Africa to 1.7 percent in the G7 countries (World Bank 2008, p. 106).

    (b) http://mospi.nic.in/reptpercent20_percent20pubn/sources_methods_2007/Chapterpercent2032.pdf.

    (c) http://www.citymayors.com/statistics/largest-cities-population-125.
    html.

3. According to UN Population Division (2007).

4. The estimates for this report are based on an economic-demographic model following Henderson and Wang (2007). No estimates are currently available for flood risk because global hazard distributions data focus on large rural floods, while most city floods are localized and result, for example, from inadequate drainage. Cyclones also cause storm surges that can devastate coastal areas. These are not considered separately here, but a recent study estimated that global (including extratropical) exposure to coastal flooding caused by storms in large port cities will rise from about 40 million people today to about 95 million by 2070, not considering the possible effects of climate change (Nicholls and others 2008).

5. The Civil War and the relative decline of water-based transportation relative to rail caused the city to lose ground, relative to northern cities, through much of the 19th century. New Orleans' population peaked at

627,000 residents in 1960 and began to decline following Hurricane Betsy in 1965 to 485,000 residents in 2000 (Glaeser 2005).

6. Nordhaus (2010), Pielke (2007), and Hallegatte (2007).

7. Narita and others (2009).

8. The models and related analyses are part of the background work conducted for the report by a joint Yale – MIT – World Bank Consortium. Details can be found in Mendelsohn and others (2010a, 2010b) and Mendelsohn, and Saher (2010).

9. WDR 2010 provides an estimate that warming of 2°C could result in an average reduction in world consumption equivalent to about 1 percent of global GDP. The forthcoming World Bank study on global adaptation estimates that it would cost between $75 to $100 billion a year between 2010 and 2050 to prevent any damages from climate change.

10. All dollar amounts are in current (2010) terms.

11. All four of the climate models lead to similar conclusions.

12. A vast literature exists on the effectiveness of international agreements. For a discussion of the climate change context, see Barrett and Toman (2010).

13. Recent research suggests that while the complete collapse of the THC is not likely, a significant weakening of the order of 25 percent in the THC is certainly conceivable in this century (IPCC 2007a).

14. Dasgupta and others (2009) use spatial analysis to determine which parts of the earth's inhabited areas would be inundated under different degrees of sea level rise and then assess the percentages of current populations and levels of economic activity at risk in developing countries as a consequence of the inundations. They find that one meter of sea level rise could expose about 1.3 percent of the developing world's current population and put at risk about 1.3 percent of total GDP in developing countries. For five meters the figures are 5.6 percent and 6.0 percent, respectively. As the authors point out, however, all these figures are calculated by superimposing alternative sea level rises on current population, economic, and other data. To the extent that future population and economic growth is more concentrated in coastal areas than elsewhere, future risks would be proportionately higher; against this effect is the potential for adaptation (including changes in coastal land use policy) to mitigate the exposures.

15. Estimates of mitigation costs always assume that mitigation measures are taken whenever and wherever they are cheapest. Violation of this "whenever wherever principle" massively increase costs. For example,

one estimate suggests that postponing all mitigation efforts in developing countries until 2020 would double the cost of stabilizing temperatures at 2°C above preindustrial temperature (Edmonds and others. 2008). With mitigation costs estimated to be anywhere between $4 trillion and $25 trillion over the century the losses implied by delays and crash scenarios are enormous. See World Bank (2009) for a discussion of this issue.

16. For a complete discussion on this point, see Barrett (2008).

References

Bahl, R., and J. Martinez-Vazquez. 2008. "The Property Tax in Developing Countries: Current Practice and Prospects." In *Toward a Vision of Land in 2015*, ed. J. Riddell and G. Cornia. Cambridge, MA: Lincoln Institute of Land and Policy.

Barrett, S. 2008. "The Incredible Economics of Geoengineering." *Environmental Resource Economics* 39: 45–54.

Barrett, S., and M. Toman. 2010. "Contrasting Future Paths for an Evolving Global Climate Regime." Policy Research Working Paper 5164, World Bank, Washington, DC.

Brecht, H., U. Deichmann, and H. Gun Wang. 2010. "Predicting future urban natural hazard exposure." Background note for the report.

Dasgupta, S., B. Laplante, S. Murray, and D. Wheeler. 2009. "Sea-Level Rise and Storm Surges: A Comparative Analysis of Impacts in Developing Countries," Policy Research Working Paper 4901, World Bank, Washington, DC.

Edmonds, J., L. Clarke, J. Lurz, and M. Wise. 2008. "Stabilizing CO2 Concentrations with Incomplete International Cooperation." *Climate Policy* 8 (4): 355–76.

Emanuel, K., R. Sundararajan, and J. Williams. 2008. "Hurricanes and Global Warming: Results from Downscaling IPCC AR4 Simulations." *American Meteorological Society* 89 (3): 347–67.

EMDAT. 2009. "The OFDA/CRED International Disaster Database." Brussels, Belgium: See chapter 1. http://www.emdat.be.

Glaeser, E. L. 2005. "Should the Government Rebuild New Orleans, or Just Give Residents Checks?" *Economists' Voice* 2 (4), article 4.

Gunawan, I. 2008. "Climate Change and Adaptation Challenges for Jakarta." Disaster Management Framework for Indonesia. Jakarta, Indonesia.

Hahm, H., and M. Fisher. 2010. "Can Jakarta Become Flood-Free: Sustainable Flood Mitigation Measures for a Coastal City." Presentation at Singapore International Water Week, June 28–July 2.

Hallegatte, S. 2007. "The Use of Synthetic Hurricane Tracks in Risk Analysis and Climate Change Damage Assessment." *Journal of Applied Meteorology and Climatology* 46 (11): 1956–66.

Henderson, J. V., and H. G. Wang. 2007. "Urbanization and City Growth: The Role of Institutions." *Regional Science and Urban Economics* 37 (3): 283–313.

IPCC (Intergovernmental Panel on Climate Change). 2000. *Special Report on Emissions Scenarios*. Cambridge, U.K.: Cambridge University Press.

———. 2007a. *The Physical Science Basis*. Cambridge, U.K.: Cambridge University Press.

———. 2007b. *Impacts, Adaptation and Vulnerability*. Cambridge, U.K.: Cambridge University Press.

Kousky, C., J. Pratt, and R. Zeckhauser. 2010. "Virgin Versus Experienced Risks." In *The Irrational Economist: Making Decisions in a Dangerous World,* ed. E. Michel-Kerjan and P. Slovic. New York: Public Affairs Books.

Mendelsohn, R., K. Emanuel, and S. Chonabayashi. 2010a. "The Impact of Climate Change on Global Tropical Storm Damages." Background paper for the report.

———. 2010b. "The Impact of Climate Change on Hurricane Damages in the United States."Background paper for the report.

Mendelsohn, R. and G. Saher. 2010. "The Global Impact of Climate Change on Extreme Events." Background paper for the report.

Montgomery, M. R. 2009: "Reshaping Economic Geography." *Population and Development Review* 35 (1): 197–208.

Narita, D., R. S. J. Tol, and D. Anthoff. 2009. "Damage Costs of Climate Change through Intensification of Tropical Cyclone Activities: An Application of FUND." *Climate Research* 39 (2): 87–97.

Nicholls, R., S. Hanson, C. Herweijer, N. Patmore, S. Hallegatte, J. Corfee-Morlot, J. Château, and R. Muir-Wood. 2008. "Ranking Port Cities with High Exposure and Vulnerability to Climate Extremes." Environment Working Paper 1, OECD, Paris.

Nordhaus, W. 2010. "The Economics of Hurricanes in the United States." *Climate Change Economics*.

Pallagst, K. 2008. "Shrinking Cities: Planning Challenges from an International Perspective." In *Cities Growing Smaller,* ed. S. Rugare and T. Schwarz. Cleveland: Kent State University, Cleveland Urban Design Collaborative.

Pearce, D., W. Cline, A. Achanta, S. Fankhauser, R. Pachauri, R. Tol, and P. Vellinga. 1996. "The Social Costs of Climate Change: Greenhouse Damage and Benefits of Control." In *Climate Change 1995: Economic and Social Dimensions of Climate Change*, J. Bruce, H. Lee, and E. Haites, eds., pp. 179–224. Cambridge Univ. Press, Cambridge, U.K.

Pielke Jr., R. A. 2007. "Future Economic Damage from Tropical Cyclones: Sensitivities to Societal and Climate Changes." *Philosophical Transactions Royal Society* 365: 1–13.

Pielke Jr., R. A., and M. Downton. 2000. "Precipitation and Damaging Floods: Trends in the United States, 1932–97." *Journal of Climate* 13 (20): 3625–37.

Pielke Jr., R. A., J. Gratz, C. W. Landsea, D. Collins, M. A. Saunders, and R. Musulin. 2008. "Normalized Hurricane Damages in the United States: 1900–2005." *Natural Hazards Review* 9 (1): 1–29.

Posner, R. 2004. *Catastrophe: Risk and Response*. New York: Oxford University Press.

Rahmstorf, S. 2007. "A Semi-empirical Approach to Projecting Future Sea-Level Rise." *Science* 315 (5810): 368–70.

Smith, J. B., S. H. Schneider, M. Oppenheimer, G. W. Yohe, W. Hare, M. D. Mastrandrea, A. Patwardhan, I. Burton, J. Corfee-Morlot, C. H. D. Magadza, H. M. Fussel, A. B. Pittock, A. Rahman, A. Suarez, J. P. van Ypersele. 2009. "Assessing Dangerous Climate Change through an Update of the Intergovernmental Panel on Climate Change (IPCC) 'Reasons for Concern.'" *Proceedings of the National Academy of Sciences* 106: 4133–7.

Stern, N. 2007. *The Economics of Climate Change*. Cambridge, U.K.: Cambridge University Press.

Swiss Re. 2006. *The Effects of Climate Change: Storm Damage in Europe on the Rise. Focus Report.*

Texier, P. 2008. "Floods in Jakarta: When the Extreme Reveals Daily Structural Constraints and Mismanagement." *Disaster Prevention and Management* 17 (3): 358–72.

Trapp, R. J., N. S. Diffenbaugh, H. E. Brooks, M. E. Baldwin, E. D. Robinson, and J. S. Pal. 2007. "Changes in Severe Thunderstorm Environment Frequency during the 21st Century Caused by Anthropogenically Enhanced Global Radiative Forcing." *Proceedings of the National Academy of Sciences* 104 (50): 19719–23.

UN Population Division. 2008. *World Urbanization Prospects 2007 Revision*. New York: United Nations Population Division.

Weitzman, M. L. 2009. "The Extreme Uncertainty of Extreme Climate Change: An Overview and Some Implications." Harvard University, Boston.

World Bank. 2008. *World Development Report 2009: Reshaping Economic Geography*. Washington, DC.

———. 2009. *World Development Report 2010: Development in a Changing Climate*. Washington, DC.

———. 2010. "The Cost to Developing Countries of Adapting to Climate Change: New Methods and Estimates." World Bank, Washington, DC.

Index